"What Is Literature?"

and Other Essays

"*What Is Literature?*"

and Other Essays

JEAN-PAUL SARTRE

Harvard University Press

Cambridge, Massachusetts

1988

This book is printed on acid-free paper, and its
binding materials have been chosen for strength
and durability.

Library of Congress Cataloging-in-Publication Data

Sartre, Jean Paul, 1905–
    [Essays. English. Selections]
    "What is literature?" and other essays / Jean-Paul
Sartre.
        p.   cm.
    Bibliography: p.
    Includes index.
    ISBN 0-674-95083-6 (alk. paper).
    ISBN 0-674-95084-4 (pbk.: alk. paper)
    1. Literature—Philosophy.   2. Authorship.   I.
Title.
PN45.S245 1988
809—dc19   87-37931
                                                 CIP

Contents

Introduction

Introduction

> *Men make their own history, but they do not make it just
> as they please; they do not make it under circumstances
> chosen by themselves, but under circumstances directly
> encountered, given and transmitted from the past.*
>
> Marx, *The Eighteenth Brumaire of Louis Bonaparte* (1852)

A WRITER as widely read as Sartre invariably suffers from a contempt bred by familiarity. Long after his death in April 1980, the reactions elicited by mention of his name range from adulation to dismissal, with many of the latter in the vein of what Sartre once described as the superiority of live dogs to dead lions. For a man who wanted above all to write for his time, dismissal is the harshest of condemnations: "It seems to be generally accepted that the Sartrean problematic has by now been essentially relegated to the past. Smiles are quick to surface whenever anyone is still interested in Sartre or still writes about him, as though the person were all but suspect of still being 'with' Sartre, of having stuck with him" (Denis Hollier, *The Politics of Prose: Essay on Sartre*, trans. Jeffrey Mehlman [Minneapolis: University of Minnesota Press, 1986], p. 92). The quick smiles are a professional hazard, a result of the notoriety Sartre maintained by choice. His detractors—many of them the "live dogs" noted above—would do well to note Sartre's awareness of this notoriety and the strategic uses to which he puts it.

Instead of asking ironically whether the Sartrean problematic is passé or whether Sartre has faded as a key figure of postwar modernity, I want to cast my comments around the question of what it might mean to read Sartre today. In so doing, I want to echo the heightened sense of history and circumstance Sartre confers on the acts of writing and reading throughout the four texts in the present volume, versions of which appeared in early issues of *Les Temps* *modernes*, the monthly Sartre started in 1945. The following pages are intended to trace the evolving concept of *littérature engagée* in the aftermath of World War II.* Chronology provides a context and a first order of specificity. Whenever possible, it serves to ground the issues of theory that Sartre's postwar writings on writing engage directly or by implication. The secondary literature on Sartre is overwhelming and I make no claims to do more than address selected issues.

> We would be hunters of meaning, we would speak the truth about the world and about our own lives.
>
> Sartre, "Merleau-Ponty" (1960)

March 1941: Jean-Paul Sartre returns to civilian life in Paris after eight months of captivity by the Germans. Almost immediately, he recruits students at the Lycée Pasteur and the Ecole Normale Supérieure for Socialisme et Liberté (Socialism and Freedom), a small cell of intellectual *résistants* including Simone de Beauvoir, Maurice Merleau-Ponty, Jacques-Laurent Bost, and Jean Pouillon. The group holds grand visions. If—as Simone de Beauvoir puts it in *The Prime of Life*—the democracies win the war, the French left will need a new program. But if, on the other hand, the Axis nations defeat the Allies, it will be necessary to see that Germany loses the peace. Party politics intervene when the Communists, fearful of a potential rival in Sartre, spread rumors that he is a German agent. After a

* I have retained the original French in place of the expression "engaged literature" used by Bernard Frechtman. My alternative translation is "committed writing." This for two reasons: First, the transitive usage of the verb "commit" denotes the conscious assertion of value that the concept is intended to convey. Second, "writing" rather than "literature" because the program set forth in "What Is Literature?" involves practices and media—journalism, radio, film—beyond traditional conceptions. On the notion of commitment and/or *engagement*, see David L. Schalk, *The Spectrum of Political Engagement: Mounier, Benda, Nizan, Brasillach, Sartre* (Princeton: Princeton University Press, 1979) and my discussion below of Theodor Adorno, "Commitment," *New Left Review* 87–88 (1974).

number of friends and contacts are arrested, Sartre feels
personally responsible and disbands the group in October
1941.

Socialisme et Liberté allows Sartre to draft a constitution
of some 120 articles mixing economics with a utopian vision
freely adapted from the writings of Marx and Proudhon.
Although none of the ten reputed copies of the constitution
survives the war, accounts by group members suggest that
it addresses concerns ranging from parliamentary representation to military service and the division between judicial
and executive branches of government. The lost constitution provides evidence that Sartre's vision of a non-
authoritarian socialism precedes the postwar period. It
supports Fredric Jameson's view that Marxism coexists with
Sartre's existentialsm; it is not something he comes to
afterward (*Marxism and Form* [Princeton: Princeton University Press, 1971], p. 207). Three years after *Nausea*, Sartre's
early attempts to lay bare the structures of consciousness articulate with issues of collective action and social
change.

In the wake of Socialisme et Liberté, Sartre's wartime
activities are increasingly devoted to writing. When *Being
and Nothingness* appears in 1943, he is writing for the theater
and working with the Comité National des Ecrivains
(National Committee of Writers), an underground group
founded with the help of Communists who have either
forgotten or repressed their accusations of two years earlier.
By September 1944, an editorial committee of Raymond
Aron, Michel Leiris, Albert Ollivier, and Jean Paulhan is
created around the nucleus of Sartre, de Beauvoir, and
Merleau-Ponty. Albert Camus and André Malraux—major
figures of the Resistance underground—are invited to join,
but turn down the invitation.*

* The 1987 Klaus Barbie trial is a reminder that full disclosure of the
Occupation has yet to occur. Survivors of the period remain the objects of
allegation and rumor. For a sense of the issues involved in such disclosure,
see Pierre Assouline's *L'Epuration des intellectuels* (Brussels: Complexe, 1985)
and Herbert Lottman's *The Purge: The Purification of French Collaborators after*

Temps modernes marks a changing of the literary guard even before its first issue appears. With the *Nouvelle Revue française* discredited because of Pierre Drieu La Rochelle's collaboration, Sartre and *TM* are prime candidates to assume the preeminence enjoyed by Gide and the *NRF* between the wars. By 1944, all indications are that at the age of seventy-five Gide is to be cast in a postwar role of gray eminence. The problem is that the role is not one of his personal choosing. Following the Liberation, ongoing and new rivalries place Sartre and *TM* in conflict with an older literary generation. The conflict goes beyond individual personalities to a change in the economy of the cultural review allying functions of production, distribution, and legitimation that usually compete with one another (Régis Debray, *Teachers, Writers, Celebrities: The Intellectuals of Modern France*, trans. David Macey [London: Verso, 1981], p. 67). Embodied respectively by writer, publisher, and critic, these functions converge in a successful marketing strategy when the *NRF* features works-in-progress it later reviews as books published by Gallimard. When the books compete for literary prizes funded by publishers, the result is a literary and economic hegemony Sartre emulates in *TM*'s program.

Initial reactions to *TM* are mixed. In *Esprit* (December 1945), Emmanuel Mounier calls it a "review-event" and notes the convergence of its vision with his own Personalism of the interwar period. Gide mixes caution with praise. Writing on *TM* in his short-lived weekly, *Terre des hommes*, he evokes the specter of Soviet art in the service of the Party.

World War II (New York: Morrow, 1986). The question of Sartre's wartime activities resurfaces in June 1985 when the Parisian daily *Libération* prints a statement by the late Vladimir Jankélévitch to the effect that Sartre's political activities after the war are an unhealthy compensation, "a remorse, a quest for the danger he did not want to run during the war" (quoted in Ronald Hayman, *Sartre: A Biography* [New York: Simon and Schuster, 1987], p. 189). My account of Sartre's wartime activities is based on Michel Contat and Michel Rybalka, *The Writings of Sartre*, trans. Richard C. McCleary (Evanston: Northwestern University Press, 1974). The recent biographies by Hayman and by Annie Cohen-Solal (*Sartre: A Life*, trans. Anna Cancogni [New York: Pantheon, 1987]) do little to substantiate Jankélévitch's purported claim.

A later issue of the weekly notes with deference that "although Sartre speaks of committing himself to our times, it is our times which are committed through him" (Anna Boschetti, *The Intellectual Enterprise: Sartre and "Les Temps Modernes,"* trans. Richard C. McCleary {Evanston, Ill.: Northwestern University Press, 1988}, p. 9). Predictably, the Communists see the new monthly as a symptom of bourgeois decadence. Jean Kanapa, an acquaintance from the Socialisme et Liberté days who joins the Communists, ranks the existentialists among the Party's major foes, alongside proponents of Surrealism ("the Trotskyism of literary cafés"). When Gabriel Marcel describes him as an existentialist, Sartre replies that his philosophy is a philosophy of existence and that he doesn't even know what Existentialism is!

October–November 1945: Just over a year after the Liberation, Sartre launches *TM* with "Introducing *Les Temps modernes*" and "The Nationalization of Literature," two statements of purpose that outline an agenda based on the program of *littérature engagée* later developed in "What Is Literature?" and "Black Orpheus." Taken as a set or unit with this common focus, all four texts extend questions of definition—what literature *is*—toward inquiry into what it *should* and *could* be. In each instance, urgency is a result of the historical immediacy from which the activity of writing derives. This sense of writing for one's time expresses what Edward Said describes as Sartre's missionary aim of upholding literature's singular capacity to disclose and reveal the present: "Literature was about the world, readers were in the world; the question was not *whether* to be but *how* to be, and this was best answered by carefully analyzing language's symbolic enactments of the various existential possibilities available to human beings" ("Opponents, Audiences, Constituencies and Community," in Hal Foster, ed., *The Anti-Aesthetic: Essays on Postmodern Culture* {Post Townsend, Wash.: Bay Press, 1983}, p. 139). The point here is that the disclosure promoted by writing and reading is intended as praxis: the action in and on history that Sartre is to expand into his theory of revolution.

Sartre draws immediate attention to the social function of writing when—in the first sentence of "Introducing *Les Temps modernes*"—he refers to the temptation of irresponsibility known by all writers of middle-class origin. In a capitalist society dominated by material value, Sartre openly addresses the issue of where the money to finance writing comes from. This might be nothing more than a jab at the low esteem in which writers—and critics, in particular—are held, were it not for the fact that *TM*'s first issue marks Sartre's decision to abandon his teaching career in order to live from his writing. No longer a civil servant in the French educational system, Sartre is in a singular position. As a graduate of the Ecole Normale Supérieure, his ties with an intellectual elite are not fully broken by his resignation. Likewise, his role in the Comité National des Ecrivains puts him on working terms with the Communists. Finally, his ability to combine the prestige of literature and philosophy holds the promise of recognition by academics and specialists as well as by the general public. In 1945, Sartre embodies the writer-intellectual as an independent agent whose removal from state institutions and political parties allows him to function as critic or mediator as circumstance dictates.*

On a sour note, Sartre's references to Flaubert and Proust are strident and abusive, as though he feels compelled to make negative examples of writers who represent views he may once have held but now condemns. When, in "Intro-

---

* While Sartre remains on the Gallimard payroll as author, reader, and special editor, *TM*'s ties with the publisher are broken after a run-in with Malraux results in eviction from the rue Sébastien-Bottin. Soon, the editorial board relocates at Editions Julliard, on the nearby rue de l'Université (Claude Francis and Fernande Gontier, *Simone de Beauvoir*, trans. Linda Nesselson [New York: St. Martin's, 1987], p. 212). Gallimard's offer to help finance *TM* is motivated in part by a desire to placate suspicions about his wartime activities. Unlike his rival publishers Bernard Grasset and Robert Denoël, Gallimard is never openly accused of collaboration despite the fact that he resumes control of his publishing interests in October 1940 and that the *NRF* under Drieu La Rochelle is a showcase of "new" Franco-German solidarity. After the war, the *NRF* does not reappear until 1954 when, with his monthly renamed the *Nouvelle Nouvelle Revue française*, Gallimard's desire to break with the past is evident.

ducing *Les Temps modernes*," he writes that Flaubert and the Goncourts are to be held responsible for their silence following the 1871 Paris Commune, his virulence recalls the ongoing purge of Nazi collaborators: "The writer is *situated* in his time; every word he utters has reverbations. As does his silence." This misplaced use of *situation* is inexcusable and embarrassing. Concering Proust, in particular, Sartre overlooks some of the very problems of subjectivity he soon explores in *Saint Genet*. In this instance, he inadvertently practices the very terrorist attitude he rejects in "The Nationalization of Literature."

"Introducing *Les Temps modernes*" also extends debate over the role of the writer as social critic in the wake of *The Treason of the Intellectuals*, Julien Benda's 1927 tract against the modern commitment to political passions. The resemblances between Benda and Sartre are striking. Both cast the writer in the role of social conscience, assert the primacy of moral concerns, and employ a rhetoric of accusation. Benda wants the writer-intellectual (*clerc*) to intervene in temporal affairs in the name of mankind: "An intellectual seems to me to betray his function by descending into the public arena only if he does so . . . to secure the triumph of a realist passion of class, race, or nation" (Benda, *La Trahison des clercs* [Paris: Grasset, 1975], p. 136). The decision to write is irreducibly historical; it constitutes an instance of a universal condition that the individual experiences in specific circumstances: "By taking part in the singularity of our era, we ultimately make contact with the eternal, and it is our task as writers to allow the eternal values implicit in such social or political debates to be perceived . . . We proclaim that man is an absolute. But he is such in his time, in his surroundings, on his parcel of earth. What is absolute, what a thousand years of history cannot destroy is *that* irreplaceable, incomparable decision which he makes at this moment concerning these circumstances ("Introducing *Les Temps modernes*," p. 254).

For Sartre, a clear sense of history is of strategic importance if he is to make commitment viable to the concerns of traditional philosophers. His use of the terms "eternal" and "absolute" in the preceding passage is unusual and conciliatory; it suggests that the differences between Benda and Sartre are differences of emphasis rather than substance. At the same time, Sartre's position clearly echoes that taken by Marx in the passage from *The Eighteenth Brumaire of Louis Bonaparte* quoted at the start of this essay. The polyvalent affinities with Benda and Marx point to Sartre's problems in establishing *littérature engagée* as a program grounded in a fully articulated philosophy of history. Only later does he accept this polyvalence as a condition rather than a consequence of his notion of commitment.

TM's literary program extends to all writings irrespective of genre. Yet Sartre confers a privileged status on the journalistic essay as the form of writing best suited to disclose the experience of freedom: "It strikes us, in fact, that journalism is one of the literary genres and that it can become one of the most important of them. The ability to grasp meanings instantly and intuitively, and a talent for regrouping them in order to offer the reader immediately comprehensible synthetic wholes, are the qualities most crucial to a reporter; they are the ones we ask of all our collaborators" ("Introducing *Les Temps modernes*," p. 266). The importance of reportage in *TM*'s program responds to the conditions of ceremony dominating French literature between the wars. "The Nationalization of Literature" describes how texts become pretexts for judgment. From the side of ceremony, each new book provides the opportunity to reassert its contribution to the interests of the Republic. The result is an empty literature of "national treasures."

"The Nationalization of Literature" also contains Sartre's views on literary terror, defined by Jean Paulhan in *The Flowers of Tarbes* (1941) as a fear of the potential of all language to betray the purity of thought prior to expression.* Paulhan ultimately assimilates the terrorist

* Paulhan's inclusion on *TM*'s editorial board reinforces Sartre's ties with Editions Gallimard. As director of the *NRF* between 1925 and 1940, Paulhan mediates between the founding group led by Gide and younger

attitude into a rhetoric of communication. For Sartre, however, terror turns literature into an alibi when it projects the meaning of a text into the future, thereby accommodating those who prefer to remain at a safe distance from the conflicts of the historical present. Sounding like a Jacques Derrida twenty years before the fact, Sartre concludes that we cannot be simultaneously inside and outside history. Concerning history, we are always (*toujours déjà!?*) *inside*!

"What Is Literature?" begins with a two-part definition of writing that opposes an instrumental prose to a poetic attitude more focused on the materiality of language. For the prose writer who *makes use* of words, language is a particular moment of action in the real world and almost an extension of the body ("a sixth finger, a third leg, in short, a pure function"). The prose writer is always looking toward the world beyond words while the poet considers them primarily as objects: "For the former, they are useful conventions, tools which gradually wear out and which one throws away when they are no longer serviceable; for the latter, they are natural things which sprout upon the earth like grass and trees" ("What Is Literature?" p. 29). For Sartre, prose and poetry are relations to language growing out of distinct attitudes and decisions. Both disclose the world, but in different ways: "For the word, which tears the writer of prose away from himself and throws him into the world, sends back to the poet his own image, like a mirror" ("What Is Literature?" p. 31). Of the two, only prose discloses the world with the intention of changing it. Only prose uses language to confer meaning on objects in the real world, thereby demonstrating that to speak is indeed to act.

Critics mistake the prose/poetry distinction as absolute when it clearly falls within a practice of writing relative to circumstance. The poetry rejected in "What Is Literature?"

contributors such as Malraux, Leiris, Sartre, and Raymond Queneau. After France falls to the Germans in June 1940, Paulhan refuses to direct the monthly under censorship. Over the next four years, he becomes a double agent who publically advocates literary publishing under the Vichy regime while he supports the underground Editions de Minuit and cofounds *Les Lettres françaises*.

is embodied by the Surrealists and by a pretension to political revolution that Sartre sees as overblown and dangerous: "They were the proclaimers of catastrophe in the time of the fat cows; in the time of the lean cows they have nothing more to say" ("What Is Literature?" p. 164). As with Flaubert and Proust, history refutes the Surrealists. In 1947, Sartre does not forget the lessons of the Occupation. If, as he argues, Surrealism is entering a period of withdrawal, it is one he is ready to advance . . . with a vengeance! Sartre's hostility is aimed at the Surrealists and at a relation to language he deems incompatible with *TM*'s ambitions. Thus Sartre displaces—rather than rejects—poetry because it does not transmit the clear and unambiguous meaning he requires for *TM*'s 1947 program. The poet's involvement with the materiality of language neglects the reader and the world. As a result, poetry does not attain the disclosure and praxis Sartre wants to promote.

"Black Orpheus," written as the preface to an anthology of works by African and West Indian poets, revises the program of *littérature engagée* in two significant ways. First, it allows for poetry to be reconsidered in the context of colonialism, thereby transposing its marginal status in "What Is Literature?" into a meaningful function tied to social change: "For once at least, the most authentic revolutionary plan and the purest poetry come from the same source" ("Black Orpheus," p. 330). Second, it allows Sartre to mediate on behalf of Senghor and the poets in order to address the white European readers for whom the anthology is intended. The conflict between colonial and native cultures converges on a practice of poetry resistant to the conventional usage imposed on the Africans by the French. The black African and Caribbean poets who appropriate the French langauge "received" under colonial rule deny the instrumentality of a dominant culture much as the Surrealists sought to deny conventions of representation and expression: "When the Negro declares in French that he rejects French culture, he accepts with one hand what he rejects with the other; he sets up the enemy's thinking-apparatus in himself, like a crusher" (p. 301).

The refusal of prose imposes a revised function for poetry as a means of generating self-awareness and liberation within an alienating culture. *Négritude* poetry does not simply export the Surrealists' spirit of revolt. Whereas Breton and his followers want poetry to help liberate the unconscious in order to overcome alienation, the poetry in the Senghor anthology grows out of an oppression whose social and economic reality is lived on a daily basis. This context inverts the relationship between prose and poetry in "What Is Literature?" In "Black Orpheus," prose is denied and poetry asserted: "Strange and decisive turn: *race* is transmuted into *historicity*" (p. 324). When *Saint-Genet* appears in 1952, Sartre's rehabilitation of poetry is complete.

> I recall, in fact, that in *littérature engagée, engagement* must in no way lead to a forgetting of *littérature,* and that our concern must be to serve literature by infusing it with new blood, even as we serve the collectivity by attempting to give it the literature it deserves.
>
> Sartre, "Introducing *Les Temps modernes*" (1945)

Sartre's advocacy of journalism extends his postwar vision of the individual as both subject and agent of history. In this context, *TM*'s early program also supports the hybrid of academic disciplines known in France as the human sciences: "We would like our journal to contribute in a modest way to the elaboration of a synthetic anthropology. But it is not, we repeat, simply a question of effecting an advance in the domain of pure knowledge: the more distant goal we are aiming at is a *liberation*" ("Introducing Les Temps modernes, p. 261). The apparent eclipse of literature and philosophy by politics points to Sartre's growing involvement with practical knowledge over other ("purer") forms after World War

II. What, then, is the synthetic anthropology announced in "Introducing *TM*" and how does it relate to the liberatory impulse behind *littérature engagée?*

For the Sartre of 1945, the study of man can be nothing other than prospective and open-ended. The project of a synthetic anthropology extends the claim in *Being and Nothingness* that existence precedes essence. In keeping with Sartre's progression toward liberation through praxis, it inscribes consideration of a human condition within a lived present that is markedly historical: *"Praxis,* then, becomes the key concept for Sartre, the linchpin in his philosophy of history and the mechanism of mediation between knowledge and being" (Michael Sprinker, *Imaginary Relations: Aesthetics and Ideology in the Theory of Historical Materialism* [New York: Verso, 1987], pp. 186–187). The priority of action over knowledge is not a simple reversal, not a rejection of the latter in favor of the former. The synthetic anthropology announced in *TM*'s first issue is Sartre's attempt to connect the ontology of *Being and Nothingness* to the philosophy of history he sets forth in his 1960 *Critique of Dialectical Reason.** As a critical project, Sartre's synthetic anthropology supplements the pure—that is, abstract and speculative—knowledge of philosophy with the lived historical dimension of the postwar present it is *TM*'s mission to disclose. In so doing, it responds to Marx's imperative— in *Theses on Feuerbach*—to transform the world that philosophers have only tried to interpret.

The centrality of praxis to Sartre's postwar position on writing represents a swing to practical politics which, in turn, entails its own problematic on the relation between thought and action. In light of Sartre's intellectual evolution, the growing importance he confers on praxis points to Martin Heidegger's inquiry into the end of philosophy.

---

* In *Sartre and "Les Temps modernes"* (New York: Cambridge University Press, 1987), Howard Davies analyzes *TM*'s attitudes toward the social sciences, anthropology in particular. His discussion of the roles of Michel Leiris and Claude Lévi-Strauss is informed and incisive. See also Terry Nichols Clark, *Prophets and Patrons: The French University and the Emergence of the Social Sciences* (Cambridge, Mass.: Harvard University Press, 1973).

Much rests on how the term "end" is understood. Some forty years after the fact, it remains unclear whether Sartre sees his move toward politics as a logical consequence ("end" as culmination) of philosophy or whether the breakdown ("end" as demise) of philosophy is a prerequisite to action. While the former sense holds true for Sartre in the immediate postwar period, a longer duration suggests in retrospect that his progression forecast a move from theory to political action more common in France some twenty years later (Vincent Descombes, *Modern French Philosophy*, trans. L. Scott-Fox and J. M. Harding [New York: Cambridge University Press, 1980], p. 136). Like others of his generation, Sartre first understands history through philosophy until he realizes that philosophy itself derives from history in the form of politics.

"What Is Literature?" addresses the question of audience—"For whom does one write?"—as a practical concern for how to incorporate potential readers into *TM*'s empirical public. To this end, Sartre sees that *littérature engagée* must adapt to the media and technology of mass communication: "The book is the noblest, the most ancient of forms; to be sure, we will always have to return to it. But there is a *literary* art of radio, film, editorial, and reporting . . . We must learn to speak in images, to transpose the ideas of our books into these new languages ("What Is Literature?" pp. 216–217). Sartre supports this imperative on a personal level with lectures, interviews and radio broadcasts as well as plays (*The Dirty Hands*), screenplays (*The Chips Are Down*), novels (*Iron in the Soul*), and essays (*Saint Genet*), all undertaken on the premise that the committed writer must contend with as many technologies and media as possible. If not, he or she can expect to be read only by the bourgeoisie. This is the barrier Sartre hopes to break when he writes "Black Orpheus" for Senghor and edits a book in support of Henri Martin, the French sailor court-martialed in 1950 for protesting the French presence in Indochina. It is this expanded sense of commitment as praxis that he embodies over the following two decades as an intellectual who takes a public stand on behalf of others who are less able to plead their own cause.

Immediate and ongoing responses to "What Is Literature?" focus on the wider sense of committed writing and the ambitions Sartre holds for it. As early as 1947, Roland Barthes answers Sartre with what later becomes the opening section of *Writing Degree Zero*. In place of the prose/poetry distinction, Barthes posits a plurality of writings removed from a unified notion of literature. A decade later, his *Mythologies* combines a Sartrean impulse to disclose the present with a systematic model of ideology in everyday life. In both cases, representation in literature and popular culture is associated with identity at the level of individual and institution. Barthes's impulse to disclose is markedly Sartrean, even if his methodology is not. Furthermore, both texts by Barthes distinguish between commitment at the level of language as opposed to commitment at the level of content. Finally, Barthes's notions of writing and scriptor suggest a problematic of the writing subject that Sartre addresses over the next three decades in his studies on Mallarmé, Genet, and Flaubert.*

If we are to render unto Sartre his due, we must contend with the fact that the questions raised by his writings outlive the answers they provide. In this sense, Theodor Adorno's critique of *littérature engagée* raises a number of substantive issues. Adorno begins by noting the confusion caused by opposing a committed art to an autonomous— and presumably uncommitted—art. He goes on to question the importance Sartre places on free choice: "The work of art becomes an appeal to subjects, because it is itself nothing other than a declaration by a subject of his own choice or failure to choose" ("Commitment," p. 78). For Adorno, Sartre's emphasis on the work of art as an appeal to freedom

* In 1965 lectures published in 1972 as "A Plea for Intellectuals," Sartre responds directly to Barthes when he notes that style is "the expression of our invisible conditioning by the world behind us." *Between Existentialism and Marxism*, trans. John Mathews (New York: Pantheon, 1974), p. 282.

is subverted by historical reality which predetermines the range of possible choices.

Unlike Sartre, Adorno is less concerned with generating specific disclosure or implementing change than with disrupting fundamental attitudes. His own aesthetic theory sees the representation ("gesture toward reality") achieved by the work of art as more meaningful than the authorial intention or motivation behind it. Setting the negative example of Brecht's theater alongside that of Sartre, Adorno rejects a committed art that ends up being neither aesthetically nor politically effective. He concludes in support of an ostensibly autonomous art—Kafka and Beckett are his examples—capable of expressing what is barred to politics: "Kafka's prose and Beckett's plays, or the truly monstrous novel *The Unnameable*, have an effect by comparison with which officially committed works look like pantomime. Kafka and Beckett arouse the fear which existentialism merely talks about" (Adorno, p. 86).

To his credit, Adorno notes that Sartre reacts against a tradition of art for art's sake in France which has no equivalent impact in postwar Germany. But what he rejects in Sartre (as in Brecht) is the pretense of a committed art's carrying a moral or political message in a culture which inevitably degrades that message into an ineffectual commodity. Such degradation is less an inherent quality of art or the artist than a condition of postwar modernity: "This is not a time for political art, but politics has migrated into autonomous art, and nowhere more so than where it seems to be politically dead" (Adorno, p. 89). In sum, the differences between Adorno and Sartre engage practice— specifically, Sartre's theater and fiction—rather than theory. Because Adorno believes that art is invariably politicized, his emphasis on the autonomous works of Kafka and Beckett is intended as sociopolitical. The Sartrean program of *littérature engagée* sets literature against politics so as to assert its inherent political value: "Proclaiming that literature is already intrinsically political is the best way of freeing it from the narrow sense of the political to which others would like to bind it" (Boschetti, p. 110). As for the pretense of a committed art, *The Words* and Sartre's 1960 essay on Merleau-Ponty acknowledge the failings of *littérature engagée*. Indeed, Adorno notes that Sartre's intellectual honesty does him credit.

> The intellectual, the product of a class-divided society, . . . is thus a product of history. In this sense, no society can complain of its intellectuals without accusing itself, for it has the intellectuals it makes.
>
> Sartre, "A Plea for Intellectuals" (1972)

Sartre's trajectory traverses all three of Debray's intellectual cycles, from university to publishing and media. In 1945, he starts *TM* as a former academic ready to extend the cultures of literature and philosophy to a wider public. After the Liberation, he remains attentive to what Adorno refers to disparagingly as the culture industry. But unlike Adorno, Sartre engages the emerging media cycle on its own terms by maintaining a high level of public visibility. By the mid-1960s, cold war politics put him at odds with both supporters and friends. During a 1966 visit to Japan, he delivers three lectures at Tokyo and Kyoto in which he reformulates committed writing on the basis of a revised notion of the intellectual as *"someone who meddles in what is not his business"* ("Plea," p. 230).

Throughout the lectures, Sartre emphasizes the particularity of historical events. On the subject of fighting against racism, for example, he refers not only to its frequency as idea or image in books, plays, and films, but also to its lived historical form in trials (the Dreyfus Affair), newspaper editorials, and political speeches: "In short, the intellectual must work to *at the level of events* to produce other concrete events that will combat pogroms or racist verdicts in the courts" (ibid., p. 251). For the Sartre of 1966, the intellectual's activist role extends the call to action expressed by the concept of praxis twenty years earlier. This activist dimension accounts for *littérature engagée*'s persistent appeal among the young and the oppressed, for whom the imperative to act in and on history—whether imposed or chosen— is experienced as the mixture of ideas and values Sartre calls the singular universal.

"A Plea for Intellectuals" also addresses issues of language and communication taken up in "What Is Literature?" but with a clear sense of the contradictions internalized by the intellectuals who, as technicians of specialized knowledge, find themselves "the instruments of ends which remain foreign to them and which they are forbidden to question" ("Plea," p. 240). Emphasis on historical particularity does not prevent Sartre from reiterating the value of the literary work as the objective model of the singular universal: "A book is necessarily a part of the world, through which the totality of the world is *made manifest*, although without ever being fully disclosed" (ibid., p. 275). In such terms, Sartre's evolution toward practical politics following "What Is Literature?" does not entail rejection of the literary work's singular capacity to disclose being-in-the-world.

The Heideggerian ring of this capacity to disclose should not be misconstrued as vaguely poetic or metaphysical. It is tempered by a clear sense of lived experience which the writer alone communicates to his or her readers. Despite the cultural privilege and isolation of Western writers—himself included—from true revolutionary activity, Sartre asserts the essential (rather than accidental) capacity of all writers to fulfill the intellectual function of disclosing the lived present. This assertion echoes the call to action in and on history set forth in *TM*'s early program. It suggests that despite its own historical particularity, the concept of committed writing is far from exhausted by its archival status as a postwar phenomenon.

Régis Debray notes in passing that all intellectual universes have their own coordinates of time and space. What might Sartre's coordinates be? For better or worse, popular memory retains the image of Henri Cartier-

Bresson's photo of a fortyish Sartre with horn-rimmed eyeglasses, philosopher's scarf, and obligatory pipe. There is, of course, more than the image. More than three decades after the Liberation, the questions Sartre raises and the ambitions he holds continue to set the agenda for literary and intellectual debate in France. Whether one sides with him or against him, the issues he addresses are the major issues of his (modern) times. As Etienne Barilier—for one—puts it in *Les Petits Camarades* (Paris: Julliard, 1987), he would rather be wrong with Sartre than right with Aron.

The four texts in the present volume point repeatedly to the interplay of thought, action, and circumstance. They evoke an age marked by war in which the consequences of writing and reading lead to issues unresolved some forty to fifty years after the fact. (It is not surprising that Claude Lanzmann, producer of the Holocaust film *Shoah,* has served on *TM*'s editorial board for over thirty years.) The Sartrean program of committed writing inscribes questions of the theory and practice of literature within a problematic of choice and accountability for which solutions are neither simple nor definitive. That remains—despite the vagaries of Sartre's career and the ambivalence of sympathizers and detractors alike—a lesson for the present which has lost little of its urgency.

Steven Ungar

What Is Literature?

'IF you want to commit yourself,' writes a young imbecile, 'what are you waiting for? Join the Communist Party.' A great writer who committed himself often and then cried off still more often, but who has forgotten, said to me, 'The worst artists are the most committed. Look at the Soviet painters.' An old critic gently complained, 'You want to murder literature. Contempt for belles-lettres is spread out insolently all through your review.' A petty mind calls me pigheaded, which for him is evidently the highest insult. An author who barely crawled from one war to the other and whose name sometimes awakens languishing memories in old men accuses me of not being concerned with immortality; he knows, thank God, any number of people whose chief hope it is. In the eyes of an American hack-journalist the trouble with me is that I have not read Bergson or Freud; as for Flaubert, who did not commit himself, it seems that he haunts me like remorse. Smart-alecks wink at me, 'And poetry? And painting? And music? You want to commit them, too?' And some martial spirits demand, 'What's it all about? Commitment in literature? Well, it's the old socialist realism, unless it's a revival of populism, only more aggressive.'

What nonsense. They read quickly, badly, and pass judgement before they have understood. So let's begin all over again. This doesn't amuse anyone, neither you nor me. But we have to hit the nail on the head. And since critics condemn me in the name of literature without ever saying what they mean by that, the best answer to give them is to examine the art of writing without prejudice. What is writing? Why does one write? For whom? The fact is, it seems that nobody has ever asked himself these questions.

What Is Writing?

No, we do not want to 'commit' painting, sculpture, and music 'too', or at least not in the same way. And why would we want to? When a writer of past centuries expressed an opinion about his craft, was he immediately asked to apply it to the other arts? But today it's the thing to 'talk painting' in the jargon of the musician or the literary man and to 'talk literature' in the jargon of the painter, as if at bottom there were only one art which expressed itself indifferently in one or the other of these languages, like the Spinozistic substance which is adequately reflected by each of its attributes.

Doubtless, one could find at the origin of every artistic calling a certain undifferentiated choice which circumstances, education, and contact with the world particularized only later. Besides, there is no doubt that the arts of a period mutually influence each other and are conditioned by the same social factors. But those who want to expose the absurdity of a literary theory by showing that it is inapplicable to music must first prove that the arts are parallel.

Now, there is no such parallelism. Here, as everywhere, it is not only the form which differentiates, but the matter as well. And it is one thing to work with colour and sound, and another to express oneself by means of words. Notes, colours, and forms are not signs. They refer to nothing exterior to themselves. To be sure, it is quite impossible to reduce them strictly to themselves, and the idea of a pure sound, for example, is an abstraction. As Merleau-Ponty has pointed out in *The Phenomenology of Perception*, there is no quality of sensation so bare that it is not penetrated with significance. But the dim little meaning which dwells within it, a light joy, a timid sadness, remains immanent or trembles about it like a heat mist; it *is* colour or sound. Who can distinguish the green apple from its tart gaiety? And aren't we already saying too much in naming 'the tart gaiety of the green apple'? There is green, there is red, and that is all. They are things, they exist by themselves.

It is true that one might, by convention, confer the value of signs upon them. Thus, we talk of the language of flowers. But if, after the agreement, white roses signify 'fidelity' to me, the fact is that I have stopped seeing them as roses. My attention cuts through them to aim beyond them at this abstract virtue. I forget them. I no longer pay attention to their mossy abundance, to their sweet stagnant odour. I have not even perceived them. That means that I have not behaved like an artist. For the artist, the colour, the bouquet, the tinkling of the spoon on the saucer, are *things*, in the highest degree. He stops at the quality of the sound or the form. He returns to it constantly and is enchanted with it. It is this colour-object that he is going to transfer to his canvas, and the only modification he will make it undergo is that he will transform it into an *imaginary* object. He is therefore as far as he can be from considering colours and signs as a *language*.[1]

What is valid for the elements of artistic creation is also valid for their combinations. The painter does not want to draw signs on his canvas, he wants to create a thing.[2] And if he puts together red, yellow, and green, there is no reason why this collection of colours should have a definable significance, that is, should refer particularly to another object. Doubtless the composition is also inhabited by a soul, and since there must have been motives, even hidden ones, for the painter to have chosen yellow rather than violet, it may be asserted that the objects thus created reflect his deepest tendencies. However, they never express his anger, his anguish, or his joy as do words or the expression of the face; they are impregnated with these emotions; and in order for them to have crept into these colours, which by themselves already had something like a meaning, his emotions get mixed up and grow obscure. Nobody can quite recognize them there.

Tintoretto did not choose that yellow rift in the sky above Golgotha to *signify* anguish or to *provoke* it. It is anguish and yellow sky at the same time. Not sky of anguish or anguished sky; it is an anguish become thing, an anguish which has turned into yellow rift of sky, and which thereby is submerged and impasted by the qualities peculiar to things, by their impermeability, their extension, their blind permanence, their externality, and that infinity of relations which they maintain with other things. That is, it is no longer *readable*. It is like an immense and vain effort, forever arrested half-way between sky and earth, to express what their nature keeps them from expressing.

Similarly, the significance of a melody—if one can still speak of significance—is nothing outside the melody itself, unlike ideas, which can be adequately rendered in several ways. Call it joyous or sad. It will always be over and above anything you can say about it. Not because its passions, which are perhaps at the origin of the invented theme, have, by being incorporated into notes, undergone a transubstantiation and a transmutation. A cry of grief is a sign of the grief which provokes it, but a song of grief is both grief itself and something other than grief. Or, if one wishes to adopt the existentialist vocabulary, it is a grief which does not *exist* any more, which *is*. But, you will say, suppose the painter portrays houses? That's just it. He *makes* them, that is, he creates an imaginary house on the canvas and not a sign of a house. And the house which thus appears preserves all the ambiguity of real houses.

The writer can guide you and, if he describes a hovel, make it seem the symbol of social injustice and provoke your indignation. The painter is mute. He presents you with *a* hovel, that's all. You are free to see in it what you like. That attic window will never be the symbol of misery; for that, it would have to be a sign, whereas it is a thing. The bad painter looks for the type. He paints the Arab, the Child, the Woman; the good one knows that neither the Arab nor the proletarian exists either in reality or on his canvas. He offers a workman, a certain workman. And what are we to think about a workman? An infinity of contradictory things. All thoughts and all feelings are there, adhering to the canvas in a state of profound undifferentiation. It is up to you to choose. Sometimes, high-minded artists try to move us. They paint long lines of workmen waiting in the snow to be hired, the emaciated faces of the unemployed, battlefields. They affect us no more than does Greuze with his 'Prodigal Son'. And that masterpiece, 'The Massacre of Guernica', does anyone think that it won over a single heart to the Spanish cause? And yet something is said that can never quite be heard and that would take an infinity of words to express. And Picasso's long harlequins, ambiguous and eternal, haunted with inexplicable meaning, inseparable from their stooping leanness and their pale diamond-shaped tights, are emotion become flesh, emotion which the flesh has absorbed as the blotter absorbs ink, and emotion which is unrecognizable, lost, strange to itself, scattered to the four corners of space and yet present to itself.

I have no doubt that charity or anger can produce other objects, but they will likewise be swallowed up; they will lose their name; there will remain only things haunted by a mysterious soul. One does not paint meanings; one does not put them to music. Under these conditions, who would dare require that the painter or musician commit himself?

On the other hand, the writer deals with meanings. Still, a distinction must be made. The empire of signs is prose; poetry is on the side of painting, sculpture, and music. I am accused of detesting it; the proof, so they say, is that *Les Temps Modernes** publishes very few poems. On the contrary, this is proof that we like it. To be convinced, all one need do is take a look at contemporary production. 'At least,' critics say triumphantly, 'you can't even dream of committing it.' Indeed. But why should I want to? Because it uses words as does prose? But it does not use them in the same way, and it does not even *use* them at all. I should

*A periodical edited by M. Sartre.—*Translator*.

rather say that it serves them. Poets are men who refuse to *utilize* language. Now, since the quest for truth takes place in and by language conceived as a certain kind of instrument, it is unnecessary to imagine that they aim to discern or expound the true. Nor do they dream of *naming* the world, and, this being the case, they name nothing at all, for naming implies a perpetual sacrifice of the name to the object named, or, as Hegel would say, the name is revealed as the inessential in the face of the thing which is essential. They do not speak, neither do they keep silent; it is something different. It has been said that they wanted to destroy the 'word' by monstrous couplings, but this is false. For then they would have to be thrown into the midst of utilitarian language and would have had to try to retrieve words from it in odd little groups, as for example 'horse' and 'butter' by writing 'horses of butter'.[3]

Besides the fact that such an enterprise would require infinite time, it is not conceivable that one can keep oneself on the plane of the utilitarian project, consider words as instruments, and at the same time contemplate taking their instrumentality away from them. In fact, the poet has withdrawn from language-instrument in a single movement. Once and for all he has chosen the poetic attitude which considers words as things and not as signs. For the ambiguity of the sign implies that one can penetrate it at will like a pane of glass and pursue the thing signified, or turn one's gaze towards its *reality* and consider it as an object. The man who talks is beyond words and near the object, whereas the poet is on this side of them. For the former, they are domesticated; for the latter they are in the wild state. For the former, they are useful conventions, tools which gradually wear out and which one throws away when they are no longer serviceable; for the latter, they are natural things which sprout naturally upon the earth like grass and trees.

But if the poet dwells upon words, as does the painter with colours and the musician with sounds, that does not mean that they have lost all meaning in his eyes. Indeed, it is meaning alone which can give words their verbal unity. Without it they are frittered away into sounds and strokes of the pen. Only, it too becomes natural. It is no longer the goal which is always out of reach and which human transcendence is always aiming at, but a property of each term, analogous to the expression of a face, to the little sad or gay meaning of sounds and colours. Having flowed into the word, having been absorbed by its sonority or visual aspect, having been thickened and defaced, it too is a thing, uncreated and eternal.

For the poet, language is a structure of the external world. The speaker is *in a situation* in langauge; he is invested by words. They are prolongations of his senses, his pincers, his antennae, his spectacles. He manœuvres them from within; he feels them as if they were his body; he is surrounded by a verbal body which he is hardly conscious of and which extends his action upon the world. The poet is outside language. He sees the reverse side of words, as if he did not share the human condition and as if he were first meeting the word as a barrier as he comes towards men. Instead of first knowing things by their name, it seems that first he has a silent contact with them, since, turning towards that other species of thing which for him is the word, touching words, testing them, fingering them, he discovers in them a slight luminosity of their own and particular affinities with the earth, the sky, the water, and all created things.

Not knowing how to use them as a *sign* of an aspect of the world, he sees in the word the *image* of one of these aspects. And the verbal image he chooses for its resemblance to the willow tree or the ash tree is not necessarily the word which we use to designate these objects. As he is already on the outside, he considers words as a trap to catch a fleeing reality rather than as indicators which throw him out of himself into the midst of things. In short, all language is for him the mirror of the world. As a result, important changes take place in the internal economy of the word. Its sonority, its length, its masculine or feminine endings, its visual aspect, compose for him a face of flesh which *represents* rather than expresses meaning. Inversely, as the meaning is *realized*, the physical aspect of the word is reflected within it, and it, in its turn, functions as an image of the verbal body. Like its sign, too, for it has lost its preeminence; since words, like things, are given, the poet does not decide whether the former exist for the latter or vice versa.

Thus, between the word and the thing signified, there is established a double reciprocal relation of magical resemblance and meaning. And the poet does not *utilize* the word, he does not choose between different senses given to it; each of them, instead of appearing to him as an autonomous function, is given to him as a material quality which merges before his eyes with the other accepted meanings.

Thus, in each word he realizes, solely by the effect of the poetic *attitude*, the metaphors which Picasso dreamed of when he wanted to do a matchbox which was completely a bat without ceasing to be a matchbox. Florence is city, flower, and woman. It is city-flower, city-woman, and girl-flower all at the same time. And the strange object which thus appears has the liquidity of the *river*, the soft, tawny ardency of *gold*, and finally gives itself up with *propriety* and, by the continuous diminution of the silent *e*, prolongs indefinitely its modest blossoming.* To that is added the insidious effect of biography. For me, Florence is also a certain woman, an American actress who played in the silent films of my childhood, and about whom I have forgotten everything except that she was as long as a long evening glove and always a bit weary and always chaste and always married and misunderstood and whom I loved and whose name was Florence.

For the word, which tears the writer of prose away from

*This sentence is not fully intelligible in translation as the author is here associating the component sounds of the word Florence with the meaning of the French words they evoke. Thus: FL-OR-ENCE, *fleuve*, *or*, and *décence*. The latter part of the sentence refers to the practice in French poetry of giving, in certain circumstances, a syllabic value to the otherwise silent terminal *e*.—*Translator*.

himself and throws him out into the world, sends back to the poet his own image, like a mirror. This is what justifies the double undertaking of Leiris who, on the one hand, in his *Glossary*, tries to give certain words a *poetic definition*, that is, one which is by itself a synthesis of reciprocal implications between the sonorous body and the verbal soul, and, on the other hand, in a still unpublished work, goes in quest of remembrance of things past, taking as guides a few words which for him are particularly charged with feeling. Thus, the poetic word is a microcosm.

The crisis of language which broke out at the beginning of this century is a poetic crisis. Whatever the social and historical factors, it showed itself in an attack of depersonalization when the writer was confronted by words. He no longer knew how to use them, and, in Bergson's famous formula, he only half recognized them. He approached them with a completely fruitful feeling of strangeness. They were no longer his; they were no longer he; but in those strange mirrors, the sky, the earth, and his own life were reflected. And, finally, they became things themselves, or rather the black heart of things. And when the poet joins several of these microcosms together the case is like that of painters when they assemble their colours on the canvas. One might think that he is composing a sentence, but this is only what it appears to be. He is creating an object. The words-things are grouped by magical associations of fitness and incongruity, like colours and sounds. They attract, repel, and '*burn*' one another, and their association composes the veritable poetic unity which is the *phrase-object*.

More often the poet first has the scheme of the sentence in his mind, and the words follow. But this scheme has nothing in common with what one ordinarily calls a verbal scheme. It does not govern the construction of a meaning. Rather, it is comparable to the creative project by which Picasso, even before touching his brush, prefigures in space the *thing* which will become a buffoon or a harlequin.

> Fuir, là-bas fuir, je sens que des oiseaux sont ivres
> Mais ô mon cœur entends le chant des matelots.

This 'but' which rises like a monolith at the threshold of the sentence does not tie the second line to the preceding one. It colours it with a certain reserved nuance, with 'private associations' which penetrate it completely. In the same way, certain poems begin with 'and'. This conjunction no longer indicates to the mind an operation which is to be carried out; it extends throughout the paragraph to give it the absolute quality of a *sequel*. For the poet, the sentence has a tonality, a taste; by means of it he tastes for their own sake the irritating flavours of objection, of reserve, of disjunction. He carries them to the absolute. He makes them real properties of the sentence, which becomes an utter objection without being an objection *to* anything precise. He finds here those relations of reciprocal implication which we pointed out a short time ago between the poetic word and its meaning; the unit made up of the words chosen functions as an *image* of the interrogative or restrictive nuance, and vice versa, the interrogation is an image of the verbal unit which it delimits.

As in the following admirable lines:

O saisons! O châteaux!
Quelle âme est sans défaut?

Nobody is questioned; nobody is questioning; the poet is absent. And the question involves no answer, or rather it is its own answer. Is it therefore a false question? But it would be absurd to believe that Rimbaud 'meant' that everybody has his faults. As Breton said of Saint-Pol Roux, 'If he had meant it, he would have said it.' Nor did he *mean* to say something else. He asked an absolute question. He conferred upon the beautiful word 'âme' an interrogative existence. The interrogation has become a thing as the anguish of Tintoretto became a yellow sky. It is no longer a meaning, but a substance. It is seen from the outside, and Rimbaud invites us to see it from the outside with him. Its strangeness arises from the fact that, in order to consider it, we place ourselves on the other side of the human condition, on the side of God.

If this is the case, one easily understands how foolish it would be to require a poetic commitment. Doubtless, emotion, even passion—and why not anger, social indignation, and political hatred?—are at the origin of the poem. But they are not *expressed* there, as in a pamphlet or in a confession. In so far as the writer of prose exhibits feelings, he illustrates them; whereas, if the poet injects his feelings into his poem, he ceases to recognize them; the words take hold of them, penetrate them, and metamorphose them; they do not signify them, even in his eyes. Emotion has become thing; it now has the opacity of things; it is compounded by the ambiguous properties of the words in which it has been enclosed. And above all, there is always much more in each phrase, in each verse, as there is more than simple anguish in the yellow sky over Golgotha. The word, the phrase-thing, inexhaustible as things, everywhere overflow the feeling which has produced them. How can one hope to provoke the indignation or the political enthusiasm of the reader when the very thing one does is to withdraw him from the human condition and invite him to consider with the eyes of God a language that has been turned inside out? Someone may say, 'You're forgetting the poets of the Resistance. You're forgetting Pierre Emmanuel.' Not a bit! They're the very ones I was going to give as examples.[4]

But even if the poet is forbidden to commit himself, is that a reason for exempting the writer of prose? What do they have in common? It is true that the prose-writer and the poet both write. But there is nothing in common between these two acts of writing except the movement of the hand which traces the letters. Otherwise, their universes are incommunicable, and what is good for one is not good for the other. Prose is, in essence, utilitarian. I would readily define the prose-writer as a man who *makes use* of words. M. Jourdan made prose so that he could ask for his slippers, and Hitler, so that he could declare war on Poland. The writer is a *speaker*; he designates, demonstrates, orders, refuses, interpolates, begs, insults, persuades, insinuates. If he does so without any effect, he does not therefore become a poet; he is a writer who is talking and saying nothing. We have seen enough of language's reverse; it is now time to look at its right side.[5]

The art of prose is employed in discourse; its substance is by nature significative—that is, the words are first of all not objects but designations for objects. It is not first of all a matter of knowing whether they please or displease in themselves; it is a matter of knowing whether they correctly indicate a certain thing or a certain notion. Thus, it often happens that we find ourselves possessing a certain idea that someone has taught us by means of words without being able to recall a single one of the words which have transmitted it to us.

Prose is first of all an attitude of mind. As Valéry would say, there is prose when the word passes across our gaze as the glass across the sun. When one is in danger or in difficulty one grabs any instrument. When the danger is past, one does not even remember whether it was a hammer or a stick; moreover, one never knew; all one needed was a prolongation of one's body, a means of extending one's hand to the highest branch. It was a sixth finger, a third leg, in short, a pure function which one assimilated. Thus, regarding language, it is our shell and our antennae; it protects us against others and informs us about them; it is a prolongation of our senses, a third eye which is going to look into our neighbour's heart. We are within language as within our body. We *feel* it spontaneously while going beyond it towards other ends, as we feel our hands and our feet; we perceive it when it is someone else who is using it, as we perceive the limbs of others. There is the word which is lived and the word which is met. But in both cases it is in the course of an undertaking, either of me acting upon others, or the others upon me. The word is a certain particular moment of action and has no meaning outside it. In certain cases of aphasia the possibilities of acting, of understanding situations, and of having normal relations with the other sex, are lost.

At the heart of this apraxia the destruction of language appears only as the collapse of one of the structures, the finest and the most apparent. And if prose is never anything but the privileged instrument of a certain undertaking, if it is only the poet's business to contemplate words in a disinterested fashion, then one has the right to ask the prosewriter from the very start, 'What is your aim in writing? What undertaking are you engaged in, and why does it require you to have recourse to writing?' In any case this undertaking cannot have pure contemplation as an end. For, intuition is silence, and the end of language is to communicate. One can doubtless *pin down* the results of intuition, but in this case a few words hastily scrawled on paper will suffice; it will always be enough for the author to recognize what he had in mind. If the words are assembled into sentences, with a concern for clarity, a decision foreign to the intuition, to the language itself, must intervene, the decision of confiding to others the results obtained. In each case one must ask how this decision can be justified. And the good sense which our pedants too readily forget never stops repeating it. Are we not in the habit of putting this basic question to young people who are thinking of writing: 'Do you have anything to say?' Which means: something which is worth the trouble of being communicated. But what do we mean by something which is 'worth the trouble' if it is not by recourse to a system of transcendent values?

Moreover, to consider only this secondary structure of the undertaking, which is what the *verbal moment* is, the serious error of pure stylists is to think that the word is a gentle breeze which plays lightly over the surface of things, grazing them without altering them, and that the speaker is a pure *witness* who sums up with a word his harmless contemplation. To speak is to act; anything which one names is already no longer quite the same; it has lost its innocence.

If you name the behaviour of an individual, you reveal it to him; he sees himself. And since you are at the same time naming it to all others, he knows that he is *seen* at the moment he *sees* himself. The furtive gesture, which he forgot while making it, begins to exist enormously, to exist for everybody; it is integrated into the objective mind; it takes on new dimensions; it is retrieved. After that, how can you expect him to act in the same way? Either he will persist in his behaviour out of obstinacy and with full knowledge of what he is doing, or he will give it up. Thus, by speaking, I reveal the situation by my very intention of changing it; I reveal it to myself and to others *in order* to change it. I strike at its very heart, I transfix it, and I display it in full view; at present I dispose of it; with every word I utter, I involve myself a little more in the world, and by the same token I emerge from it a little more, since I go beyond it towards the future.

Thus, the prose-writer is a man who has chosen a certain method of secondary action which we may call action by disclosure. It is therefore permissible to ask him this second question: 'What aspect of the world do you want to disclose? What change do you want to bring into the world by this disclosure?' The 'committed' writer knows that words are action. He knows that to reveal is to change and that one can reveal only by planning to change. He has given up the impossible dream of giving an impartial picture of Society and the human condition. Man is the being towards whom no being can be impartial, not even God. For God, if He existed, would be, as certain mystics have seen Him, in a *situation* in relationship to man. And He is also the being Who cannot even see a situation without changing it, for His gaze congeals, destroys, or sculpts, or, as does eternity, changes the object in itself. It is in love, in hate, in anger, in fear, in joy, in indignation, in admiration, in hope, in despair, that man and the world reveal themselves *in their truth*. Doubtless, the committed writer can be mediocre; he can even be conscious of being so; but as one cannot write without the intention of succeeding perfectly, the modesty with which he envisages his work should not divert him from constructing it *as if* it were to have the greatest celebrity. He should never say to himself, 'Bah! I'll be lucky if I have three thousand readers,' but rather, 'What would happen if everybody read what I wrote?' He remembers what Mosca said beside the coach which carried Fabrice and Sanseverina away: 'If the word Love comes up between them, I'm lost.' He knows that he is the man who names what has not yet been named or what dares not tell its name. He knows that he makes the word 'love' and the word 'hate' *surge up* and with them love and hate between men who had not yet decided upon their feelings. He knows that words, as Brice Parain says, are 'loaded pistols'. If he speaks, he fires. He may be silent, but since he has chosen to fire, he must do it like a man, by aiming at targets, and not like a child, at random, by shutting his eyes and firing merely for the pleasure of hearing the shot go off.

Later on we shall try to determine what the goal of literature may be. But from this point on we may conclude that the writer has chosen to reveal the world and particularly to reveal man to other men so that the latter may assume full responsibility before the object which has been thus laid bare. It is assumed that no one is ignorant of the law because there is a code and because the law is written down; thereafter, you are free to violate it, but you know the risks you run. Similarly, the function of the writer is to act in such a way that nobody can be ignorant of the world and that nobody may say that he is innocent of what it's all about. And since he has once committed himself in the universe of language, he can never again pretend that he cannot speak. Once you enter the universe of meanings, there is nothing you can do to get out of it. Let words organize themselves freely and they will make sentences, and each sentence contains language in its entirety and refers back to the whole universe. Silence itself is defined in relationship to words, as the pause in music receives its meaning from the group of notes round it. This silence is a moment of language; being silent is not being dumb; it is to refuse to speak, and therefore to keep on speaking. Thus, if a writer has chosen to remain silent on any aspect whatever of the world, or, according to an expression which says just what it means, to *pass over* it in silence, one has the right to ask him a third question: 'Why have you spoken of this rather than that, and—since you speak in order to bring about change—why do you want to change this rather than that?'

All this does not prevent there being a manner of writing. One is not a writer for having chosen to say certain things, but for having chosen to say them in a certain way. And, to be sure, the style makes the value of the prose. But it should pass unnoticed. Since words are transparent and since the gaze looks through them, it would be absurd to slip in among them some panes of rough glass. Beauty is in this case only a gentle and imperceptible force. In a painting it shines forth at the very first sight; in a book it hides itself; it acts by persuasion like the charm of a voice or a face. It does not coerce; it inclines a person without his suspecting it, and he thinks that he is yielding to arguments when he is really being solicited by a charm that he does not see. The ceremonial of the Mass is not faith; it disposes. The harmony of words, their beauty, the balance of the phrases, *dispose* the passions of the reader without his being aware and order them like the Mass, like music, like the dance. If he happens to consider them by themselves, he loses the meaning; there remains only a boring seesaw of phrases.

In prose the aesthetic pleasure is pure only if it is thrown in into the bargain. I blush at recalling such simple ideas, but it seems that today they have been forgotten. If that were not the case, would we be told that we are planning the murder of literature, or, more simply, that commitment is harmful to the art of writing? If the contamination of a certain kind of prose by poetry had not confused the ideas of our critics, would they dream of attacking us on the matter of form, when we have never spoken of anything but the content? There is nothing to be said about form in advance, and we have said nothing. Everyone invents his own, and one judges it afterwards. It is true that the subjects suggest the style, but they do not order it. There are no styles ranged *a priori* outside the literary art. What is more 'committed', what is more boring, than the idea of attacking the Jesuits? Yet, out of this Pascal made his *Provincial Letters*. In short, it is a matter of knowing what one wants to write about, whether butterflies or the condition of the Jews. And when one knows, then it remains to decide how one will write about it.

Often the two choices are only one, but among good writers the second choice never precedes the first. I know that Giraudoux has said that 'the only concern is finding one's style; the idea comes afterwards'; but he was wrong. The idea did not come. On the contrary, if one considers subjects as problems which are always open, as solicitations, as expectations, it will be easily understood that art loses nothing by being committed. On the contrary, just as physics submits to mathematicians new problems which require them to produce a new symbolism, in like manner the always new requirements of the social and the metaphysical involve the artist in finding a new language and new techniques. If we no longer write as they did in the eighteenth century, it is because the language of Racine and Saint-Evremond does not lend itself to talking about locomotives or the proletariat. After that, the purists will perhaps forbid us to write about locomotives. But art has never been on the side of the purists.

If that is the principle of commitment, what objection can one have to it? And above all *what objection has been made to it*? It has seemed to me that my opponents have not had their hearts in their work very much and that their articles contain nothing more than a long scandalized sigh which drags on over two or three columns. I should have liked to know *in the name of what*, with what conception of literature, they condemned commitment. But they have not said; they themselves have not known. The most reasonable thing would have been to support their condemnation on the old theory of art for art's sake. But none of them can accept it. That is also disturbing. We know very well that pure art and empty art are the same thing and that aesthetic purism was a brilliant manœuvre of the bourgeois of the last century who preferred to see themselves denounced as philistines rather than as exploiters. Therefore, they themselves admitted that the writer had to speak about something. But about what? I believe that their embarrassment would have been extreme if Fernandez had not found for them, after the other war, the notion of the *message*. The writer of today, they say, should in no case occupy himself with temporal affairs. Neither should he set up lines without meaning, or seek only beauty of phrase and of imagery. His function is to deliver messages to his readers. Well, what is a message?

It must be borne in mind that most critics are men who have not had much luck and who, just about the time they were growing desperate, found quiet little jobs as cemetery watchmen. God knows whether cemeteries are peaceful; none of them are more cheerful than a library. The dead are there; the only thing they have done is write. They have long since been washed clean of the sin of living, and besides, their lives are known only through other books which other dead men have written about them. Rimbaud is dead. So are Paterne Berrichon and Isabelle Rimbaud. The trouble makers have disappeared; all that remains are the little coffins that are stacked on shelves along the walls like urns in a columbarium. The critic lives badly; his wife does not appreciate him as she ought to; his children are ungrateful; the first of the month is hard on him. But it is always possible for him to enter his library, take down a book from the shelf, and open it. It gives off a slight odour of the cellar, and a strange operation begins which he has decided to call reading. From one point of view it is a possession; he lends his body to the dead in order that they may come back to life. And from another point of view it is a contact with the beyond. Indeed, the book is by no means an object; neither is it an act, or even a thought. Written by a dead man about dead things, it no longer has any place on this earth; it speaks of nothing which interests us directly. Left to itself, it falls back and collapses; there remain only ink spots on musty paper. And when the critic reanimates these spots, when he makes letters and words of them, they speak to him of passions which he does not feel, of bursts of anger without objects, of dead fears and hopes. It is a whole disembodied world which surrounds him, where human feelings, because they are no longer affecting, have passed on to the status of exemplary feelings and, in short, of *values*. So he persuades himself that he has entered into relations with an intelligible world which is like the truth of his daily sufferings. And their reason for being. He thinks that nature imitates art, as for Plato the world of the senses imitates that of the archetypes. And during the time he is reading, his everyday life becomes an appearance. His nagging wife, his hunchbacked son, they too are appearances. And he will put up with them because Xenophon has drawn the portrait of Xantippe, and Shakespeare that of Richard the Third.

It is a holiday for him when contemporary authors do him the favour of dying. Their books, too raw, too living, too urgent, pass on to the other shore; they become less and less affecting and more and more beautiful. After a short stay in Purgatory they go on to people the intelligible heaven with new values. Bergotte, Swann, Siegfried and Bella, and M. Teste are recent acquisitions. He is waiting for Nathanaël and Ménalque. As for the writers who persist in living, he asks them only not to move about too much, and to make an effort to resemble from now on the dead men they will be. Valéry, who for twenty-five years had been publishing posthumous books, managed the matter very nicely. That is why, like some highly exceptional saints, he was canonized during his lifetime. But Malraux is scandalous.

Our critics are Catharists. They don't want to have anything to do with the real world except eat and drink in it, and since it is absolutely necessary to have relations with our fellow-creatures, they have chosen to have them with the defunct. They get excited only about classified matters, closed quarrels, stories whose ends are known. They never bet on uncertain issues, and since history has decided for them, since the objects which terrified or angered the authors they read have disappeared, since bloody disputes seem futile at a distance of two centuries, they can be charmed with balanced periods, and everything happens for them as if all literature were only a vast tautology and as if every new prose-writer had invented a new way of speaking only for the purpose of saying nothing.

To speak of archetypes and 'human nature'—is that speaking in order to say nothing? All the conceptions of our critics oscillate from one idea to the other. And, of course, both of them are false. Our great writers wanted to destroy, to edify, to demonstrate. But we no longer retain the proofs which they have advanced because we have no concern with what they mean to prove. The abuses which they denounced are no longer those of our time. There are others which rouse us which they did not suspect. History has given the lie to some of their predictions, and those which have been fulfilled became true so long ago that we have forgotten that at first they were flashes of their genius. Some of their thoughts are utterly dead, and there are others which the whole human race has taken up to its advantage and which we now regard as commonplace. It follows that the best arguments of these writers have lost their effectiveness. We admire only their order and rigour. Their most compact composition is in our eyes only an ornament, an elegant architecture of exposition, with no more practical application than such architectures as the fugues of Bach and the arabesques of the Alhambra.

We are still moved by the passion of these impassioned geometries when the geometry no longer convinces us. Or rather, by the representation of the passion. In the course of centuries the ideas have turned flat, but they remain the little personal objectives of a man who was once flesh and bone; behind the reasons of reason, which wither, we perceive the reasons of the heart, the virtues, the vices, and that great pain that men have in living. Sade does his best to win us over, but we hardly find him scandalous. He is no longer anything but a soul eaten by a beautiful disease, a pearl-oyster. The *Letter on the Theatre* no longer keeps anyone from going to the theatre, but we find it piquant that Rousseau detested the art of the drama. If we are a bit versed in psycho-analysis, our pleasure is perfect. We shall explain the *Social Contract* by the Oedipus complex and *The Spirit of the Laws* by the inferiority complex. That is, we shall fully enjoy the well-known superiority of live dogs to dead lions. Thus, when a book presents befuddled thoughts which have only the appearance of being reasons before melting under our scrutiny and dwindling into the beatings of a heart, when the teaching that one can draw from it is radically different from what its author intended, the book is called a message. Rousseau, the father of the French Revolution, and Gobineau, the father of racism, both sent us messages. And the critic considers them with equal sympathy. If they were alive, he would have to choose between the two, to love one and hate the other. But what brings them together, above all, is that they are both profoundly and deliciously wrong, and in the same way: they are dead.

Thus, contemporary writers should be advised to deliver messages, that is, voluntarily to limit their writing to the involuntary expression of their souls. I say involuntary because the dead, from Montaigne to Rimbaud, have portrayed themselves completely, but without having meant to—it is something they have simply thrown into the bargain. The surplus which they have given us unintentionally should be the primary and professed goal of living writers. They are not to be forced to give us confessions without any affectation, nor are they to abandon themselves to the too-naked lyricism of the romantics. But since we find pleasure in foiling the ruses of Chateaubriand or Rousseau, in surprising them in the secret places of their being at the moment they are playing at being the public man, in distinguishing the private motives from their most universal assertions, we shall ask newcomers to procure us this pleasure deliberately. So let them reason, assert, deny, refute, and prove; but the cause they are defending must be only the apparent aim of their discourse; the deeper goal is to yield themselves without seeming to do so. They must first disarm themselves of their arguments as time has done for those of the classic writers; they must bring them to bear upon subjects which interest no one or on truths so general that readers are convinced in advance. As for their ideas, they must give them an air of profundity, but with an effect of emptiness, and they must shape them in such a way that they are obviously explained by an unhappy childhood, a class hatred, or an incestuous love. Let them not presume to think in earnest; thought conceals the man, and it is the man alone who interests us. A bare tear is not lovely. It offends. A good argument also offends, as Stendhal well observed. But an argument that masks a tear —that's what we're after. The argument removes the obscenity from the tears; the tears, by revealing their origin in the passions, remove the aggressiveness from the argument. We shall be neither too deeply touched nor at all convinced, and we shall be able to yield ourselves safely to that moderate pleasure which, as everyone knows, we derive from the contemplation of works of art. Thus, this is 'true', 'pure' literature, a subjective thing which reveals itself under the aspect of the objective, a discourse so curiously contrived that it is equivalent to silence, a thought which debates with itself, a reason which is only the mask of madness, an Eternal which lets it be understood that it is only a moment of History, a historical moment which, by the hidden side which it reveals, suddenly sends back a perpetual lesson to the eternal man, but which is produced against the express wishes of those who do the teaching.

When all is said and done, the message is a soul which is made object. A soul, and what is to be done with a soul? One contemplates it at a respectful distance. It is not customary to show one's soul in society without a powerful motive. But, with certain reservations, convention permits some individuals to put theirs into commerce, and all adults may procure it for themselves. For many people today, works of the mind are thus little wandering souls which one acquires at a modest price; there is good old Montaigne's, dear La Fontaine's, and that of Jean-Jacques and of Jean-Paul and of delicious Gérard. What is called literary art is the sum of the treatments which make them inoffensive. Tanned, refined, chemically treated, they provide their acquirers with the opportunity of devoting some moments of a life completely turned outwards to the cultivation of subjectivity. Custom guarantees it to be without risk. Montaigne's scepticism? Who can take it seriously since the author of the *Essays* got frightened when the plague ravaged Bordeaux? Or Rousseau's humanitarianism, since 'Jean-Jacques' put his children into an orphanage? And the strange revelations of *Sylvie*, since Gérard de Nerval was mad? At the very most, the professional critic will set up infernal dialogues between them and will inform us that French thought is a perpetual colloquy between Pascal and Montaigne. In so doing he has no intention of making Pascal and Montaigne more alive, but of making Malraux and Gide more dead. Finally, when the internal contradictions of the life and the work have made both of them useless, when the message, in its imponderable depth, has taught us these capital truths, 'that man is neither good nor bad', 'that there is a great deal of suffering in human life', 'that genius is only great patience', this dismal bungling will have achieved its ultimate purpose, and the reader, as he lays down the book, will be able to cry out with a tranquil soul, 'All this is only literature.'

But since, for us, writing is an enterprise; since writers are alive before being dead; since we think that we must try to be as right as we can in our books; and since, even if afterwards the centuries show us to be in the wrong, this is no reason why they should prove us wrong in advance; since we think that the writer should commit himself completely in his works, and not in an abjectly passive rôle by putting forward his vices, his misfortunes, and his weaknesses, but as a resolute will and as a choice, as this total enterprise of living that each one of us is, it is then proper that we take up this problem at its beginning and that we, in our turn, ask ourselves: '*Why* does one write?'

Why Write?

ACH has his reasons: for one, art is a flight; for another
a means of conquering. But one can flee into a hermit-
age, into madness, into death. One can conquer by
arms. Why does it have to be *writing*, why does one have to
manage one's escapes and conquests by *writing*? Because,
behind the various aims of authors, there is a deeper and
more immediate choice which is common to all of us. We
shall try to elucidate this choice, and we shall see whether
it is not in the name of this very choice of writing that the
self-commitment of writers must be required.

Each of our perceptions is accompanied by the consciousness that human reality is a 'revealer', that is, it is
through human reality that 'there is' being, or, to put it
differently, that man is the means by which things are manifested. It is our presence in the world which multiplies
relations. It is we who set up a relationship between this
tree and that bit of sky. Thanks to us, that star which has
been dead for millennia, that quarter moon, and that dark
river are disclosed in the unity of a landscape. It is the speed
of our car and our aeroplane which organizes the great
masses of the earth. With each of our acts, the world reveals
to us a new face. But, if we know that we are directors of
being, we also know that we are not its producers. If we
turn away from this landscape, it will sink back into its
dark permanence. At least, it will sink back; there is no one
mad enough to think that it is going to be annihilated. It is
we who shall be annihilated, and the earth will remain in
its lethargy until another consciousness comes along to
awaken it. Thus, to our inner certainty of being 'revealers'
is added that of being inessential in relation to the thing
revealed.

One of the chief motives of artistic creation is certainly

the need of feeling that we are essential in relationship to the world. If I fix on canvas or in writing a certain aspect of the fields or the sea or a look on someone's face which I have disclosed, I am conscious of having produced them by condensing relationships, by introducing order where there was none, by imposing the unity of mind on the diversity of things. That is, I feel myself essential in relation to my creation. But this time it is the created object which escapes me; I cannot reveal and produce at the same time. The creation becomes inessential in relation to the creative activity. First of all, even if it appears finished to others, the created object always seems to us in a state of suspension; we can always change this line, that shade, that word. Thus, it never *forces itself*. A novice painter asked his teacher, 'When should I consider my painting finished?' And the teacher answered, 'When you can look at it in amazement and say to yourself *"I'm* the one who did *that!"* '

Which amounts to saying 'never'. For that would be virtually to consider one's work with someone else's eyes and to reveal what one has created. But it is self-evident that we are proportionally less conscious of the thing produced and more conscious of our productive activity. When it is a matter of pottery or carpentry, we work according to traditional patterns, with tools whose usage is codified; it is Heidegger's famous 'they' who are working with our hands. In this case, the result can seem to us sufficiently strange to preserve its objectivity in our eyes. But if we ourselves produce the rules of production, the measures, the criteria, and if our creative drive comes from the very depths of our heart, then we never find anything but ourselves in our work. It is we who have invented the laws by which we judge it. It is our history, our love, our gaiety that we recognize in it. Even if we should look at it without touching it any further, we never *receive* from it that gaiety of love. We put them into it. The results which we have obtained on canvas or paper never seem to us *objective*. We are too familiar with the processes of which they are the effects. These processes remain a subjective discovery; they are ourselves, our inspiration, our trick, and when we seek to *perceive* our work, we create it again, we repeat mentally the operations which produced it; each of its aspects appears as a result. Thus, in the perception, the object is given as the essential thing and the subject as the inessential. The latter seeks essentiality in the creation and obtains it, but then it is the object which becomes the inessential.

This dialectic is nowhere more apparent than in the art of writing, for the literary object is a peculiar top which exists only in movement. To make it come into view a concrete act called reading is necessary, and it lasts only as long as this act can last. Beyond that, there are only black marks on paper. Now, the writer cannot read what he writes, whereas the shoemaker can put on the shoes he has just made if they are his size, and the architect can live in the house he has built. In reading, one foresees; one waits. One foresees the end of the sentence, the following sentence, the next page. One waits for them to confirm or disappoint one's foresights. The reading is composed of a host of hypotheses, of dreams followed by awakenings, of hopes and deceptions. Readers are always ahead of the sentence they are reading in a merely probable future which partly collapses and partly comes together in proportion as they progress, which withdraws from one page to the next and forms the moving horizon of the literary object. Without waiting, without a future, without ignorance, there is no objectivity.

Now the operation of writing involves an implicit quasi-reading which makes real reading impossible. When the words form under his pen, the author doubtless sees them, but he does not see them as the reader does, since he knows them before writing them down. The function of his gaze is not to reveal, by brushing against them, the sleeping words which are waiting to be read, but to control the sketching of the signs. In short, it is a purely regulating mission, and the view before him reveals nothing except for slight slips of the pen. The writer neither foresees nor conjectures; he *projects*. It often happens that he awaits, as they say, the inspiration. But one does not wait for oneself the way one waits for others. If he hesitates, he knows that the future is not made, that he himself is going to make it, and if he still does not know what is going to happen to his hero, that simply means that he has not thought about it, that he has not decided upon anything. The future is then a blank page, whereas the future of the reader is two hundred pages filled with words which separate him from the end. Thus, the writer meets everywhere only *his* knowledge, *his* will, *his* plans, in short, himself. He touches only his own subjectivity; the object he creates is out of reach; he does not create it *for himself*. If he re-reads himself, it is already too late. The sentence will never quite be a thing in his eyes. He goes to the very limits of the subjective but without crossing it. He appreciates the effect of a touch, of an epi-gram, of a well-placed adjective, but it is the effect they will have on others. He can judge it, not feel it. Proust never discovered the homosexuality of Charlus, since he had decided upon it even before starting on his book. And if a day comes when the book takes on for its author a sem-blance of objectivity, it is because years have passed, because he has forgotten it, because its spirit is quite foreign to him, and doubtless he is no longer capable of writing it. This was the case with Rousseau when he re-read the *Social Contract* at the end of his life.

Thus, it is not true that one writes for oneself. That would be the worst blow. In projecting one's emotions on paper, one barely manages to give them a languid extension. The creative act is only an incomplete and abstract moment in the production of a work. If the author existed alone he would be able to write as much as he liked; the work as *object* would never see the light of day and he would either have to put down his pen or despair. But the operation of writing implies that of reading as its dialectical correlative and these two connected acts necessitate two distinct agents. It is the joint effort of author and reader which brings upon the scene that concrete and imaginary object which is the work of the mind. There is no art except for and by others.

Reading seems, in fact, to be the synthesis of perception and creation.[6] It posits the essentiality of both the subject and the object. The object is essential because it is strictly transcendent, because it imposes its own structures, and because one must wait for it and observe it; but the subject is also essential because it is required not only to disclose the object (that is, to make it possible for there to *be* an object) but also so that this object might exist absolutely (that is, to produce it). In a word, the reader is conscious of disclosing in creating, of creating by disclosing. In reality, it is not necessary to believe that reading is a mechanical operation and that signs make an impression upon him as light does on a photographic plate. If he is inattentive, tired, stupid, or thoughtless, most of the relations will escape him. The object will never 'catch' with him (in the sense in which we say that fire 'catches' or 'doesn't catch'). He will draw some phrases out of the shadow, but they will seem to have appeared at random. If he is at his best, he will project beyond the words a synthetic form, each phrase of which will be no more than a partial function: the 'theme', the 'subject', or the 'meaning'. Thus, from the very beginning, the meaning is no longer contained in the words, since it is he, on the contrary, who allows the significance of each of them to be understood; and the literary object, though realized *through* language, is never given *in* language. On the contrary, it is by nature a silence and an opponent of the word. In addition, the hundred thousand words aligned in a book can be read one by one so that the meaning of the work does not emerge. Nothing is accomplished if the reader does not put himself from the very beginning and almost without a guide at the height of this silence; if, in short, he does not invent it and does not then place there, and hold on to, the words and sentences which he awakens. And if I am told that it would be more fitting to call this operation a re-invention or a discovery, I shall answer that, first, such a re-invention would be as new and as original an act as the first invention. And, especially, when an object has never existed before, there can be no question of re-inventing it or discovering it. For if the silence about which I am speaking is really the goal at which the author is aiming, he has, at least, never been familiar with it; his silence is subjective and anterior to language. It is the absence of words, the undifferentiated and lived silence of inspiration, which the word will then particularize, whereas the silence produced by the reader is an object. And at the very interior of this object there are more silences—which the author does not mention. It is a question of silences which are so particular that they could not retain any meaning outside the object which the reading causes to appear. However, it is these which give it its density and its particular face.

To say that they are unexpressed is hardly the word; for they are precisely the inexpressible. And that is why one does not come upon them at any definite moment in the reading; they are everywhere and nowhere. The quality of the marvellous in *Le Grand Meaulnes*, the grandioseness of *Armance*, the degree of realism and truth of Kafka's mythology, these are never given. The reader must invent them all in a continual exceeding of the written thing. To be sure, the author guides him, but all he does is guide him. The landmarks he sets up are separated by the void. The reader must unite them; he must go beyond them. In short, reading is directed creation.

On the one hand, the literary object has no other substance than the reader's subjectivity; Raskolnikov's waiting is *my* waiting which I lend him. Without this impatience of the reader he would remain only a collection of signs. His hatred of the police magistrate who questions him is my hatred which has been solicited and wheedled out of me by signs, and the police magistrate himself would not exist without the hatred I have for him via Raskolnikov. That is what animates him, it is his very flesh.

But on the other hand, the words are there like traps to arouse our feelings and to reflect them towards us. Each word is a path of transcendence; it shapes our feelings, names them, and attributes them to an imaginary personage who takes it upon himself to live them for us and who has no other substance than these borrowed passions; he confers objects, perspectives, and a horizon upon them.

Thus, for the reader, all is to do and all is already done; the work exists only at the exact level of his capacities; while he reads and creates, he knows that he can always go further in his reading, can always create more profoundly, and thus the work seems to him as inexhaustible and opaque as things. We would readily reconcile that 'rational intuition' which Kant reserved to divine Reason with this absolute production of qualities, which, to the extent that they emanate from our subjectivity, congeal before our eyes into impenetrable objectivities.

Since the creation can find its fulfilment only in reading, since the artist must entrust to another the job of carrying out what he has begun, since it is only through the consciousness of the reader that he can regard himself as essential to his work, all literary work is an appeal. To write is to make an appeal to the reader that he lead into objective existence the revelation which I have undertaken by means of language. And if it should be asked *to what* the writer is appealing, the answer is simple. As the sufficient reason for the appearance of the aesthetic object is never found either in the book (where we find merely solicitations to produce the object) or in the author's mind, and as his subjectivity, which he cannot get away from, cannot give a reason for the act of leading into objectivity, the appearance of the work of art is a new event which cannot *be explained* by anterior data. And since this directed creation is an absolute beginning, it is therefore brought about by the freedom of the reader, and by what is purest in that freedom. Thus, the writer appeals to the reader's freedom to collaborate in the production of his work.

It will doubtless be said that all tools address themselves to our freedom since they are the instruments of a possible action, and that the work of art is not unique in that. And it is true that the tool is the congealed outline of an operation. But it remains on the level of the hypothetical imperative. I may use a hammer to nail up a case or to hit my neighbour over the head. In so far as I consider it in itself, it is not an appeal to my freedom; it does not put me face to face with it; rather, it aims at using it by substituting a set succession of traditional procedures for the free invention of means. The book does not serve my freedom; it requires it. Indeed, one cannot address oneself to freedom as such by means of constraint, fascination, or entreaties. There is only one way of attaining it: first, by recognizing it, then, by having confidence in it, and finally, by requiring of it an act, an act in its own name—that is, in the name of the confidence that one brings to it.

Thus, the book is not, like the tool, a means for any end whatever; the end to which it offers itself is the reader's freedom. And the Kantian expression 'finality without end' seems to me quite inappropriate for designating the work of art. In fact, it implies that the aesthetic object presents only the appearance of a finality and is limited to soliciting the free and ordered play of the imagination. It forgets that the imagination of the spectator has not only a regulating function, but a constitutive one. It does not play; it is called upon to recompose the beautiful object beyond the traces left by the artist. The imagination cannot revel in itself any more than can the other functions of the mind; it is always on the outside, always engaged in an enterprise. There would be finality without end if some object offered such a well-arranged composition that it would lead us to suppose that it has an end even though we cannot ascribe one to it. By defining the beautiful in this way one can—and this is Kant's aim—liken the beauty of art to natural beauty, since a flower, for example, presents so much symmetry, such harmonious colours, and such regular curves, that one is immediately tempted to seek a finalist explanation for all these properties and to see them as just so many means at the disposal of an unknown end. But that is exactly the error. The beauty of nature is in no way comparable to that of art. The work of art *does not have* an end; there we agree with Kant. But the reason is that it *is* an end. The Kantian formula does not account for the appeal which resounds at the basis of each painting, each statue, each book. Kant believes that the work of art first exists as fact and that it is then seen. Whereas it exists only if one *looks* at it and if it is first pure appeal, pure exigence to exist. It is not an instrument whose existence is manifest and whose end is undetermined. It presents itself as a task to be discharged; from the very beginning it places itself on the level of the categorical imperative. You are perfectly free to leave that book on the table. But if you open it, you assume responsibility for it. For freedom is experienced not in the enjoyment of free subjective functioning, but in a creative act required by an imperative. The absolute end, this imperative which is transcendent yet acquiesced in, which freedom itself adopts as its own, is what we call a value. The work of art is a value because it is an appeal.

If I appeal to my reader so that we may carry to a successful conclusion the enterprise which I have begun, it is self-evident that I consider him as a pure freedom, as an unconditioned activity; thus, in no case can I address myself to his passiveness, that is, try to *affect* him, to communicate to him, from the very first, emotions of fear, desire, or anger. There are, doubtless, authors who concern themselves solely with arousing these emotions because they are foreseeable, manageable, and because they have at their disposal sure-fire means for provoking them. But it is also true that they are reproached for this kind of thing, as Euripides has been since antiquity because he had children appear on the stage. Freedom is alienated in the state of passion; it is abruptly engaged in partial enterprises; it loses sight of its task, which is to produce an absolute end. And the book is no longer anything but a means for feeding hate or desire. The writer should not seek to *overwhelm*; otherwise he is in contradiction with himself; if he wishes to *make demands* he must propose only the task to be fulfilled.

Hence, the character of pure presentation which appears essential to the work of art. The reader must be able to make a certain aesthetic withdrawal. This is what Gautier foolishly confused with 'art for art's sake' and the Parnassians with the imperturbability of the artist. It is simply a matter of precaution, and Genet more justly calls it the author's politeness towards the reader. But that does not mean that the writer makes an appeal to some sort of abstract and conceptual freedom. One certainly creates the aesthetic object with feelings; if it is touching, it appears through our tears; if it is comic, it will be recognized by laughter. However, these feelings are of a particular kind. They have their origin in freedom; they are loaned. The belief which I accord the tale is freely assented to. It is a Passion, in the Christian sense of the word, that is, a freedom which resolutely puts itself into a state of passiveness to obtain a certain transcendent effect by this sacrifice. The reader renders himself credulous; he descends into credulity which, though it ends by enclosing him like a dream, is at every moment conscious of being free. An effort is sometimes made to force the writer into this dilemma: 'Either one believes in your story, and it is intolerable, or one does not believe in it, and it is ridiculous'. But the argument is absurd because the characteristic of aesthetic consciousness is to be a belief by means of commitment, by oath, a belief sustained by fidelity to one's self and to the author, a perpetually renewed choice to believe. I can awaken at every moment, and I know it; but I do not want to; reading is a free dream. So that all feelings which are exacted on the basis of this imaginary belief are like particular modulations of my freedom. Far from absorbing or masking it, they are so many different ways it has chosen to reveal itself to itself. Raskolnikov, as I have said, would only be a shadow, without the mixture of repulsion and friendship which I feel for him and which makes him live. But, by a reversal which is the characteristic of the imaginary object, it is not his behaviour which excites my indignation or esteem, but my indignation and esteem which give consistency and objectivity to his behaviour. Thus, the reader's feelings are never dominated by the object, and as no external reality can condition them, they have their permanent source in freedom; that is, they are all generous —for I call a feeling generous which has its origin and its end in freedom. Thus, reading is an exercise in generosity, and what the writer requires of the reader is not the application of an abstract freedom but the gift of his whole person, with his passions, his prepossessions, his sympathies, his sexual temperament, and his scale of values. Only this person will give himself generously; freedom goes through and through him and comes to transform the darkest masses of his sensibility. And just as activity has rendered itself passive in order for it better to create the object, conversely, passiveness becomes an act; the man who is reading has raised himself to the highest degree. That is why we see people who are known for their toughness shed tears at the recital of imaginary misfortunes; for the moment, they have become what they would have been if they had not spent their lives hiding their freedom from themselves.

Thus, the author writes in order to address himself to the freedom of readers, and he requires it in order to make his work exist. But he does not stop there; he also requires that they return this confidence which he has given them, that they recognize his creative freedom, and that they in turn solicit it by a symmetrical and inverse appeal. Here there appears the other dialectical paradox of reading; the more we experience our freedom, the more we recognize that of the other; the more he demands of us, the more we demand of him.

When I am enchanted with a landscape, I know very well that it is not I who create it, but I also know that without me the relations which are established before my eyes among the trees, the foliage, the earth, and the grass would not exist at all. I know that I can give no reason for the appearance of finality which I discover in the assortment of hues and in the harmony of the forms and movements created by the wind. Yet, it exists; there it is before my eyes, and I can make something more out of what is already there. But even if I believe in God, I cannot establish any passage, unless it be purely verbal, between the divine, universal solicitude and the particular spectacle which I am considering. To say that He made the landscape in order to charm me or that He made me the kind of person who is pleased by it is to take a question for an answer. Is the marriage of this blue and that green deliberate? How can I know? The idea of a universal providence is no guarantee of any particular intention, especially in the case under consideration, since the green of the grass is explained by biological laws, specific constants, and geographical determinism, while the reason for the blue of the water is accounted for by the depth of the river, the nature of the soil and the swiftness of the current. The assorting of the shades, if it is willed, can only be something *thrown into the bargain*; it is the meeting of two causal series, that is to say, at first sight, a fact of chance. At best, the finality remains problematic. All the relations we establish remain hypotheses; no end is proposed to us in the manner of an imperative, since none is expressly revealed as having been willed by a creator. Thus, our freedom is never *called forth* by natural beauty. Or rather, there is an appearance of order in the whole which includes the foliage, the forms, and the movements, hence, the illusion of a calling forth which seems to solicit this freedom and which disappears immediately when one looks at it. Hardly have we begun to run our eyes over this arrangement, than the appeal disappears; we remain alone, free to tie one colour with another or with a third, to set up a relationship between the tree and the water, or between the tree and the sky, or between the tree, the water, and the sky. My freedom becomes caprice. To the extent that I establish new relationships, I remove myself further from the illusory objectivity which solicits me. I *muse* about certain motifs which are vaguely outlined by the things; the natural reality is no longer anything but a pretext for musing. Or, in that case, because I have deeply regretted that this arrangement which was momentarily perceived was not offered to me by somebody and consequently is not *real,* the result is that I fix my dream, that I transpose it to canvas or in writing. Thus, I interpose myself between the finality without end which appears in the natural spectacles and the gaze of other men. I transmit it to them. It becomes human by this transmission. Art here is a ceremony of the *gift*, and the gift alone brings about the metamorphosis. It is something like the transmission of titles and powers in the matriarchate, where the mother does not possess the names but is the indispensable intermediary between uncle and nephew. Since I have captured this illusion in flight, since I lay it out for other men and have disentangled it and rethought it for them, they can consider it with confidence. It has become intentional. As for me, I remain, to be sure, at the border of the subjective and the objective without ever being able to contemplate the objective arrangement which I transmit.

The reader, on the contrary, progresses in security. However far he may go, the author has gone further. Whatever connections he may establish among the different parts of the book—among the chapters or the words—he has a guarantee, namely, that they have been expressly willed. As Descartes says, he can even pretend that there is a secret order among parts which seem to have no connection. The creator has preceded him along the way, and the most beautiful disorders are effects of art, that is, again order. Reading is induction, interpolation, extrapolation, and the basis of these activities rests on the reader's will, as for a long time it was believed that that of scientific induction rested on the divine will. A gentle force accompanies us and supports us from the first page to the last. That does not mean that we fathom the artist's intentions easily. They constitute, as we have said, the object of conjectures, and there is an *experience* of the reader; but these conjectures are supported by the great certainty we have that the beauties which appear in the book are never accidental. In nature, the tree and the sky harmonize only by chance; if, on the contrary, in the novel, the protagonists find themselves in a *certain* tower, in a *certain* prison, if they stroll in a *certain* garden, it is a matter both of the restitution of independent causal series (the character had a certain state of mind which was due to a succession of psychological and social events; on the other hand, he betook himself to a determined place and the layout of the city required him to cross a certain park) and of the expression of a deeper finality, for the park came into existence only *in order to* harmonize with a certain state of mind, to express it by means of things or to put it into relief by a vivid contrast, and the state of mind itself was conceived in connection with the landscape. Here it is causality which is appearance and which might be called 'causality without cause', and it is the finality which is the profound reality. But if I can thus in all confidence put the order of ends under the order of causes, it is because by opening the book I am asserting that the object has its source in human freedom.

If I were to suspect the artist of having written out of passion and in passion, my confidence would immediately vanish, for it would serve no purpose to have supported the order of causes by the order of ends. The latter would be supported in its turn by a psychic causality and the work of art would end by re-entering the chain of determinism. Certainly I do not deny when I am reading that the author may be impassioned, nor even that he might have conceived the first plan of his work under the sway of passion. But his decision to write supposes that he withdraws somewhat from his feelings, in short, that he has transformed his emotions into free emotions as I do mine while reading him, that is, that he is in an attitude of generosity.

Thus, reading is a pact of generosity between author and reader. Each one trusts the other; each one counts on the other, demands of the other as much as he demands of himself. For this confidence is itself generosity. Nothing can force the author to believe that his reader will use his freedom; nothing can force the reader to believe that the author has used his. Both of them make a free decision.

There is then established a dialectical going-and-coming; when I read, I make demands; if my demands are met, what I am then reading provokes me to demand more of the author, which means to demand of the author that he demand more of me. And, vice versa, the author's demand is that I carry my demands to the highest pitch. Thus, my freedom, by revealing itself, reveals the freedom of the other.

It matters little whether the aesthetic object is the product of 'realistic' art (or supposedly such) or 'formal' art. At any rate, the natural relations are inverted; that tree in the foreground of the Cézanne painting appears initially as the product of a causal chain. But the causality is an illusion; it will doubtless remain as a proposition as long as we look at the painting, but it will be supported by a deep finality; if the tree is placed in such a way it is because the rest of the painting *requires* that this form and those colours be placed in the foreground. Thus, through the phenomenal causality, our gaze attains finality as the deep structure of the object, and, beyond finality, it attains human freedom as its source and original basis. Vermeer's realism is carried so far that at first it might be thought to be photographic. But if one considers the splendour of his texture, the pink and velvety glory of his little brick walls, the blue thickness of a branch of woodbine, the glazed darkness of his vestibules, the orange-coloured flesh of his faces, which are as polished as the stone of holy-water basins, one suddenly feels, in the pleasure that he experiences, that the finality is not so much in the forms or colours as in his material imagination. It is the very substance and temper of the things which here give the forms their reason for being. With this realist we are perhaps closest to absolute creation, since it is in the very passiveness of the matter that we meet the unfathomable freedom of man.

The work is never limited to the painted, sculpted, or narrated object. Just as one perceives things only against the background of the world, so the objects represented by art appear against the background of the universe. In the background of Fabrice's adventures are the Italy of 1820, Austria, France, the sky and stars which the Abbé Blanis consults, and finally the whole earth. If the painter presents us with a field or a vase of flowers, his paintings are windows that open onto the whole world. We follow the red path which is buried among the wheat much farther than Van Gogh has painted it, among other wheat fields, under other clouds, to the river which empties into the sea, and we extend to infinity, to the other end of the world, the deep finality which supports the existence of the field and the earth. So that, through the various objects which it produces or reproduces, the creative act aims at a total renewal of the world. Each painting, each book, is a recovery of the totality of being. Each of them presents this totality to the freedom of the spectator. For this is quite the final goal of art: to recover this world by giving it to be seen as it is, but as if it had its source in human freedom. But, since what the author creates takes on objective reality only in the eyes of the spectator, this recovery is consecrated by the ceremony of the spectacle—and particularly of reading. We are already in a better position to answer the question we raised a while ago: the writer chooses to appeal to the freedom of other men so that, by the reciprocal implications of their demands, they may re-adapt the totality of being to man and may again enclose the universe within man.

If we wish to go still further, we must bear in mind that the writer, like all other artists, aims at giving his reader a certain feeling that is customarily called aesthetic pleasure, and which I would very much rather call aesthetic joy, and that this feeling, when it appears, is a sign that the work is achieved. It is therefore fitting to examine it in the light of the preceding considerations. In effect, this joy, which is denied to the creator, in so far as he creates, becomes one with the aesthetic consciousness of the spectator, that is, in the case under consideration, of the reader. It is a complex feeling but one whose structures and condition are inseparable from one another. It is identical, at first, with the recognition of a transcendent and absolute end which,

for a moment, suspends the utilitarian round of ends-means
and means-ends,[7] that is, of an appeal or, what amounts
to the same thing, of a value. And the positional consciousness which I take of this value is necessarily accompanied
by the non-positional consciousness of my freedom, since
my freedom is manifested to itself by a transcendent exigency. The recognition of freedom by itself is joy, but this
structure of non-thetical consciousness implies another:
since, in effect, reading is creation, my freedom does not
only appear to itself as pure autonomy but as creative
activity, that is, it is not limited to giving itself its own law
but perceives itself as being constitutive of the object. It is
on this level that the phenomenon specifically is manifested,
that is, a creation wherein the created object is given *as
object* to its creator. It is the sole case in which the creator
gets any enjoyment out of the object he creates. And the
word enjoyment which is applied to the positional consciousness of the work read indicates sufficiently that we
are in the presence of an essential structure of aesthetic joy.
This positional enjoyment is accompanied by the non-
positional consciousness of being essential in relation to an
object perceived as essential. I shall call this aspect of
aesthetic consciousness the feeling of security; it is this
which stamps the strongest aesthetic emotions with a sovereign calm. It has its origin in the authentication of a strict
harmony between subjectivity and objectivity. As, on the
other hand, the aesthetic object is properly the world in so
far as it is aimed at through the imaginary, aesthetic joy
accompanies the positional consciousness that the world is
a value, that is, a task proposed to human freedom. I shall
call this the aesthetic modification of the human project,
for, as usual, the world appears as the horizon of our situation, as the infinite distance which separates us from ourselves, as the synthetic totality of the given, as the undifferentiated whole of obstacles and implements—but never
as a demand addressed to our freedom. Thus, aesthetic joy
proceeds to this level of the consciousness which I take of
recovering and internalizing that which is non-ego *par*

excellence, since I transform the given into an imperative and the fact into a value. The world is *my task*, that is, the essential and freely accepted function of my freedom is to make that unique and absolute object which is the universe come into being in an unconditioned movement. And, thirdly, the preceding structures imply a pact between human freedoms, for, on the one hand, reading is a confident and exacting recognition of the freedom of the writer, and, on the other hand, aesthetic pleasure, as it is itself experienced in the form of a value, involves an absolute exigence in regard to others; every man, in so far as he is a freedom, feels the same pleasure in reading the same work. Thus, all mankind is present in its highest freedom; it sustains the being of a world which is both *its* world and the 'external' world. In aesthetic joy the positional consciousness is an *image-making* consciousness of the world in its totality both as being and having to be, both as totally ours and totally foreign, and the more ours as it is the more foreign. The non-positional consciousness *really* envelops the harmonious totality of human freedoms in so far as it makes the object of a universal confidence and exigency.

To write is thus both to disclose the world and to offer it as a task to the generosity of the reader. It is to have recourse to the consciousness of others in order to make one's self be recognized as *essential* to the totality of being; it is to wish to live this essentiality by means of interposed persons; but, on the other hand, as the real world is revealed only by action, as one can feel oneself in it only by exceeding it in order to change it, the novelist's universe would lack depth if it were not discovered in a movement to transcend it. It has often been observed that an object in a story does not derive its density of existence from the number and length of the descriptions devoted to it, but from the complexity of its connections with the different characters. The more often the characters handle it, take it up, and put it down, in short, go beyond it towards their own ends, the more real will it appear. Thus, of the world of the novel, that is, the totality of men and things, we may say that in order for it to offer its maximum density the disclosure-creation by which the reader discovers it must also be an imaginary participation in the action; in other words, the more disposed one is to change it, the more alive it will be. The error of realism has been to believe that the real reveals itself to contemplation, and that consequently one could draw an impartial picture of it. How could that be possible, since the very perception is partial, since by itself the naming is already a modification of the object? And how could the writer, who wants himself to be essential to this universe, want to be essential to the injustice which this universe comprehends? Yet, he must be; but if he accepts being the creator of injustices, it is in a movement which goes beyond them towards their abolition. As for me who read, if I create and keep alive an unjust world, I cannot help making myself responsible for it. And the author's whole art is bent on obliging me to *create* what he *discloses*, therefore to compromise myself. So both of us bear the responsibility for the universe. And precisely because this universe is supported by the joint effort of our two freedoms, and because the author, with me as medium, has attempted to integrate it into the human, it must appear truly *in itself*, in its very marrow, as being shot through and through with a freedom which has taken human freedom as its end, and if it is not really the city of ends that it ought to be, it must at least be a stage along the way; in a word, it must be a becoming and it must always be considered and presented not as a crushing mass which weighs us down, but from the point of view of its going beyond towards that city of ends. However bad and hopeless the humanity which it paints may be, the work must have an air of generosity. Not, of course, that this generosity is to be expressed by means of edifying discourses and virtuous characters; it must not even be premeditated, and it is quite true that fine sentiments do not make fine books. But it must be the very warp and woof of the book, the stuff out of which the people and things are cut; whatever the subject, a sort of essential lightness must appear everywhere and remind us that the work is never a natural datum, but an *exigence* and a *gift*. And if I am given this world with its injustices, it is not so that I may contemplate them coldly, but that I may animate them with my indignation, that I may disclose them and create them with their nature as injustices, that is, as abuses to be suppressed. Thus, the writer's universe will only reveal itself in all its depth to the examination, the admiration, and the indignation of the reader; and the generous love is a promise to maintain, and the generous indignation is a promise to change, and the admiration a promise to imitate; although literature is one thing and morality a quite different one, at the heart of the aesthetic imperative we discern the moral imperative. For, since the one who writes recognizes, by the very fact that he takes the trouble to write, the freedom of his readers, and since the one who reads, by the mere fact of his opening the book, recognizes the freedom of the writer, the work of art, from whichever side you approach it, is an act of confidence in the freedom of men. And since readers, like the author, recognize this freedom only to demand that it manifest itself, the work can be defined as an imaginary presentation of the world in so far as it demands human freedom. The result of which is that there is no 'gloomy literature', since, however dark may be the colours in which one paints the world, one paints it only so that free men may feel their freedom as they face it. Thus, there are only good and bad novels. The bad novel aims to please by flattering, whereas the good one is an exigence and an act of faith. But above all, the unique point of view from which the author can present the world to those freedoms whose concurrence he wishes to bring about is that of a world to be impregnated always with more freedom. It would be inconceivable that this unleashing of generosity provoked by the writer could be used to authorize an injustice, and that the reader could enjoy his freedom while reading a work which approves or accepts or simply abstains from condemning the subjection of man by man. One can imagine a good novel being written by an American negro even if hatred of the whites were spread all over it, because it is the freedom of his race that he demands through this hatred. And, as he invites me to assume the attitude of generosity, the moment I feel myself a pure freedom I cannot bear to identify myself with a race of oppressors. Thus, I require of all freedoms that they demand the liberation of coloured people against the white race and against myself in so far as I am a part of it, but nobody can suppose for a moment that it is possible to write a good novel in praise of anti-Semitism.[8] For, the moment I feel that my freedom is indissolubly linked with that of all other men, it cannot be demanded of me that I use it to approve the enslavement of a part of these men. Thus, whether he is an essayist, a pamphleteer, a satirist, or a novelist, whether he speaks only of individual passions or whether he attacks the social order, the writer, a free man addressing free men, has only one subject—freedom.

Hence, any attempt to enslave his readers threatens him in his very art. A blacksmith can be affected by fascism in his life as a man, but not necessarily in his craft; a writer will be affected in both, and even more in his craft than in his life. I have seen writers, who before the war called for fascism with all their hearts, smitten with sterility at the very moment when the Nazis were loading them with honours. I am thinking of Drieu la Rochelle in particular; he was mistaken, but he was sincere. He proved it. He had agreed to direct a Nazi-inspired review. The first few months he reprimanded, rebuked, and lectured his countrymen. No one answered him because no one was free to do so. He became irritated; he no longer *felt* his readers. He became more insistent, but no sign appeared to prove that he had been understood. No sign of hatred, nor of anger either; nothing. He seemed to have lost his bearings, the victim of a growing distress. He complained bitterly to the Germans. His articles had been superb; they became shrill. The moment arrived when he struck his breast; no echo, except among the bought journalists whom he despised. He handed in his resignation, withdrew it, again spoke, still in the desert. Finally, he said nothing, gagged by the silence of others. He had demanded the enslavement of others, but in his crazy mind he must have imagined that it was voluntary, that it was still free. It came; the man in him congratulated himself mightily, but the writer could not bear it. While this was going on, others, who, happily, were in the majority, understood that the freedom of writing implies the freedom of the citizen. One does not write for slaves. The art of prose is bound up with the only régime in which prose has meaning, democracy. When one is threatened, the other is too. And it is not enough to defend them with the pen. A day comes when the pen is forced to stop, and the writer must then take up arms. Thus, however you might have come to it, whatever the opinions you might have professed, literature throws you into battle. Writing is a certain way of wanting freedom; once you have begun, you are committed, willy-nilly.

Committed to what? Defending freedom? That's easy to say. Is it a matter of acting as a guardian of ideal values like Benda's 'clerk' before the betrayal,* or is it concrete everyday freedom which must be protected by our taking sides in political and social struggles? The question is tied up with another one, one very simple in appearance but which nobody ever asks himself: 'For whom does one write?'

---

* The reference here is to Benda's *La Trahison des clercs*, translated into English as *The Great Betrayal.*—*Translator.*

For Whom
Does One Write?

Aᴛ first sight, there doesn't seem to be any doubt: one
writes for the universal reader, and we have seen,
in effect, that the exigency of the writer is, as a rule,
addressed to *all* men. But the preceding descriptions are
ideal. As a matter of fact the writer knows that he speaks
for freedoms which are swallowed up, masked, and unavail-
able; and his own freedom is not so pure; he has to clean it.
It is dangerously easy to speak too readily about eternal
values; eternal values are very, very fleshless. Even freedom,
if one considers it *sub specie aeternitatis*, seems to be a
withered branch; for, like the sea, there is no end to it. It is
nothing else but the movement by which one perpetually
uproots and liberates oneself. There is no given freedom.
One must win an inner victory over one's passions, one's
race, one's class, and one's nation and must conquer other
men along with oneself. But what counts in this case is the
particular form of the obstacle to be surmounted, of the
resistance to be overcome. That is what gives form to freedom
in each circumstance. If the writer has chosen, as Benda has
it, to talk drivel, he can speak in fine, rolling periods of that
eternal freedom which National Socialism, Stalinist communism, and the capitalist democracies all lay claim to. He
won't disturb anybody; he won't address anybody. Everything he asks for is granted him in advance. But it is an
abstract dream. Whether he wants to or not, and even if he
has his eyes on eternal laurels, the writer is speaking to his
contemporaries and brothers of his class and race.

As a matter of fact, it has not been sufficiently observed
that a work of the mind is by nature *allusive*. Even if the
author's aim is to give the fullest possible representation of
his object, there is never any question as to whether he is
telling *everything*. He knows far more than he tells. This is

so because language is elliptical. If I want to let my neighbour know that a wasp has got in by the window, there is
no need for a long speech. 'Look out!' or 'Hey!'—a word
is enough, a gesture—as soon as he sees the wasp, everything
is clear. Imagine a gramophone record reproducing for us,
without comment, the everyday conversations of a house-
hold in Provins or Angoulême—we wouldn't understand a
thing; the *context* would be lacking, that is, memories and
perceptions in common, the situation and the enterprises of
the couple; in short, the world such as each of the speakers
knows it to appear to the other.

The same with reading: people of the same period and
community, who have lived through the same events, who
have raised or avoided the same questions, have the same
taste in their mouth; they have the same complicity, and
there are the same corpses among them. That is why it is
not necessary to write so much; there are key-words. If I
were to tell an audience of Americans about the German
occupation, there would have to be a great deal of analysis
and precaution. I would waste twenty pages in dispelling
preconceptions, prejudices, and legends. Afterwards, I
would have to be sure of my position at every step; I
would have to look for images and symbols in American
history which would enable them to understand ours; I
would always have to keep in mind the difference between
our old man's pessimism and their childlike optimism. If I
were to write about the same subject for Frenchmen, we
would be *entre nous*. For example, it would be enough to say:
'A concert of German military music in the band-stand of a
public garden.' Everything is there: a raw spring day, a park
in the provinces, men with shaven skulls blowing away at
their brasses, blind and deaf passers-by who quicken their
steps, two or three sullen-looking listeners under the trees,
this useless serenade to France which drifts off into the sky,
our shame and our anguish, our anger, and our pride too.
Thus, the reader I am addressing is neither Micromégas nor
L'Ingénu; nor is he God the Father either. He has not the
ignorance of the noble savage to whom everything has to be

explained on the basis of principles; he is not a spirit or a *tabula rasa*. Neither has he the omniscience of an angel or of the Eternal Father. I reveal certain aspects of the universe to him; I take advantage of what he knows to attempt to teach him what he does not know. Suspended between total ignorance and omniscience, he has a definite stock of knowledge which varies from moment to moment and which is enough to reveal his *historical* character. In actual fact, he is not an instantaneous consciousness, a pure timeless affirmation of freedom, nor does he soar above history; he is involved in it.

Authors too are historical. And that is precisely the reason why some of them want to escape from history by a leap into eternity. The book, serving as a go-between, establishes an historical contact among the men who are steeped in the same history and who likewise contribute to its making. Writing and reading are two facets of the same historical fact, and the freedom to which the writer invites us is not a pure abstract consciousness of being free. Strictly speaking, it *is not*; it wins itself in an historical situation; each book proposes a concrete liberation on the basis of a particular alienation. Hence, in each one there is an implicit recourse to institutions, customs, certain forms of oppression and conflict, to the wisdom and the folly of the day, to lasting passions and passing stubbornness, to superstitions and recent victories of common sense, to evidence and ignorance, to particular modes of reasoning which the sciences have made fashionable and which are applied in all domains, to hopes, to fears, to habits of sensibility, imagination, and even perception, and finally, to customs and values which have been handed down, to a whole world which the author and the reader have in common. It is this familiar world which the writer animates and penetrates with his freedom. It is on the basis of this world that the reader must bring about his concrete liberation; it is alienation, situation, and history. It is this world which I must change or preserve for myself and others. For if the immediate aspect of freedom is negativity, we know that it is not a matter of the abstract power of saying no, but of a concrete negativity which retains within itself (and is completely coloured by) what it denies. And since the freedoms of the author and reader seek and affect each other through a world, it can just as well be said that the author's choice of a certain aspect of the world determines the reader and, vice versa, that it is by choosing his reader that the author decides upon his subject.

Thus, all works of the mind contain within themselves the image of the reader for whom they are intended. I could draw the portrait of Gide's Nathanaël on the basis of *Fruits of the Earth*: I can see that the alienation from which he is urged to free himself is the family, the property he owns or will own by inheritance, the utilitarian project, a conventional morality, a narrow theism; I also see that he is cultured and has leisure, since it would be absurd to offer Ménalque as an example to an unskilled labourer, a man out of work, or an American negro; I know that he is not threatened by any external danger—by hunger, war, or class or racial oppression; the only danger is that of being the victim of his own milieu. Therefore, he is a rich white Aryan, the heir of a great bourgeois family that lives in a period which is still relatively stable and easy, in which the ideology of the possessing class is barely beginning to decline: the image of that Daniel de Fontanin whom Roger Martin du Gard later presented to us as an enthusiastic admirer of André Gide.

To take a still more recent example, it is striking that *The Silence of the Sea*, a work written by a man who was a member of the resistance from the very beginning and whose aim is perfectly evident, was received with hostility in the *émigré* circles of New York, London, and sometimes even Algiers, and they even went so far as to tax its author with collaboration. The reason is that Vercors did not aim at *that* public. In the occupied zone, on the other hand, nobody doubted the author's intentions or the efficacy of his writing; he was writing for us. As a matter of fact, I do not think that one can defend Vercors by saying that his German is real or that his old Frenchman and French girl are real. Koestler has written some very fine pages about this question; the silence of the two French characters has no psychological verisimilitude; it even has a slight taste of anachronism; it recalls the stubborn muteness of Maupassant's patriotic peasants during another occupation, *an other* occupation with other hopes, other anguish, and other customs. As to the German officer, his portrait does not lack life, but, as is self-evident, Vercors, who at the time refused to have any contact with the occupying army, did it 'without a model', by combining the probable elements of his character. Thus, it is not in the name of *truth* that these images should be preferred to those which Anglo-Saxon propaganda was shaping each day. But for a Frenchman of continental France, Vercors' story, in 1941, was *effective*. When the enemy is separated from you by a barrier of fire, you have to judge him as a whole, as the incarnation of evil; all war is a form of Manichaeism. It is therefore understandable that the English newspapers did not waste their time distinguishing the wheat from the chaff in the German army. But, conversely, the conquered and occupied populations, who mingled with their conquerors, re-learned by familiarization and the effects of clever propaganda to consider them as men. Good men and bad men; good *and* bad at the same time. A work which in '41 would have presented the German soldiers to them as ogres would have made them laugh and would have failed in its purpose.

As early as the end of '42 *The Silence of the Sea* had lost its effectiveness; the reason is that the war was starting again on our soil. On one side, underground propaganda, sabotage, derailment of trains, and acts of violence; and on the other, curfew, deportations, imprisonment, torture, and execution of hostages. An invisible barrier of fire once again separated Germans and Frenchmen. We no longer wished to know whether the Germans who plucked out the eyes and ripped off the nails of our friends were accomplices or victims of Nazism; it was no longer enough to maintain a lofty silence before them; besides, they would not have tolerated it. At this point in the war it was necessary to be either for them or against them. In the midst of bombardments and massacres, of burned villages and deportations, Vercors' story seemed like an idyll; it had lost its public. Its public was the man of '41 humiliated by defeat but astonished at the studied courtesy of the occupiers, desiring peace, terrified by the spectre of Bolshevism and misled by the speeches of Pétain. It would have been fruitless to present the Germans to this man as bloodthirsty brutes. On the contrary, you had to admit to him that they might be polite and even likeable, and since he had discovered with surprise that most of them were 'men like us,' he had to be re-shown that even if such were the case, fraternizing was impossible, that the more likeable they seemed, the more unhappy and impotent they were, and that it was necessary to fight against a régime and an ideology even if the men who brought it to us did not seem bad. And, in short, as one was addressing a passive crowd, as there were still rather few important organizations, and as these showed themselves to be highly cautious in their recruiting, the only form of opposition that could be required of the population was silence, scorn, and an obedience which was forced and which showed it.

Thus, Vercors' story defined its public; by defining it, it defined itself. It wanted to combat within the mind of the French bourgeoisie of 1941 the effects of Pétain's interview with Hitler at Montoire. A year and a half after the defeat it was alive, virulent, and effective. In a half-century it will no longer excite anyone. An ill-informed public will still read it as an agreeable and somewhat languid tale about the war of 1939. It seems that bananas have a better taste when they have just been picked. Works of the mind should likewise be eaten on the spot.

One might be tempted to accuse any attempt to explain a work of the mind by the public to which it is addressed for its vain subtlety and its indirect character. Is it not more simple, direct, and rigorous to take the condition of the author himself as the determining factor? Shouldn't one be satisfied with Taine's notion of the 'milieu'? I answer that the explanation by the milieu is, in effect, *determinative*: the milieu *produces* the writer; that is why I do not believe in it. On the contrary, the public calls to him, that is, it puts questions to his freedom. The milieu is a *vis a tergo*; the public, on the contrary, is a waiting, an emptiness to be filled in, *an aspiration*, figuratively and literally. In a word, it is the *other*. And I am so far from rejecting the explanation of the work by the situation of the man that I have always considered the project of writing as the free exceeding of a certain human and *total* situation. In which, moreover, it is not different from other undertakings. Étiemble in a witty but superficial article writes,[9] 'I was going to revise my little dictionary when chance put three lines of Jean-Paul Sartre right under my nose: "In effect, for us the writer is neither a Vestal nor an Ariel. Do what he may, he's in the thick of it, marked and compromised down to his deepest refuge." To be in the thick of it, up to the ears. I recognized, in a way, the words of Blaise Pascal: "We are embarked." But at once I saw commitment lose all its value, reduced suddenly to the most ordinary of facts, the fact of the prince and the slave, to the human condition.'

That's what I said all right. But Étiemble is being silly. If every man is embarked, that does not at all mean that he is fully conscious of it. Most men pass their time in hiding their commitment from themselves. That does not necessarily mean that they attempt evasions by lying, by artificial paradises, or by a life of make-believe. It is enough for them to dim their lanterns, to see the foreground without the background and, vice versa, to see the ends while passing over the means in silence, to refuse solidarity with their kind, to take refuge in the spirit of pompousness, to remove all value from life by considering it from the point of view of someone who is dead, and at the same time, all horror from death by fleeing from it in the commonplaceness of everyday existence, to persuade themselves, if they belong to an oppressing class, that they are escaping their class by the loftiness of their feelings, and, if they belong to the oppressed, to conceal from themselves their complicity with oppression by asserting that one can remain free while in chains if one has a taste for the inner life. Writers can have recourse to all this just like anyone else. There are some, and they are the majority, who furnish a whole arsenal of tricks to the reader who wants to go on sleeping quietly.

I shall say that a writer is committed when he tries to achieve the most lucid and the most complete consciousness of being embarked, that is, when he causes the commitment of immediate spontaneity to advance, for himself and others, to the reflective. The writer is, *par excellence*, a mediator and his commitment is to mediation. But, if it is true that we must account for his work on the basis of his condition, it must also be borne in mind that his condition is not only that of a man in general but precisely that of a writer as well. Perhaps he is a Jew, and a Czech, and of peasant family, but he is a Jewish *writer*, a Czech *writer* and of rural stock. When, in another article, I tried to define the situation of the Jew, the best I could do was this: 'The Jew is a man whom other men consider as a Jew and who is obliged to choose himself on the basis of the situation which is made for him.' For there are qualities which come to us solely by means of the judgement of others. In the case of the writer, the case is more complex, for no one is obliged to choose himself as a writer. Hence, freedom is at the origin. I am an author, first of all, by my free intention to write. But at once it follows that I become a man whom other men consider as a writer, that is, who has to respond to a certain demand and who has been invested, whether he likes it or not, with a certain social function. Whatever game he may want to play, he must play it on the basis of the representation which others have of him. He may want to modify the character that one attributes to the man of letters in a given society; but in order to change it, he must first slip into it. Hence, the public intervenes, with its customs, its vision of the world, and its conception of society and of literature within that society. It surrounds the writer, it hems him in, and its imperious or sly demands, its refusals and its flights, are the given facts on whose basis a work can be constructed.

Let us take the case of the great negro writer, Richard Wright. If we consider only his condition as a *man*, that is, as a Southern 'nigger' transported to the North, we shall at once imagine that he can only write about Negroes or Whites *seen through the eyes of Negroes*. Can one imagine for a moment that he would agree to pass his life in the contemplation of the eternal True, Good, and Beautiful when ninety per cent. of the negroes in the South are practically deprived of the right to vote? And if anyone speaks here about the treason of the clerks, I answer that there are no clerks among the oppressed. Clerks are necessarily the parasites of oppressing classes or races. Thus, if an American negro finds that he has a vocation as a writer, he discovers his subject at the same time. He is the man who sees the whites from the outside, who assimilates the white culture from the outside, and each of whose books will show the alienation of the black race within American society. Not objectively, like the realists, but passionately, and in a way that will compromise his reader. But this examination leaves the nature of his work undetermined; he might be a pamphleteer, a blues-writer, or the Jeremiah of the Southern negroes.

If we want to go further, we must consider his public. To whom does Richard Wright address himself? Certainly not to the universal man. The essential characteristic of the notion of the universal man is that he is not involved in any particular age, and that he is no more and no less moved by the lot of the negroes of Louisiana than by that of the Roman slaves in the time of Spartacus. The universal man can think of nothing but universal values. He is a pure and abstract affirmation of the inalienable right of man. But neither can Wright think of intending his books for the white racialists of Virginia or South Carolina whose minds are made up in advance and who will not open them. Nor to the black peasants of the bayous who cannot read. And if he seems to be happy about the reception his books have had in Europe, still it is obvious that at the beginning he had not the slightest idea of writing for the European public. Europe is far away. Its indignation is ineffectual and hypocritical. Not much is to be expected from the nations which have enslaved the Indies, Indo-China, and negro Africa. These considerations are enough to define his readers. He is addressing himself to the cultivated negroes of the North and the white Americans of goodwill (intellectuals, democrats of the left, radicals, C.I.O. workers).

It is not that he is not aiming through them at all men but it is *through them* that he is thus aiming. Just as one can catch a glimpse of eternal freedom at the horizon of the historical and concrete freedom which it pursues, so the human race is at the horizon of the concrete and historical group of its readers. The illiterate negro peasants and the Southern planters represent a margin of abstract possibilities around its real public. After all, an illiterate may learn to read. *Black Boy* may fall into the hands of the most stubborn of negrophobes and may open his eyes. This merely means that every human project exceeds its actual limits and extends itself step by step to the infinite.

Now, it is to be noted that there is a fracture at the very heart of this *actual public*. For Wright, the negro readers represent the subjective. The same childhood, the same difficulties, the same complexes: a mere hint is enough for them; they understand with their hearts. In trying to become clear about his own personal situation, he clarifies theirs for them. He mediates, names, and shows them the life they lead from day to day in its immediacy, the life they suffer without finding words to formulate their sufferings. He is their conscience, and the movement by which he raises himself from the immediate to the reflective recapturing of his condition is that of his whole race. But whatever the goodwill of the white readers may be, for a negro author they represent the *Other*. They have not lived through what he has lived through. They can understand the negro's condition only by an extreme stretch of the imagination and by relying upon analogies which at any moment may deceive them. On the other hand, Wright does not completely know them. It is only from without that he conceives their proud security and that tranquil certainty, common to all white Aryans, that the world is white and that they own it. The words he puts down on paper have not the same context for whites as for negroes. They must be chosen by guess-work, since he does not know what resonances they will set up in those strange minds. And when he speaks to them, their very aim is changed. It is a matter of implicating them and making them take stock of their responsibilities. He must make them indignant and ashamed.

Thus, each of Wright's works contains what Baudelaire would have called 'a double simultaneous postulation'; each word refers to two contexts; two forces are applied simul-taneously to each phrase and determine the incomparable tension of his tale. Had he spoken to the whites alone, he might have turned out to be more prolix, more didactic, and more abusive; to the negroes alone, still more elliptical, more of a confederate, and more elegiac. In the first case, his work might have come close to satire; in the second, to prophetic lamentations. Jeremiah spoke only to the Jews. But Wright, a writer for a split public, has been able both to maintain and go beyond this split. He has made it the pretext for a work of art.

The writer consumes and does not produce, even if he has decided to serve the community's interests with his pen. His works remain gratuitous; thus no price can be set on their value. Their market value is fixed arbitrarily. In some periods he is pensioned and in others he gets a percentage of the sales of the book. But there is no more common measure between the work of the mind and percentage remuneration in modern society than there was between the poem and the royal pension under the old régime. Actually, the writer is not paid; he is fed, well or badly, according to the period. The system cannot work any differently, for his activity is *useless*. It is not at all *useful*; it is sometimes *harmful* for society to become self-conscious. For the fact is that the useful is defined within the framework of an established society and in relationship to institutions, values, and ends which are already fixed. If society sees itself and, in particular, sees itself as *seen*, there is, by virtue of this very fact, a contesting of the established values of the régime. The writer presents it with its image; he calls upon it to assume it or to change itself. At any rate, it changes; it loses the equilibrium which its ignorance had given it; it wavers between shame and cynicism; it practises dishonesty; thus, the writer gives society *a guilty conscience*; he is thereby in a state of perpetual antagonism towards the conservative forces which are maintaining the balance he tends to upset. For the transition to the mediate which can be brought about only by a negation of the immediate is a perpetual revolution.

Only the governing classes can allow themselves the luxury of remunerating so unproductive and dangerous an activity, and if they do so, it is a matter both of tactics and of misapprehension. Misapprehension for the most part: free from material cares, the members of the governing *élite* are sufficiently detached to want to have a reflective knowledge of themselves. They want to retrieve themselves, and they charge the artist with presenting them with their image without realizing that he will then make them assume it. A tactic on the part of some who, having recognized the danger, pension the artist in order to control his destructive power. Thus, the writer is a parasite of the governing *élite*. But, functionally, he moves in opposition to the interests of those who keep him alive.[10] Such is the original conflict which defines his condition.

Sometimes the conflict is obvious. We still talk about the courtiers who made the success of the *Marriage of Figaro* though it sounded the death-knell of the régime. Other times, it is masked, because to name is to show, and to show is to change. And as this challenging activity, which is harmful to the established interests, ventures, in its very modest way, to concur in a change of régime, as, on the other hand, the oppressed classes have neither the leisure nor the taste for reading, the objective aspect of the conflict may express itself as an antagonism between the conserva-

tive forces, or the real public of the writer, and the progressive forces, or the virtual public.

In a classless society, one whose internal structure would
be permanent revolution, the writer might be a mediator *for
all*, and his challenge on principle might precede or accompany the changes in fact. In my opinion this is the deeper
meaning we should give to the notion of *self-criticism*. The
expanding of the real public up to the limits of his virtual
public would bring about within his mind a reconciliation
of hostile tendencies. Literature, entirely liberated, would
represent *negativity* in so far as it is a necessary moment in
reconstruction. But to my knowledge this type of society
does not for the moment exist, and it may be doubted
whether it is possible. Thus, the conflict remains. It is at
the origin of what I would call the writer's ups and downs
and his bad conscience.

It is reduced to its simplest expression when the virtual
public is practically nil and when the writer, instead of remaining on the margin of the privileged class, is absorbed
by it. In that case literature identifies itself with the ideology
of the directing class; reflection takes place within the class;
the challenge deals with details and is carried on in the
name of uncontested principles. For example, that is what
happened in Europe in about the twelfth century; the clerk
wrote exclusively for clerks. But he could keep a good
conscience because there was a divorce between the spiritual
and the temporal. The Christian Revolution brought in the
spiritual, that is, the spirit itself, as a negation, a challenge,
and a transcendence, a perpetual construction, beyond the
realm of Nature, of the *anti-natural* city of freedoms. But it
was necessary that this universal power of surpassing the
object be first encountered as an object, that this perpetual
negation of Nature appear, in the first place, as nature, that
this faculty of perpetually creating ideologies and of leaving
them behind along the way be embodied, to begin with, in
a particular ideology. In the first centuries of our era the
spiritual was a captive of Christianity, or, if you prefer,
Christianity was the spiritual itself but *alienated*. It was the

spirit made object. Hence, it is evident that instead of appearing as the common and forever renewed experience of all
men, it manifested itself at first as the specialty of a few.
Medieval society had spiritual needs, and, to serve them, it
set up a body of specialists who were recruited by co-option.
Today we consider reading and writing as human rights
and, at the same time, as means for communicating with
others which are almost as natural and spontaneous as oral
language. That is why the most uncultured peasant is a
potential reader. In the time of the clerks, they were techniques which were reserved strictly for professionals. They
were not practised for their own sake, like spiritual exercises.
Their aim was not to obtain access to that large and vague
humanism which was later to be called 'the humanities'.
They were means solely of preserving and transmitting
Christian ideology. To be able to read was to have the
necessary tool for acquiring knowledge of the sacred texts
and their innumerable commentaries; to be able to write
was to be able to comment. Other men no more aspired to
possess these professional techniques than we aspire today
to acquire that of the cabinet-maker or the palaeographer if
we practise other professions. The barons counted on the
clerks to produce and watch over spirituality. By themselves
they were incapable of exercising control over writers as
the public does today, and they were unable to distinguish
heresy from orthodox beliefs if they were left without help.
They got excited only when the pope had recourse to the
secular arm. Then they pillaged and burned everything, but
only because they had confidence in the pope, and they
never turned up their noses at a chance to pillage. It is true
that the ideology was ultimately intended for them, for
them and the people, but it was communicated to them
orally by preaching, and the church very early made use of a
simpler language than writing: the image. The sculpture of
the cloisters and the cathedrals, the stained glass windows,
the paintings, and the mosaics speak of God and the Holy
Story. The clerk wrote his chronicles, his philosophical
works, his commentaries, and his poems on the margin of

this vast illustrating enterprise of faith. He intended them for his peers; they were controlled by his superiors. He did not have to be concerned with the effects which his works would produce upon the masses, since he was assured in advance that they would have no knowledge of them. Nor did he want to introduce remorse into the conscience of a feudal plunderer or caitiff; violence was unlettered. Thus, for him it was neither a question of reflecting its own image back to the temporal, nor of taking sides, nor of disengaging the spiritual from historical experience by a continuous effort. Quite the contrary, as the writer was of the Church, as the Church was an immense spiritual college which proved its dignity by its resistance to change, as history and the temporal were one and spirituality was radically distinct from the temporal, as the aim of his clerkship was to maintain this distinction, that is, to maintain itself as a specialized body in the face of the century, as, in addition, the economy was so divided up and as means of communication were so few and slow that events which occurred in one province had no effect upon the neighbouring province and as a monastery could enjoy its individual peace, like the hero of the *Acharnians*, while its country was at war, the writer's mission was to prove his autonomy by delivering himself to the exclusive contemplation of the Eternal. He incessantly affirmed the Eternal's existence and demonstrated it precisely by the fact that his only concern was to regard it. In this sense, he realized, in effect, the ideal of Benda, but one can see under what conditions: spirituality and literature had to be alienated, a particular ideology had to triumph, a feudal pluralism had to make the isolation of the clerks possible, virtually the whole population had to be illiterate, and the only public of the writer could be the college of other writers. It is inconceivable that one can practise freedom of thought, write for a public which coincides with the restricted collectivity of specialists, and restrict oneself to describing the content of eternal values and *a priori* ideas. The good conscience of the medieval clerk flowered on the death of literature.

However, in order for writers to preserve this happy conscience it is not quite necessary that their public be reduced to an established body of professionals. It is enough for them to be steeped in the ideology of the privileged classes, to be completely permeated by it, and to be unable even to conceive any others. But in this case their function is modified; they are no longer asked to be the *guardians* of dogma but merely not to make themselves its detractors. As a second example of the adherence of writers to established ideology, one might, I believe, choose the French seventeenth century.

The secularization of the writer and his public was in process of being completed in that age. It certainly had its origin in the expansive force of the written thing, its monumental character, and the appeal to freedom which is hidden away in any work of the mind. But external circumstances contributed, such as the development of education, the weakening of the spiritual power, and the appearance of new ideologies which were expressly intended for the temporal. However, secularization does not mean universalization. The writer's public still remained strictly limited. Taken as a whole, it was called *society*, and this name designated a fraction of the court, the clergy, the magistracy, and the rich bourgeoisie. Considered individually, the reader was called a 'gentleman' (*honnête homme*) and he exercised a certain function of censorship which was called *taste*. In short, he was both a member of the upper classes and a specialist. If he criticized the writer, it was because he himself could write. The public of Corneille, Pascal, and Descartes was Mme de Sévigné, the Chevalier de Méré, Mme de Grignan, Mme de Rambouillet, and Saint-Évremonde. Today the public, in relation to the writer, is in a state of passiveness: it waits for ideas or a new art form to be imposed upon it. It is the inert mass wherein the idea will assume flesh. Its means of control is indirect and negative; one cannot say that it gives its opinion; it simply buys or does not buy the book; the relationship between author and reader is analogous to that of male and female: reading has become a simple means of information and writing a very general means of communication. In the seventeenth century being able to write already meant really being able to write well. Not that Providence divided the gift of style equally among all men, but because the reader, if not strictly identical with the writer, was a potential writer. He belonged to a parasitical *élite* for whom the art of writing was, if not a profession, at least the mark of its superiority. He read because he could write; with a little luck he might have been able to write what he read. The public was active; productions of the mind were really *submitted* to it. It judged them by a scale of values which it helped to maintain. A revolution analogous to romanticism is not conceivable in this period because there would have to have been the concurrence of an indecisive mass, which one surprises, overwhelms, and suddenly animates by revealing to it ideas or feelings of which it was ignorant, and which, lacking firm convictions, constantly requires being ravished and fecundated. In the seventeenth century convictions were unshakeable; the religious ideology went hand in hand with a political ideology which the temporal itself secreted; no one publicly questioned the existence of God or the divine right of kings. 'Society' had its language, its graces, and its ceremonies which it expected to find in the books it read. Its conception of time, too. As the two historical facts which it constantly pondered—original sin and redemption—belonged to a remote past, as it was also from this past that the great governing families drew their pride and the justification of their privileges, as the future could bring nothing new, since God was too perfect to change, and since the two great earthly powers, the Church and the Monarchy, aspired only to immutability, the active element of temporality was the past, which is itself a phenomenal degradation of the Eternal; the present is a perpetual sin which can find an excuse for itself only if it reflects, with the least possible unfaithfulness, the image of a completed era. For an idea to be received, it must prove its antiquity; for a work of art to please, it must have been inspired by an ancient model.

Again we find writers expressly making themselves the guardians of this ideology. There were still great clerks who belonged to the Church and who had no other concern than to defend dogma. To them were added the 'watchdogs' of the temporal, historians, court poets, jurists, and philosophers who were concerned with establishing and maintaining the ideology of the absolute monarchy. But we see appearing at their side a third category of writers, strictly secular, who, for the most part, *accepted* the religious and political ideology of the age without thinking that they were bound to prove it or preserve it. They did not write about it, they accepted it implicitly. For them, it was what we called a short time ago the context or the whole body of the presuppositions common to readers and author which are necessary to make the writings of the latter intelligible to the former. In general, they belonged to the bourgeoisie; they were pensioned by the nobility. As they consumed without producing, and as the nobility did not produce either but lived off the work of others, they were the parasites of a parasitic class. They no longer lived in a college but formed an implicit corporation in that highly integrated society, and to remind them constantly of their collegiate origin and their former clerkship the royal power chose some of them and grouped them in a sort of symbolic college, the French Academy. Fed by the king and read by an *élite*, they were concerned solely with responding to the demands of this limited public. They had as good or almost as good a conscience as the twelfth-century clerks. It is impossible to speak of a virtual public as distinguished from a real public in this age. La Bruyère happened to speak *about* peasants, but he did not speak *to* them, and if he took note of their misery, it was not for the sake of drawing an argument against the ideology he accepted, but in the name of that ideology: it was a disgrace for enlightened monarchs and good Christians. Thus, one spoke about the masses above their heads and without even conceiving the notion that one might help them become self-conscious. And the homogeneity of the public banished all contradiction from the authors' souls. They were not pulled between real but detestable readers and readers who were virtual and desirable but out of reach; they did not ask themselves questions about their rôle in the world, for the writer questions himself about his mission only in ages when it is not clearly defined and when he must invent or re-invent it, that is, when he notices, beyond the *élite* who read him, an amorphous mass of possible readers whom he may or may not choose to win, and when he must himself decide, in the event that he has the opportunity to reach them, what his relations with them are to be. The authors of the seventeenth century had a definite function because they addressed an enlightened, strictly limited, and active public which exercised permanent control over them. Unknown by the people, their job was to reflect back its own image to the *élite* which supported them. But there are many ways of reflecting an image: certain portraits are by themselves challenges because they have been made from without and without passion by a painter who refuses any complicity with his model. However, for a writer merely to conceive the idea of drawing a portrait-challenge of his real reader, he must have become conscious of a contradiction between himself and his public, that is, he must come to his readers *from without* and must consider them with astonishment, or he must feel the astonished regard of unfamiliar minds (ethnic minorities, oppressed classes, etc.) weighing upon the little society which he forms with them. But in the seventeenth century, since the virtual public did not exist, since the artist accepted without criticism the ideology of the *élite*, he made himself an accomplice of his public. No unfamiliar stare came to trouble him in his games. Neither the prose writer nor even the poet was accursed. They did not have to decide with each work what the meaning and value of literature were, since its meaning and value were fixed by tradition. Well integrated in a hierarchical society, they knew neither the pride nor the anguish of being 'different'; in short, they were *classical*. There is classicism when a society has taken on a relatively stable

form and when it has been permeated with the myth of its
perpetuity, that is, when it confounds the present with the
eternal and historicity with traditionalism, when the hierarchy of classes is such that the virtual public never exceeds
the real public and when each reader is for the writer a
qualified critic and a censor, when the power of the religious
and political ideology is so strong and the prohibitions so
rigorous that in no case is there any question of discovering
new countries of the mind, but only of putting into shape
the *commonplaces* adopted by the *élite*, in such a way that
reading—which, as we have seen, is the concrete relation
between the writer and his public—is a ceremony of *recognition* analogous to the bow of salutation, that is, the cere-
monious affirmation that author and reader are of the same
world and have the same opinions about everything. Thus,
each production of the mind is at the same time an act of
courtesy, and style is the supreme courtesy of the author
towards his reader, and the reader, for his part, never tires
of finding the same thoughts in the most diverse of books
because these thoughts are his own and he does not ask to
acquire others but only to be offered with magnificence
those which he already has. Hence, it is in a spirit of complicity that the author presents and the reader accepts a
portrait which is necessarily abstract; addressing a parasitical
class, he cannot show man at work or, in general, the relations between man and external nature. As, on the other
hand, there are bodies of specialists who, under the control
of the Church and the Monarchy, are concerned with maintaining the spiritual and secular ideology, the writer does
not even suspect the importance of economic, religious,
metaphysical, and political factors in the constitution of the
person; and as the society in which he lives confounds the
present with the eternal he cannot even imagine the slightest
change in what he calls human nature. He conceives history
as a series of accidents which affect the eternal man on the
surface without deeply modifying him, and if he had to
assign a meaning to historical duration he would see in it
both an eternal repetition, so that previous events can and

ought to provide lessons for his contemporaries, and a process of slight degeneration, since the fundamental events of history are long since *passed* and since, perfection in letters having been attained in Antiquity, his ancient models seem beyond rivalry. And in all this he is once again fully in harmony with his public, which considers work as a curse, which does not *feel* its situation in history and in the world for the simple reason that it is privileged and because its only concern is faith, respect for the Monarch, passion, war, death, and courtesy. In short, the image of classical man is purely psychological because the classical public is conscious only of his psychology. Furthermore, it must be understood that this psychology is itself traditionalist, it is not concerned with discovering new and profound truths about the human heart or with setting up hypotheses. It is in unstable societies when the public exists on several social levels, that the writer, torn and dissatisfied, invents explanations for his anguish. The psychology of the seventeenth century is purely descriptive. It is not based so much upon the author's personal experience as it is the aesthetic expression of what the *élite* thinks about itself. La Rochefoucauld borrows the form and the content of his maxims from the diversions of the salons. The casuistry of the Jesuits, the etiquette of the Précieuses, the portrait game, the ethics of Nicole, and the religious conception of the passions are at the origin of a hundred other works. The comedies draw their inspiration from ancient psychology and the plain common sense of the upper bourgeoisie. Society is thoroughly delighted at seeing itself mirrored in them because it recognizes the notions it has about itself; it does not ask to be shown what it is, but it asks rather for a reflection of what it thinks it is. To be sure, some satires are permitted, but it is the *élite* which, through pamphlets and comedies, carries on, in the name of its morality, the cleansings and the purges necessary for its health. The ridiculous marquis, the litigants, or the Précieuses are never made fun of from a point of view *external* to the governing class; it is always a matter of eccentrics who are inassimilable in a civilized society and who live on the margin of the collective life. The Misanthrope is twitted because he lacks courtesy, Cathos and Madelon, because they have too much. Philaminte goes counter to the accepted ideas about women; the bourgeois gentleman is odious to the rich bourgeois who have a lofty modesty and who know the greatness and the humbleness of their condition, and, at the same time, to the gentlemen because he wants to push his way into the nobility. This internal and, so to speak, physiological satire has no connection with the great satire of Beaumarchais, P. L. Courier, J. Vallès, and Céline; it is less courageous and much more severe because it exhibits the repressive action which the collectivity practises upon the weak, the sick, and the maladjusted. It is the pitiless laughter of a gang of street-urchins at the awkwardness of their scapegoat.

Bourgeois in origin and outlook, more like Oronte and Chrysale in his home life than like his brilliant and restless confrères of 1780 or 1830, yet accepted in the Society of the Great and pensioned by them, slightly unclassed from above, yet convinced that talent is no substitute for birth, docile to the reprimands of the clergy, respectful of the royal power, happy to occupy a modest place in the immense structure of which the Church and the Monarchy are the pillars, somewhat above the merchants and the scholars, below the nobles and the clergy, the writer practises his profession with a good conscience, convinced that he has come too late, that everything has been said, and that the only proper thing to do is to re-say it agreeably. He conceives the glory which awaits him as a feeble reflection of hereditary titles and if he expects it to be eternal it is because he does not even suspect that the society of his readers may be overthrown by social changes. Thus, the permanence of the royal family seems to him a guarantee of that of his renown.

Yet, almost in spite of himself, the mirror which he modestly offers to his readers is magical: it enthrals and compromises. Even though everything has been done to offer them only a flattering and complaisant image, more subjective than objective and more internal than external, this image remains none the less a work of art, that is, it has its basis in the freedom of the author and is an appeal to the freedom of the reader. Since it is beautiful, it is made of glass; aesthetic distance puts it out of reach. Impossible to be delighted with it, to find any comfortable warmth in it, any discrete indulgence. Even though it is made up of the commonplaces of the age and that smug complacency which unite contemporaries like an umbilical cord, it is supported by a freedom and thereby another kind of objectivity. It is *itself*, to be sure, that the *élite* finds in the mirror, but itself as it would see itself if it went to the very extremes of severity. It is not congealed into an object by the gaze of the Other, for neither the peasant nor the working-man has yet become the *Other* for it, and the art of reflective presentation which characterizes the art of the seventeenth century is a strictly internal process; however, it pushes to the limits each one's efforts to see into himself clearly; it is a perpetual *cogito*. To be sure, it does not call idleness, oppression, or parasitism into question, because these aspects of the governing class are revealed only to observers who place themselves outside it; hence, the image which is reflected back to it is strictly psychological. But spontaneous behaviour, by passing to the reflective state, loses its innocence and the excuse of immediacy; it must be assumed or changed. It is, to be sure, a world of courtesy and ceremony which is offered to the reader, but he is already emerging from this world since he is invited to know it and to recognize himself in it. In this sense, Racine was not wrong when he said in regard to *Phèdre* that 'the passions are presented before your eyes only to show all the disorder of which they are the cause'. On condition that one does not take that to mean that his express purpose was to inspire a horror of love. But to paint passion is already to go beyond it, already to shed it. It is not a matter of chance that, about the same time, philosophers were suggesting the idea of curing one's self of it by knowledge. And as the reflective practice of freedom when confronted by the passions is usually adorned with the name of *morals*, it must be recognized that the art of the seventeenth century is eminently a moralizing art. Not that its avowed aim is to teach virtue, nor that it is poisoned by the good intentions which produce bad literature, but by the mere fact that it quietly offers the reader his own image, it makes it unbearable for him. Moralizing: this is both a definition and a limit. It is not moralizing *only*; if it proposes to man that he transcend the psychological towards the moral, it is because it regards religious, metaphysical, political, and social problems as solved; but its action is none the less 'orthodox'. As it confounds universal man with the particular men who are in power, it does not dedicate itself to the liberation of any concrete category of the oppressed; however, the writer, though completely assimilated by the oppressing class, is by no means its accomplice; his work is unquestionably a liberator since its effect, within this class, is to free man from himself.

Up to this point we have been considering the case in which the writer's potential public was nil, or just about, and in which his real public was not torn by any conflict. We have seen that he could then accept the current ideology with a good conscience and that he launched his appeals to freedom within the ideology itself. If the potential public suddenly appears, or if the real public is broken up into hostile factions, everything changes. We must now consider what happens to literature when the writer is led to reject the ideology of the ruling classes.

The eighteenth century was the palmy time, unique in history, and the soon-to-be-lost paradise, of French writers. Their social condition had not changed. Bourgeois in origin, with very few exceptions, they were unclassed by the favours of the great. The circle of their real readers had grown perceptibly larger because the bourgeoisie had begun to read, but they were still unknown to the 'lower' classes, and if the writers spoke of them more often than did La Bruyère and Fénelon, they never addressed them, even in spirit. However, a profound upheaval had broken their public in two; they had to satisfy contradictory demands.

Their situation was characterized from the beginning by *tension*. This tension was manifested in a very particular way. The governing class had in fact lost confidence in its ideology. It had put itself into a position of defence; it tried, to a certain extent, to retard the diffusion of new ideas, but it could not keep from being penetrated by these ideas. It understood that its religious and political principles were the best instruments for establishing its power, but the fact is that as it saw them only as instruments, it ceased to believe in them completely. *Pragmatic* truth had replaced revealed truth. If censorship and prohibitions were more visible, they covered up a secret weakness and a cynicism of despair. There were no more *clerks*; church literature was empty apologetics, a fist holding on to dogmas which were breaking loose; it was turning against freedom; it addressed itself to respect, fear, and self-interest, and by ceasing to be a free appeal to free men, it was ceasing to be literature. This distraught *élite* turned to the genuine writer and asked him to do the impossible, not to spare his severity, if he was bent on it, but to breathe at least a bit of freedom into a wilting ideology, to address himself to his readers' reason and to persuade them to adopt dogmas which, with time, had become irrational. In short, to turn propagandist without ceasing to be a writer. But it was playing a losing game. Since its principles were no longer a matter of immediate and unformulated evidence and since it had to *present* them to the writer so that he might come to their defence, since there was no longer any question of saving them for their own sake but rather of maintaining order, it contested their validity by its very effort to re-establish them. The writer who consented to buttress this shaky ideology at least *consented* to do so, and this voluntary adherence to principles which, in the past, had governed minds without being noticed now freed him from them. He was already going beyond them. In spite of himself he was emerging into solitude and freedom. The bourgeoisie, on the other hand, which constituted what in Marxist terms is called the rising class, was trying at this same time to disengage itself from the ideology that was being imposed upon it and to construct one better suited to its own purpose.

Now, this 'rising class', which was soon to claim the right to participate in affairs of State, was subject only to *political* oppression. Confronted with a ruined nobility, it was in the process of very calmly attaining economic pre-eminence. It already had money, culture, and leisure. Thus, for the first time an oppressed class was presenting itself to the writer as a real public. But the conjunction was still more favourable; for this awakening class, which was reading and trying to think, had not yet produced an organized revolutionary party which would secrete its own ideology as did the Church in the Middle Ages. The writer was not yet wedged, as we shall see that he was later to be, between the dying ideology of a declining class and the rigorous ideology of the rising class. The bourgeoisie wanted light; it felt vaguely that its thought was alienated, and it wanted to become conscious of itself. One could probably find some traces of organization: materialist societies, groups of intellectuals, freemasonry. But they were chiefly associations for inquiry which were waiting for ideas rather than producing them. To be sure, a form of popular and spontaneous writing was spreading: the secret and anonymous tract. But this literature of amateurs did not compete with the professional writer; rather, it goaded and solicited him by informing him about the confused aspirations of the collectivity. Thus, the bourgeoisie—as opposed to a public of half-specialists, which with difficulty held on to its position and which was always recruited at Court and from the upper circles of society—offered the rough draft of a mass public. In regard to literature, it was in a state of relative *passivity* since it had no experience in the art of writing, no preconceived opinion about style and literary genres, and was awaiting everything, form and content, from the genius of the writer.

Solicited by both sides, the writer found himself between the two hostile factions of his public as the arbiter of their conflict. He was no longer a clerk; the ruling class was not the only one supporting him. It is true that it was still pensioning him, but it was the bourgeoisie which was buying his books. He was collecting at both ends. His father had been a bourgeois and his son would be as well; one might thus be tempted to see in him a bourgeois more gifted than others but similarly oppressed, a man who had attained knowledge of his state under the pressure of historical circumstances, in short, an inner mirror by means of which the whole bourgeoisie became conscious of itself and its demands. But this would be a superficial view. It has not been sufficiently pointed out that a class can acquire class consciousness only if it sees itself from within and without at the same time; in other words, if it profits by external competition; that is where the intellectuals, the perpetually unclassed, come into the picture.

The essential characteristic of the eighteenth-century writer was precisely an objective and subjective unclassing. Though he still remembered his bourgeois attachments, yet the favour of the great drew him away from his milieu; he no longer felt any concrete solidarity with his cousin the lawyer or his brother the village curé because he had privileges which they had not. It was from the court and nobility that he borrowed his manners and the very graces of his style. Glory, his dearest hope and his consecration, had become for him a slippery and ambiguous notion; a fresh idea of glory was rising up in which a writer was truly rewarded if an obscure doctor in Bruges or a briefless lawyer in Rheims devoured his books almost in secret.

But the diffuse recognition of this public which he hardly knew only half touched him. He had received from his elders a traditional conception of fame. According to this conception, it was the monarch who consecrated his genius. The visible sign of his success was for Catherine or Frederick to invite him to their table. The recompense given to him and the dignities conferred from above did not yet have the official impersonality of the prizes and decorations awarded by our republics. They retained the quasi-feudal character of man to man relations. And since he was, above all, an eternal consumer in a society of producers, a parasite of a parasitic

class, he treated money like a parasite. He did not *earn* it
since there was no common measure between his work and
his remuneration; he only *spent* it. Therefore, even if he was
poor, he lived in luxury. Everything was a luxury to him,
including, and in fact particularly so, his writing. Yet, even
in the king's chamber he retained a rough force, a potent
vulgarity; Diderot, in the heat of a philosophical conversation, pinched the thigh of the Empress of Russia until the
blood flowed. And then, if he went too far, he could always
be made to feel that he was only a scribbler. The life of
Voltaire, from his beating, his imprisonment, and his flight
to London, to the insolence of the King of Prussia was a
succession of triumphs and humiliations. At times the writer
enjoyed the passing favours of a marquise, but he married
his maid or a bricklayer's daughter. Hence, his mind, as well
as his public, was torn apart. But this did not cause him to
suffer; on the contrary, this original contradiction was the
source of his pride. He thought that he had no obligations
to anyone, that he could choose his friends and opponents,
and that it was enough for him to take his pen in hand to free
himself from the conditioning of milieu, nation, or class. He
flew, he soared, he was pure thought, pure observation. He
chose to write to vindicate his unclassing which he assumed
and transformed into solitude. From the outside, he con-
templated the great with the eyes of the bourgeois and the
bourgeois with the eyes of the nobility, and he retained
enough complicity with both to understand them equally
from within. Hence, literature, which up to then had been
only a conservative and purifying function of an integrated
society, became conscious in him and by him of its autonomy. Placed by an extreme chance between confused aspirations and an ideology in ruins—like the writer between the
bourgeoisie, the Court, and the Church—literature suddenly
asserted its independence. It was no longer to reflect the
commonplaces of the collectivity; it identified itself with
Mind, that is, with the permanent power of forming and
criticizing ideas.

Of course, this taking over of literature by itself was

abstract and almost purely formal, since the literary works were not the concrete expression of any class; and as the writers began by rejecting any deep solidarity with the milieu from which they came as well as the one which adopted them, literature became confused with Negativity, that is, with doubt, refusal, criticism, and opposition. But as a result of this very fact, it led to the setting up, against the ossified spirituality of the Church, of the rights of a new spirituality, one in movement, which was no longer identified with any ideology and which manifested itself as the power of continually surpassing the given, whatever it might be. When, in the shelter of the structure of the very Christian monarchy, it was imitating wonderful models, it hardly fussed about truth because truth was only a very crude and very concrete quality of the ideology which had been nourishing it; according to the dogmas of the Church, to be true or, quite simply, to be, was all one, and truth could not be conceived apart from the system. But now that spirituality had become this abstract movement which cut through all ideologies and then left them along the wayside like empty shells, truth, in its turn, was disentangled from all concrete and particular philosophy; it was revealed in its abstract independence; it became the regulating idea of literature and the distant limit of the critical movement.

Spirituality, literature, and truth: these notions were bound up in that abstract and negative moment of becoming conscious of the world. Their instrument was analysis, a negative and critical method which perpetually dissolves concrete data into abstract elements and the products of history into combinations of universal concepts. An adolescent chooses to write in order to escape an oppression from which he suffers and a solidarity he is ashamed of; as soon as he has written a few words, he thinks he has escaped from his milieu and class and from all milieus and all classes and that he has broken through his historical situation by the mere fact that he has attained reflective and critical knowledge. Above the confusion of those bourgeois and nobles, locked up in their particular age by their prejudices, he has, on taking up his pen, discovered himself as a timeless and unlocalized consciousness, in short, as *universal man*. And literature, which has delivered him, is an abstract function and an *a priori* power of human nature; it is the movement whereby at every moment man frees himself from history; in short, it is the exercise of freedom.

In the seventeenth century a man, by choosing to write, embraced a definite profession, with the tricks of the trade, its rules and customs, its rank in the hierarchy of the professions. In the eighteenth century, the moulds were broken; everything remained to be done; works of the mind, instead of being put together according to established patterns and more or less by luck, were each a particular invention and were a kind of decision of the author regarding the nature, value, and scope of belles-lettres; each one brought its own rules and the principles by which it was to be judged; each one aspired to engage the whole of literature and to blaze new paths. It is not by chance that the worst works of the period are also those which claimed to be the most traditional; tragedy and epic were the exquisite fruits of an integrated society; in a collectivity which was torn apart, they could subsist only in the form of survivals and pastiches.

What the eighteenth-century writer tirelessly demanded in all his works was the right to practise an anti-historical reason against history, and in this sense all he did was to reveal the essential requirements of abstract literature. He was not concerned with giving his readers a clearer class consciousness. Quite the contrary, the urgent appeal which he addressed to his bourgeois public was an invitation to forget humiliations, prejudices, and fears; the one he directed to his noble public was a solicitation to strip itself of its pride of caste and its privileges. As he had made himself universal, he could have only universal readers, and what he required of the freedom of his contemporaries was that they cut their historical ties in order to join him in universality.

What is the origin of this miracle by which, at the very moment he was setting up abstract freedom against concrete oppression and Reason against History, he was going along in the very direction of historical development? First, the bourgeoisie, by a tactic which was characteristic of it and which it was to repeat in 1830 and 1848, joined forces, on the eve of taking power, with those oppressed classes which were not in a condition to push their demands. And since the bonds which united social groups so different from one another could only be very general and very abstract, it aimed not so much to acquire a clear consciousness of itself, which would have opposed it to the workingmen and peasants, as to have its right to lead the opposition recognized on the grounds that it was in a better position to let the established powers know the demands of universal human nature. On the other hand, the revolution being prepared was a *political* one; there was no revolutionary ideology and no organized party. The bourgeoisie wanted to be enlightened; it wanted the ideology which for centuries had mystified and alienated man to be liquidated. There would be time later on to replace it. For the time being, it aimed at freedom of opinion as a step towards political power. Hence, by demanding *for himself* and *as a writer* freedom of thinking and of expressing his thought, the author necessarily served the interests of the bourgeois class. No more was asked of him and there was nothing more he could do. In later periods, as we shall see, the writer could demand his freedom to write with a bad conscience; he might be aware that the oppressed classes wanted something other than that freedom. Freedom of thinking could then appear as a privilege; in the eyes of some it could pass for a means of oppression, and the position of the writer risked becoming untenable. But on the eve of the Revolution he enjoyed an extraordinary opportunity, that is, it was enough for him to defend his profession in order to serve as a guide to the aspirations of the rising class.

He knew it. He considered himself a guide and a spiritual chief. He took chances. As the ruling *élite*, which grew increasingly nervous, lavished its graces upon him one day only to have him locked up the next, he had none of that tranquillity, that proud mediocrity, which his predecessors

had enjoyed. His glorious and eventful life, with its sunlit
crests and its dizzying steeps, was that of an adventurer.
The other evening I was reading the dedication of Blaise
Cendrars' *Rhum*: 'To the young people of today who are tired
of literature, to prove to them that a novel can also be an
act', and I thought that we are quite unfortunate and quite
guilty, since we have to prove what in the eighteenth century was self-evident. A work of the mind was then doubly
an act since it produced ideas which were to lead to social
upheavals and since it exposed its author to danger. And
this act, whatever the book we may be considering, was
always defined in the same way; it was a *liberator*. And,
doubtless, in the seventeenth century too, literature had a
liberating function, though one which remained veiled and
implicit. In the time of the Encyclopaedists, it was no longer
a question of freeing the gentleman from his passions by
reflecting them back to him without complaisance, but of
helping with the pen to bring about the political freedom
simply of man. The appeal which the writer addressed to his
bourgeois public was, whether he meant it or not, an incite-
ment to revolt; the one which he directed to the ruling class
was an invitation to lucidity, to critical self-examination, to
the giving up of its privileges. The condition of Rousseau
was much like that of Richard Wright when he writes for
both enlightened negroes and whites. Before the nobility he
bore witness and at the same time was inviting his fellow
commoners to become conscious of themselves. It was not
only the taking of the Bastille which his writings and those
of Diderot and Condorcet were preparing at long range; it
was also the night of August the fourth.

And as the writer thought that he had broken the bonds
which united him to his class of origin, as he spoke to his
readers from above about universal human nature, it seemed
to him that the appeal he made to them and the part he took
in their misfortunes were dictated by pure generosity. To
write is to give. In this way he accepted and excused what
was unacceptable in his situation as a parasite in an industrious society; this was also how he became conscious of

that absolute freedom, that gratuity, which characterize literary creation. But though he constantly had in view universal man and the abstract rights of human nature, there is no reason to believe that he was an incarnation of the 'clerk' as Benda has described him. Since his position was, in essence, *critical*, he certainly had to have *something* to criticize; and the objects which first presented themselves to criticism were the institutions, superstitions, traditions, and acts of a traditional government.

In other words, as the walls of Eternity and the Past which had supported the ideological structure of the seventeenth century cracked and gave way, the writer perceived a new dimension of temporality in its purity: the Present. The Present, which preceding centuries had sometimes conceived as a perceptible figuration of Eternity and sometimes as a degraded emanation of Antiquity. He had only a confused notion of the future, but he knew that the fleeting hour which he was living was unique and that it was his, that it was in no way inferior to the most magnificent hours of Antiquity, since they too had begun by being the present. He knew that it was his chance and that he must not waste it. That was why he considered the fight he had to wage not so much as a preparation for the society of the future but rather as a short-term enterprise, one of immediate efficacy. It was *this* institution that had to be denounced and at once, *that* superstition that had to be destroyed immediately, *that* particular injustice that had to be rectified. This impassioned sense of the present saved him from idealism; he did not confine himself to contemplating the eternal ideas of Freedom or Equality. For the first time since the Reformation, writers intervened in public life, protested against an unjust decree, asked for the review of a trial, and, in short, decided that the spiritual was in the street, at the fair, in the market place, at the tribunal, and that it was by no means a matter of turning away from the temporal, but, on the contrary, that one had to come back to it incessantly and go on beyond it in each particular circumstance.

Thus, the overthrow of his public and the crisis of the European consciousness had invested the writer with a new function. He conceived literature to be the permanent practice of magnanimity. He still submitted to the strict and severe control of his peers, but below him he caught a glimpse of an unformed and passionate waiting, a more feminine, more undifferentiated kind of desire which freed him from their censorship. He had disembodied the spiritual and had separated his cause from that of a dying ideology; his books were free appeals to the freedom of his readers.

The political triumph of the bourgeoisie which writers had so eagerly desired convulsed their condition from top to bottom and put the very essence of literature into question. It might be said that the result of all their efforts was merely a preparation for their certain ruin. There is no doubt that by identifying the cause of belles-lettres with that of political democracy they helped the bourgeoisie to come to power, but by the same token they ran the risk of seeing the disappearance of the object of their demands, that is, the constant and almost the only subject of their writing. In short, the miraculous harmony which united the essential demands of literature with that of the oppressed bourgeoisie was broken as soon as both were realized. So long as millions of men were burning to be able to express their feelings it was fine to demand the right to write freely and to examine everything, but once freedom of thought and confession and equality of political rights were gained, the defence of literature became a purely formal game which no longer amused anyone; something else had to be found.

Now, at the same time writers had lost their privileged position whose origin had been the split which had torn apart their public and which had allowed them to have a foot in both camps. These two halves had knitted together; the bourgeoisie had absorbed the nobility or very nearly. Authors had to meet the demands of a unified public. There was no hope of getting away from their class of origin. Born of bourgeois parents, read and paid by bourgeois, they had to remain bourgeois; the bourgeoisie had closed round them like a prison. It was to take them a century to get over their keen regret for the flighty and parasitic class which had indulged them out of caprice and whom they had remorselessly undermined in their rôle of double agent. It seemed to them that they had killed the goose which laid the golden eggs. The bourgeoisie introduced new forms of oppression; however, it was not parasitic. Doubtless, it had taken over the means of work, but it was highly diligent in regulating the production and distribution of its products. It did not conceive literary work as a gratuitous and disinterested creation but as a paid service.

The justifying myth of this industrious and unproductive class was *utilitarianism*; in one way or another the function of the bourgeois was that of intermediary between producer and consumer; it was the *middleman* raised to omnipotence. Thus, in the indissoluble yoke of means and end, he had chosen to give primary importance to the means. The end was implied; one never looked it in the face but passed over it in silence. The goal and dignity of a human life was to spend itself in the ordering of means. It was not *serious* to occupy oneself without intermediary in producing an absolute end. It was as if one aspired to see God face to face without the help of the Church. The only enterprises to be credited were those whose end was the perpetually withdrawing horizon of an infinite series of means. If the work of art entered the utilitarian round, if it hoped to be taken seriously, it had to descend from the heaven of unconditioned ends and resign itself to becoming useful in its turn, that is, to presenting itself as a means of ordering means. In particular, as the bourgeois was not quite sure of himself, because his power was not based on a decree of Providence, literature had to help it feel bourgeois by divine right. Thus, after having been the bad conscience of the privileged in the eighteenth century it ran the risk in the nineteenth century of becoming the good conscience of an oppressing class.

Well and good, if the writer could have kept that spirit of free criticism which in the preceding century had been his fortune and his pride. But his public was opposed to that.

So long as the bourgeoisie had been struggling against the privileges of the nobility it had given assent to destructive negativity. But now that it had power, it passed on to construction and asked to be helped in constructing. Opposition had remained possible within the religious ideology because the believer referred his obligations and the articles of faith back to the will of God. He thereby established a concrete and feudal person-to-person bond with the Almighty. This recourse to the divine free will introduced, although God was perfect and chained to His perfection, an element of gratuity into Christian ethics and consequently a bit of freedom into literature. The Christian hero was always Jacob wrestling with the angel; the saint *contested* the divine will even if he did so in order to submit to it even more narrowly. But bourgeois ethics did not derive from Providence; its universal and abstract procedures were inscribed in things. They were not the effect of a sovereign and quite amiable but personal will; rather, they resembled the uncreated laws of physics. At least, so one supposed, for it was not prudent to look at them too closely. The serious man kept from examining them precisely because their origin was obscure. Bourgeois art either would be a means or would not be; it would forbid itself to lay hands on principles, for fear they might collapse,[11] and to probe the human heart too deeply for fear of finding disorder in it. Its public feared nothing so much as talent, that gay and menacing madness which uncovers the disturbing roots of things by unforeseeable words and which, by repeated appeals to freedom, stirs the still more disturbing roots of men. *Facility* sold better; it was talent in leash, turned against itself, the art of reassuring readers by harmonious and expected discourse, in a tone of good fellowship, that man and the world were quite ordinary, transparent, without surprises, without threats, and without interest.

There was more: as the only relationship which the bourgeois had with natural forces was through intermediaries, as material reality appeared to him in the form of manufactured products, as he was surrounded as far as the eye could see by an already humanized world which reflected back to him his own image, as he limited himself to gleaning on the surface of things the meaning that other men had put forward, as his job was essentially that of handling abstract symbols, words, figures, plans, and diagrams for determining methods whereby his employees would share in consumer's goods, as his culture, quite as much as his trade, inclined him to consider ideas, he was convinced that the universe was reducible to a system of ideas; he dissolved effort, difficulty, needs, oppression, and wars into ideas; there was no evil, only pluralism; certain ideas lived in a free state; they had to be integrated into the system. Thus, he conceived human progress as a vast movement of assimilation; ideas assimilated each other and so did minds. At the end of this immense digestive process, thought would find its unification and society its total integration.

Such optimism was at the opposite extreme of the writer's conception of his art: the artist needs an unassimilable matter because beauty is not resolved into ideas. Even if he is a prose-writer and assembles signs, his style will have neither grace nor force if it is not sensitive to the material character of the word and its irrational resistances. And if he wishes to build the universe in his work and to support it by an inexhaustible freedom, the reason is that he radically distinguishes things from thought. His freedom and the thing are homogeneous only in that both are unfathomable, and if he wishes to readapt the desert or the virgin forest to the Mind, he does so not by transforming them into ideas of desert and forest, but by having Being sparkle as Being, with its opacity and its coefficient of adversity, by the indefinite spontaneity of Existence. That is why the work of art is reducible to an idea: first, because it is a production or a reproduction of a *being*, that is, of something which never quite allows itself to be *thought*; then, because this being is totally penetrated by an *existence*, that is, by a freedom which decides on the very fate and value of thought. That is also

why the artist has always had a special understanding of
Evil, which is not the temporary and remediable isolation of
an idea, but the irreducibility of man and the world of
Thought.

The bourgeois could be recognized by the fact that he
denied the existence of social classes and particularly of the
bourgeoisie. The gentleman wished to command because he
belonged to a caste. The bourgeois based his power and his
right to govern on the exquisite ripening which comes from
the secular possession of the goods of this world. Moreover, he admitted only synthetic relationships between the
owner and the thing possessed; for the rest, he demonstrated
by analysis that all men are alike because they are unvarying
elements of social combinations and because each one of
them, whatever his rank, completely possesses *human nature*.
Hence, inequalities appeared as fortuitous and passing accidents which could not alter the permanent characteristics of
the social atom. There was no proletariat, that is, no synthetic class of which each worker was a passing mode; there
were only proletarians, each isolated in his human nature,
who were not united by internal solidarity but only by
external bonds of resemblance.

The bourgeois saw only *psychological* relations among the
individuals whom his analytical propaganda circumvented
and separated. That is understandable: as he had no direct
hold on things, as his work was concerned essentially with
men, it was purely a matter, for him, of pleasing and intim-
idating. Ceremony, discipline, and courtesy ruled his behaviour; he regarded his fellow-men as marionettes, and if
he wished to acquire some knowledge of their emotions and
character, it was because it seemed to him that each passion
was a wire that could be pulled. The breviary of the ambitious bourgeois was 'The Art of Making Good'; the
breviary of the rich was 'The Art of Commanding'. Thus,
the bourgeoisie considered the writer as an expert. If he
started reflecting on the social order, he annoyed and frightened it. All it asked of him was to share his practical experience of the human heart. So, as in the seventeenth century,

literature was reduced to psychology. All the same, the psychology of Corneille, Pascal and Vauvenargues was a cathartic appeal to freedom. But the merchant distrusted the freedom of the people he dealt with and the prefect that of the sub-prefect. All they wanted was to be provided with infallible recipes for winning over and dominating. Man had to be governable as a matter of course and by modest means. In short, the laws of the heart had to be rigorous and without exceptions. The bourgeois bigwig no more believed in human freedom than the scientist believes in a miracle. And as his ethics were utilitarian, the chief motive of his psychology was self-interest. For the writer it was no longer a matter of addressing his work as an appeal to absolute freedoms, but of exhibiting the psychological laws which determined him to readers who were likewise determined.

Idealism, psychologism, determinism, utilitarianism, the spirit of seriousness—this was what the bourgeois writer had to reflect to his public first of all. He was no longer asked to restore the strangeness and opacity of the world, but to dissolve it into elementary subjective impressions which made it easier to digest; nor was he asked to discover the most intimate movements of his heart at the very depths of his freedom, but to bring his 'experience' face to face with that of his readers. All his works were at once inventories of bourgeois appurtenances, psychological reports of an expert which invariably tended to ground the rights of the *élite* and to show the wisdom of institutions, and handbooks of civility. The conclusions were decided in advance; the degree of depth permitted to the investigation was also established in advance; the psychological motives were selected; the very style was regulated. The public feared no surprise. It could buy with its eyes closed. But literature had been assassinated. From Émile Augier to Marcel Prévost and Edmond Jaloux, including Dumas *fils*, Pailleron, Ohnet, Bourget, and Bordeaux, authors were found to do the job and, if I may say so, to honour their signature to the very end. It is not by chance that they wrote bad books; if they had talent, they were forced to hide it.

The best refused. This refusal saved literature but fixed its traits for fifty years. Indeed, from 1848 on, and until the war of 1914, the radical unification of his public led the author to write on principle *against all his readers*. However, he sold his productions, but he despised those who bought them and forced himself to disappoint their wishes. It was taken for granted that it was better to be unknown than famous, that success—if the writer ever got it in his lifetime—was to be explained by a misunderstanding. And if, by chance, the book one published did not offend sufficiently, one added an insulting preface. This fundamental conflict between the writer and his public was an unprecedented phenomenon in literary history. In the seventeenth century the harmony between the man of letters and his readers was perfect; in the eighteenth century the author had two equally real publics at his disposal and could rely upon one or the other as he pleased. In its early stages, romanticism had been a vain attempt to avoid open conflict by restoring this duality and by depending upon the aristocracy against the liberal bourgeoisie. But after 1850 there was no longer any means of covering up the profound contradiction which opposed bourgeois ideology to the requirements of literature. About the same time a virtual public was beginning to take form in the deeper layers of society; it was already waiting to be revealed to itself because the cause of free and compulsory education had made some progress. The Third Republic was soon to sanction the right of all men to read and write. What was the writer going to do? Would he choose the masses against the *élite*, and would he attempt to re-create for his own profit the duality of publics?

At first sight, it seemed so. By means of the great movement of ideas which from 1830 to 1848 were brewing in the marginal zones of the bourgeoisie, certain writers had the revelation of their virtual public. They adorned this public, under the name of 'The People', with mystic graces. It would be the instrument of salvation. But, as much as they loved it, they hardly knew it and above all they did not come from it. Sand was Baronne Dudevant; Hugo, the son of a general of the Empire; even Michelet, the son of a printer, was still far removed from the silk-weavers of Lyons or the textile-weavers of Lille. Their socialism—when they were socialists—was a by-product of bourgeois idealism. And then the people were much more the subject of certain of their works than their chosen public. Hugo, to be sure, had the rare fortune of penetrating everywhere. He was one of the few—perhaps the only one—of our writers who was really popular. But the others had incurred the hostility of the bourgeoisie without creating a working-class public in compensation. To convince oneself of this fact all one need do is compare the importance which the bourgeois University accorded to Michelet, an authentic genius and a first-rate prose-writer, and to Taine, who was only a cheap pedant, or to Renan, whose 'fine style' offers all the examples one could want of meanness and ugliness. This purgatory in which the bourgeois class let Michelet vegetate was without compensation; the 'people' that he loved read him for a while, and then the success of Marxism pushed him into oblivion. In short, most of these authors were the losers in a revolution that didn't come off. They attached their name and their destiny to it. None of them, except Hugo, really left their mark on literature.

The others, all the others, backed away from the perspective of an unclassing from below which would have made them sink straight down as if a stone had been tied round their necks. They had no lack of excuses: the time wasn't ripe, there was no real bond which attached them to the proletariat, that oppressed class couldn't absorb their work, it didn't know how much it needed them; their decision to defend it had remained abstract; whatever their sincerity might have been, they had 'brooded' over miseries which they had understood with their heads without feeling them in their hearts. Fallen from their class of origin, haunted by the memory of an affluence which they should have refused to accept, they ran the risk of forming 'a white-collar proletariat' on the margin of the real proletariat, suspect to the workers and spurned by the bourgeois, whose demands had been dictated by bitterness and resentment rather than large-mindedness and who had ended by turning against both groups.[12]

Besides, in the eighteenth century, the necessary liberties required by literature were not distinguished from the political liberties which the citizen wanted to win; all that was necessary for the writer to become a revolutionary was to explore the arbitrary essence of his art and to make himself the interpreter of its formal demands; when the revolution which was in the making was bourgeois, literature was naturally revolutionary because the first discovery which it made of itself revealed to it its connections with political democracy. But the formal liberties which the essayist, the novelist, and the poet were to defend had nothing in common with the deeper needs of the proletariat. The latter was not dreaming of demanding political freedom, which, after all, it did enjoy, and which was only a mystification.[13] As for freedom of thought, for the time being the proletariat was not concerned with it. What it asked for was quite different from these abstract liberties. It wanted material improvement of its lot, and more deeply, and more obscurely too, the end of man's exploitation by man. We shall see later that these demands were of the same kind made by the art of writing conceived as a concrete and historical phenomenon; that is, as the particular and timely appeal which, by agreeing to historicize himself, a man launches in regard to all mankind to the men of his time.

But in the nineteenth century literature had just disengaged itself from religious ideology and refused to serve bourgeois ideology. Thus, it set itself up as being, in principle, independent of any sort of ideology. As a result, it retained its abstract aspect of pure negativity. It had not yet understood that it *was itself* ideology; it wore itself out asserting its autonomy, which no one contested. This amounted to saying that it claimed it had no privileged subject and could treat any matter whatever. There was no doubt about the fact that one might write felicitously about the condition of the working class; but the choice of this

subject depended upon circumstances, upon a free decision
of the artist. One day one might talk about a provincial
bourgeoise, another day, about Carthaginian mercenaries.
From time to time, a Flaubert would affirm the identity of
form and content, but he drew no practical conclusion from
it. Like all his contemporaries, he drew his definition of
beauty from what the Winckelmanns and Lessings had said
almost a hundred years earlier and which in one way or
other boiled down to presenting it as multiplicity in unity.
It was a matter of capturing the iridescence of the various
and imposing a strict unity upon it by means of style. The
'artistic style' of the Goncourts had no other meaning. It
was a formal method of unifying and embellishing any
materials, even the most beautiful. How could anyone have
then conceived that there might be an internal relationship
between the demands of the lower classes and the principles
of the art of writing? Proudhon seems to have been the only
one to have surmised it. And of course Marx. But they were
not men of letters. Literature, still completely absorbed by
the discovery of its autonomy, was to itself its own subject.
It had passed to the reflective period; it tried out its methods,
broke its former moulds, and tried to determine experiment-
ally its own laws and to forge new techniques. It advanced
step by step towards the current forms of the drama and the
novel, free verse, and the criticism of language. Had it discovered a specific content, it would have had to tear itself
away from its meditation on itself and derive its aesthetic
rules from the nature of this content.

At the same time, by choosing to write for a virtual
public, authors would have had to adapt their art to the
capacities of the readers, which would have amounted to
determining it according to external demands and not
according to its own essence. It would have had to give up
some of the exquisite forms of narrative, poetry, and even
reasoning, for the sole reason that they would be inaccessible
to readers without culture. It seemed, therefore, that literature would be running the risk of relapsing into alienation.
Hence, the writer, in all honesty, refused to enslave literature

to a public and a determined subject. But he did not perceive the divorce which was taking place between the concrete revolution trying to be born and the abstract games he was indulging in. This time it was the masses who wanted power, and as the masses had no culture or leisure, any would-be literary revolution, by refining its technique, put the works it inspired out of their range and served the interests of social conservatism.

Thus, he had to revert to the bourgeois public. The writer tried hard to break all relations with it, but by refusing to be unclassed from below, his break was condemned to remain symbolic; he played at it tirelessly; he showed it by his clothes, his food, the way he furnished his home, and the manners he adopted, but he did not do it. It was the bourgeoisie which read him. It was the bourgeoisie alone which maintained him and decided his fame. In vain did he pretend that he was getting perspective in order to consider it as a whole. Had he wanted to judge it, he would first have had to leave it, and there was no other way to leave it than by trying out the interests and way of life of another class. Since he did not bring himself to do this, he lived in a state of contradiction and dishonesty since he both knew and did not want to know *for whom* he was writing. He was fond of speaking of his *solitude*, and rather than assume responsibility for the public which he had slyly chosen, he concocted the notion that one writes for oneself alone or for God. He made of writing a metaphysical occupation, a prayer, an examination of conscience, everything but a communication. He frequently likened himself to one possessed, because, if he spewed up words under the sway of an inner necessity, at least he was not *giving* them. But that did not keep him from carefully polishing his writings. And moreover, he was so far from wishing harm to the bourgeoisie that he did not even dispute its right to govern.

Quite the contrary. Flaubert recognized its right and mentioned it by name, and his correspondence after the Commune, which frightened him so, abounds in disgraceful abuse of the workers. [14] And, as the artist, submerged in his milieu, was unable to judge it from without, as his rejections were ineffectual states of mind, he did not even notice that the bourgeoisie was an oppressing class; in fact, he did not at all consider it as a class, but rather as a natural species, and if he ventured to describe it, he did so in strictly psychological terms.

Thus the bourgeois writer and the 'damned' (*maudit*) writer moved on the same level; their only difference was that the first practised white psychology and the second, black psychology. For example, when Flaubert declared that he called 'anyone who thought basely bourgeois', he was defining the bourgeois in psychological and idealistic terms, that is, in the perspective of the ideology which he pretended to reject. As a result, he rendered a signal service to the bourgeoisie. He led back to the fold the rebellious and the maladjusted, who might have gone over to the proletariat, by convincing them that one could cast off the bourgeois in oneself by a simple inner discipline. All they had to do was to practise high thinking in private and they could continue to enjoy their goods and prerogatives with a peaceful conscience. They could still live in bourgeois fashion, and enjoy their incomes in bourgeois fashion, and frequent bourgeois drawing-rooms, but that would all be nothing but appearance. They had raised themselves above their kind by the nobility of their feelings. By the same token he taught his confrères the trick which could allow them, at any rate, to maintain a good conscience; for magnanimity finds its most fitting practice in the practice of the arts.

The solitude of the artist was doubly a fake: it covered up not only a real relationship with the great public but also the restoration of an audience of specialists. Since the government of men and goods was abandoned to the bourgeoisie, the spiritual was once again separated from the temporal. A sort of priesthood once again sprang up. Stendhal's public was Balzac, Baudelaire's was Barbey d'Aurevilly; and Baudelaire, in turn, made himself the public of Poe. These literary salons took on a vague collegiate atmosphere; one 'talked literature' in a hushed voice, with an infinite respect; one debated whether the musician derived more aesthetic joy from his music than the writer from his books. Art again became sacred to the extent that it turned aside from life. It even set up for itself a sort of communion of saints; one joined hands across the centuries with Cervantes, Rabelais, and Dante. One identified oneself with this monastic society. The priesthood, instead of being a concrete and, so to speak, geographical organism, became a hereditary institution, a club, all of whose members were dead except one, the last in point of time, who represented the others upon earth and who epitomized the whole college.

These new believers, who had their saints in the past, also had their future life. The divorce of the temporal and spiritual led to a deep modification of the idea of glory. From the time of Racine on, it had been not so much the revenge of the misunderstood writer as the natural prolongation of success in an immutable society. In the nineteenth century it functioned as a mechanism of overcompensation. 'I shall be understood in 1880', 'I shall win my trial on appeal'; these famous words prove that the writer had not lost the desire to practise a direct and universal action within the framework of an integrated collectivity. But as this action was not possible in the present, one projected into an indefinite future the compensatory myth of a reconciliation between the writer and his public. Moreover, all this remained quite vague; none of these lovers of glory asked himself in what sort of society he would be able to find his recompense. They merely took pleasure in dreaming that their grandnephews would profit from an internal betterment for having come at a later time into an older world. That was the way Baudelaire, who didn't worry about contradictions, often dressed his wounded pride, by considering his posthumous renown, although he held that society had entered a period of decadence which would end only with the disappearance of the human race.

Thus, for the present, the writer relied on an audience of

specialists; as for the past, he concluded a mystic pact with the great dead; as to the future, he made use of the myth of glory. He neglected nothing in wrenching himself free from his class. He was up in the air, a stranger to his century, out of his element, damned. All this play-acting had but one goal: to integrate the writer into a symbolic society which would be like an image of the aristocracy of the old régime. Psycho-analysis is familiar with these processes of identification of which artistic thinking offers numerous examples: the sick person who needs the key of the asylum in order to escape and finally comes to believe that he himself is the key. Thus, the writer, who needed the favour of the great to unclass himself, ended by taking himself for the incarnation of the whole nobility, and as the latter was characterized by its parasitism it was the ostentation of parasitism which he chose for his style of living. He made himself the martyr of pure consumption. As we have pointed out, he saw no objection to using the goods of the bourgeoisie, but on condition that he was to spend them, that is, transform them into unproductive and useless objects. He burned them, so to speak, because fire purifies everything. Moreover, as he was not always rich, and as he had to live well, he composed a strange life for himself, both extravagant and needy, in which a calculated improvidence symbolized the mad liberality which was denied him. Outside of art, he found nobility in only three kinds of occupation. First, in love, because it is a useless passion and because women, as Nietzsche said, are the most dangerous game. Also in travel, because the traveller is a perpetual witness who passes from one society to another without ever remaining in any and because, as a *foreign* consumer in an industrious collectivity, he is the very image of parasitism. Sometimes, in war too, because it is an immense consumption of men and goods.

The contempt with which trade was regarded in aristocratic and warlike societies was again met with in the writer. He was not satisfied with being useless, like the courtiers of the Old Régime; he wanted to be able to trample on utilitarian work, to smash it, burn it, damage it; he wanted to imitate the unconstraint of the lords whose hunting parties rode across the ripe wheat. He cultivated in himself those destructive impulses of which Baudelaire has spoken in *The Glass-maker*. A little later he was to have a particular liking for instruments which were defective, worthless or no longer in use, half retrieved by nature, and which were like caricatures of instruments. It was not a rare thing for him to consider his own life as a tool to be destroyed. In any event, he risked it and played to lose: alcohol, drugs, everything served his purpose. The height of uselessness, of course, was beauty. From 'art for art's sake' to symbolism, including realism and the Parnassians, all schools agreed that art was the highest form of pure consumption. It taught nothing, it reflected no ideology, and above all, it refrained from moralizing. Long before Gide wrote it, Flaubert, Gautier, the Goncourts, Renard, and Maupassant had in their own way said that 'it is with good sentiments that one produces bad literature'.

For some, literature was subjectivity carried to the absolute, a bonfire in which the black vines of their sufferings and vices writhed and twisted. Lying at the bottom of a world as in a dungeon, they passed beyond it and dispelled it by their dissatisfaction, which revealed other worlds to them. It seemed to them that their heart was different enough so that the picture of it which they drew might be resolutely barren. Others set themselves up as the impartial witnesses of their age, but nobody noticed that they were testifying. They raised testimony and witness to the absolute; they offered to the empty sky the tableau of the society about them. Circumvented, transposed, unified, and caught in the trap of an artistic style, the events of the universe were neutralized and, so to speak, put in parentheses; realism was an *epochē*. Here impossible truth joined hands with inhuman Beauty 'beautiful as a marble dream'. Neither the author, in so far as he wrote, nor the reader, in so far as he read, belonged to this world any longer: they were transformed into pure beholding; they considered man from without; they strove to see him from the point of view of God, or, if you like, of the absolute void. But after all, I can still recognize myself in the purest lyricist's description of his particularities. And if the experimental novel imitated science, was it not utilizable as science was? Could it not likewise have its social *applications?*

The extremists wished, for fear of being serviceable, that their works should not even enlighten the reader about his own heart; they refused to transmit their experience. In the last analysis the work would be entirely gratuitous only if it were entirely inhuman. The logical conclusion of all this was the hope of an absolute creation, a quintessence of luxury and prodigality, not utilizable in this world because it *was not of the world* and because it recalled nothing in it. Imagination was conceived as an unconditioned faculty of *denying* the real and the *objet d'art* was set up on the collapsing of the universe. There was the heightened artificiality of Des Esseintes, the systematic deranging of all the senses, and finally the concerted destruction of language. There was also silence: that icy silence, the work of Mallarmé—or the silence of M. Teste for whom all communication was impure.

The extreme point of this brilliant and mortal literature was nothingness. Its extreme point and its deeper essence. There was nothing positive in the new spirituality. It was a pure and simple negation of the temporal. In the Middle Ages it was the temporal which was the Inessential in relation to spirituality; in the nineteenth century the opposite occurred: the Temporal was primary and the spiritual was the inessential parasite which gnawed away at it and tried to destroy it. It was a question of denying the world or consuming it. Of denying it by consuming it. Flaubert wrote to disentangle himself from men and things. His sentence surrounds the object, seizes it, immobilizes it and breaks its back, changes into stone and petrifies the object as well. It is blind and deaf, without arteries; not a breath of life. A deep silence separates it from the sentence which follows; it falls into the void, eternally, and drags its prey along in this infinite fall. Once described, any reality is stricken from the inventory; one moves on to the next. Realism was nothing else but this great gloomy chase. It was a matter of setting one's mind at rest before anything else. Wherever one went, the grass stopped growing. The determinism of the naturalistic novel crushed out life and replaced human actions by one-way mechanisms. It had virtually but one subject: the slow disintegration of a man, an enterprise, a family, or a society. It was necessary to return to zero. One took nature in a state of productive disequilibrium and one wiped out this disequilibrium; one returned to an equilibrium of death by annulling the forces with which one was confronted. When, by chance, he shows us the success of an ambitious man, it is only in appearance; Bel Ami does not take the strongholds of the bourgeoisie by assault; he is a gauge whose rise merely testifies to the collapse of a society. And when symbolism discovered the close relationship between beauty and death, it was merely making explicit the theme of the whole literature of a half century. The beauty of the past, because it is gone; the beauty of young people dying and of flowers which fade; the beauty of all erosions and all ruins; the supreme dignity of consumption, of the disease which consumes, of the love which devours, of the art which kills; death is everywhere, before us, behind us, even in the sun and the perfumes of the earth. The art of Barrès is a meditation on death: a thing is beautiful only when it is 'consumable', that is, it dies when one has enjoyed it.

The temporal structure which was particularly appropriate for those princely games was the moment. Because it passes and because in itself it is the image of eternity, it is the negation of human time, that three-dimensional time of work and history. A great deal of time is needed to build; a moment is enough to hurl everything to the ground. When one considers the work of Gide in this perspective, one cannot help seeing in it an ethic strictly reserved for the writer-consumer. What is his gratuitous act if not the culmination of a century of bourgeois comedy and the

imperative of the author-gentleman: Philoctète gives away
his bow, the millionaire squanders his banknotes, Bernard
steals, Lafcadio kills and Ménalque sells his belongings.

This destructive movement was to go to its logical consequence: 'The simplest surrealist act', Breton was to write
twenty years later, 'consists of going down into the street,
revolver in hand, and firing into the crowd at random as
long as you can.' It was the last stage of a long dialectical
process. In the eighteenth century literature had been a
negativity; in the reign of the bourgeoisie it passed on to a
state of absolute and hypostasized Negation. It became a
multicoloured and glittering process of annihilation. 'Surrealism is not interested in paying much attention . . . to
anything whose end is not the annihilation of being and its
transformation into an internal and blind brilliance which is
no more the soul of ice than it is of fire,' writes Breton once
again. In the end there is nothing left for literature to do but
to challenge itself. That is what it did in the name of
surrealism. For seventy years writers had been working
to consume the world; after 1918 one wrote in order
to consume literature: one squandered literary traditions,
hashed together words, threw them against each other to
make them shatter. Literature as Negation became Anti-
literature; never had it been more *literary*: the circle was
completed.

During the same time, the writer, in order to imitate the
lighthearted squandering of an aristocracy of birth, had no
greater concern than that of establishing his irresponsibility.
He began by setting up the rights of genius which replaced
the divine right of the authoritarian monarchy. Since Beauty
was luxury carried to the extreme, since it was a pyre with
cold flames which lit up and consumed everything, since it
was fed by all forms of deterioration and destruction, in
particular suffering and death, the artist, who was its priest,
had the right to demand in its name and to provoke, if need
be, the unhappiness of those close to him. As for him, he
had been burning for a long time; he was in ashes; other
victims were needed to feed the flames. Women in particular:

they would make him suffer and he would pay them back
with interest. He wanted to be able to bring bad luck to
everyone around him. And if there were no means of setting off catastrophes, he would accept offerings. Admirers,
male and female, were there so that he might set fire to their
hearts or spend their money without gratitude or remorse.
Maurice Sachs reports that his maternal grandfather, who
had a fanatical admiration for Anatole France, spent a
fortune furnishing the Villa Saïd. When he died, Anatole
France uttered this funeral eulogy: 'Too bad! He was
decorative.' By taking money from the bourgeois, the writer
was practising his priesthood, since he was diverting a part
of their wealth in order to send it up in smoke. And by the
same token he placed himself above all responsibilities:
whom could he be responsible to? And in the name of what?
If his work aimed at constructing, he could be asked to give
an account. But since it declared itself to be pure destruction,
it escaped judgement.

At the end of the century all this remained somewhat
confused and contradictory. But when literature, with surrealism, made itself a provocation to murder, one saw the
writer, by a paradoxical but logical sequence, explicitly
setting up the principle of his total irresponsibility. To tell
the truth, he did not make his reasons clear; he took refuge
in the bushes of automatic writing. But the motives are
evident: a parasitic aristocracy of pure consumption, whose
function was to keep burning the goods of an industrious
and productive society, could not come under the jurisdiction of the collectivity he was destroying. And as this
systematic destruction never went any further than *scandal*,
this amounted in the last analysis to saying that the primary
duty of the writer was to provoke scandal and that his
inalienable right was to escape its consequences.

The bourgeoisie let him carry on; it smiled at these pranks.
What did it matter if the writer scorned it? This scorn
wouldn't lead to anything since the bourgeoisie was his only
public. It was the only one to whom he spoke about it; it
was a secret between them; in a way, it was the bond which

united them. And even if he won the popular audience, what likelihood was there of stirring up the discontent of the masses by showing that bourgeois thinking was contemptible? There was not the slightest chance that a doctrine of absolute consumption could fool the working classes. Besides, the bourgeoisie knew very well that the writer secretly took its part: he needed it for his aesthetic of opposition and resentment; it provided him with the goods he consumed; he wanted to preserve the social order so that he could feel that as a stranger there he was a permanent fixture. In short, he was a rebel, not a revolutionary.

As for rebels, they were right in the bourgeoisie's line. In a sense, the bourgeoisie even became their accomplice; it was better to keep the forces of negation within a vain aestheticism, a rebellion without effect; if they were free, they might have interested themselves on behalf of the oppressed classes. And then, bourgeois readers understood, in their way, what the writer called the *gratuitousness* of his work: for the latter, this was the very essence of spirituality and the heroic manifestation of his break with the temporal; for the former, a gratuitous work was fundamentally inoffensive, an amusement. They doubtless preferred the literature of Bordeaux and Bourget but they did not think it bad if there were useless books. Such books distracted the mind from serious preoccupations; they provided it with the recreation it needed for its general well-being. Thus, even while recognizing that the work of art could serve no purpose, the bourgeois public still found means of utilizing it.

The writer's success was built upon this misunderstanding; as he rejoiced in being misunderstood, it was normal for his readers to be mistaken. Since literature had become in his hands an abstract negation which fed on itself, he must have expected them to smile at his most cutting insults and say 'it's only literature'; and since it was a pure challenge to the spirit of seriousness, he must have been pleased that they refused on principle to take him seriously. Thus, they found themselves, even though it was with scandal and without quite realizing it, in the most 'nihilistic' works of the age.

The reason was that even though the writer might have put all his efforts into concealing his readers from himself, he could never completely escape their insidious influence. A shame-faced bourgeois, writing for bourgeois without admitting it to himself, he was able to launch the maddest ideas; the ideas were often only bubbles which popped up on the surface of his mind. But his technique betrayed him because he did not watch over it with the same zeal. It expressed a deeper and truer choice, an obscure metaphysic, a genuine relationship with contemporary society. Whatever the cynicism and the bitterness of the chosen subject, nineteenth-century narrative technique offered the French public a reassuring image of the bourgeoisie. Our authors, to be sure, inherited it, but they were responsible for having perfected it.

Its appearance, which dates from the end of the Middle Ages, coincided with the first reflective meditation by which the novelist became conscious of his art. At first he told his story without putting himself on the stage or meditating on his function because the subjects of his tales were almost always of folk or, at any rate, collective origin, and he limited himself to making use of them. The social character of the matter he worked with as well as the fact that it existed before he came to be concerned with it conferred upon him the rôle of intermediary and was enough to justify him; he was the man who knew the most charming stories and who, instead of telling them orally, set them down in writing. He invented little; he gave them style; he was the historian of the imaginary. When he himself started contriving the fiction which he published, he found himself. He discovered simultaneously his almost guilty solitude and unjustifiable gratuitousness, the subjectivity of literary creation. In order to mask them from the eyes of others and from his own as well, in order to establish his right to tell these stories, he wanted to give his inventions the appearance of truth. Lacking the power to preserve the almost material opacity which characterized them when they emanated from the collective imagination, he pretended that at least they did not originate with him, and he managed to give them out as memories. To do that he had represented himself in his works by means of a narrator of oral tradition and at the same time he inserted into them a fictitious audience which represented his real public, such as the characters in the *Decameron* whom their temporary exile puts curiously in the position of learned people and who in turn take up the rôle of narrator, audience, and critic. Thus, after the age of objective and metaphysical realism, when the words of the tale were taken for the very things which they named and when its substance was the universe, there came that of literary idealism in which the word has existence only in someone's mouth or on someone's pen and refers back in essence to a speaker to whose presence it bears witness, where the substance of the tales is the subjectivity which perceives and thinks the universe, and where the novelist, instead of putting the reader directly into contact with the object, has become conscious of his rôle of mediator and embodies the mediation in a fictitious recital.

Since that time the chief characteristic of the story which one gives to the public has been that of being already thought, that is, achieved, set in order, pruned, and clarified; or rather, of yielding itself only through the thoughts which one retrospectively forms about it. That is why the tense of the novel is almost always the past, whereas that of the epic, which is of collective origin, is frequently the present.

Passing from Boccaccio to Cervantes and then to the French novels of the seventeenth and eighteenth centuries, the proceedings grow complicated and become episodic because the novel picks up along the way and incorporates the satire, the fable, and the character sketch.[15] The novelist appears in the first chapter; he announces, he questions his readers, admonishes them, and assures them of the truth of his story. I shall call this 'primary subjectivity'. Then, secondary characters intervene along the way, characters whom the narrator has met and who interrupt the course of the plot to tell the story of their own misfortunes. These are the 'secondary subjectivities' supported and restored by the primary subjectivity. Thus, certain stories are re-thought and intellectualized to the second degree.[16] The readers never experience the direct onrush of the event; if the narrator has been surprised by it at the moment of its occurrence, he does not *communicate* his surprise to them; he simply *informs* them of it. As to the novelist, since he is convinced that the only reality of the word lies in its being said, since he lives in a polite century in which there still exists an art of conversation, he introduces conversationalists into his book in order to justify the words which are read there; but since it is by words that he represents the characters whose function is to talk, he does not escape the vicious circle.[17]

Of course, the authors of the nineteenth century brought their efforts to bear on the narration of the event. They tried to restore part of its freshness and violence, but for the most part they again took up the idealistic technique and adapted it to their needs. Authors as dissimilar as Barbey d'Aurevilly and Fromentin make use of it constantly. In *Dominique*, for example, one finds a primary subjectivity which manipulates the levels of a secondary subjectivity and it is the latter which makes the tale. The procedure is nowhere more manifest than in Maupassant. The structure of his short stories is almost invariable; we are first presented with the audience, a brilliant and wordly society which has assembled in a drawing-room after dinner. It is night-time, which dispels fatigue and passion. The oppressed are asleep, as are the rebellious; the world is enshrouded; the story unfolds. In a bubble of light surrounded by nothing there remains this *élite* which stays awake, completely occupied with its ceremonies. If there are intrigues or love or hate among its members, we are not told of them, and desire and anger are likewise stilled; these men and women are occupied in *preserving* their culture and manners and in *recognizing* each other by the rites of politeness. They represent order in its most exquisite form; the calm of night, the silence of the passions, everything concurs in symbolizing the stable bourgeoisie of the end of the century which thinks that nothing more will happen and which believes in the eternity of capitalist organization. Thereupon, the narrator is introduced. He is a middle-aged man who has 'seen much, read much, and retained much', a professional man of experience, a doctor, a military man, an artist, or a Don Juan. He has reached the time of life when, according to a respectful and comfortable myth, man is freed from the passions and considers with an indulgent clear sightedness those he has experienced. His heart is calm, like the night. He tells his story with detachment. If it has caused him suffering, he has made honey from this suffering. He looks back upon it and considers it as it really was, that is, *sub specie aeternitatis*. There was difficulty to be sure, but this difficulty ended long ago; the actors are dead or married or comforted. Thus, the adventure was a brief disturbance which is over with. It is told from the viewpoint of experience and wisdom; it is listened to from the viewpoint of order. Order triumphs; order is everywhere; it contemplates an old disorder as if the still waters of a summer day have preserved the memory of the ripples which have run through it. Moreover, had there even been this disturbance? The evocation of an abrupt change would frighten this bourgeois society. Neither the general nor the doctor confides his recollections in the raw state; they are experiences from which they have extracted the quintessence, and they warn us, from the moment they start talking, that their tale has a moral. Besides, the story is explanatory; it aims at producing a psychological law on the basis of this example. A law, or, as Hegel says, the calm image of change. And the change itself, that is, the individual aspect of the anecdote, is it not an appearance? To the extent that one explains it, one reduces the entire effect to the entire cause, the unforeseen to the expected and the new to the old. The narrator brings the same workmanship to bear upon the human event as, according to Myerson, the nineteenth-century scientist brought to bear upon the scientific fact. He reduces the diverse to the identical. And if, from time to time, he maliciously desires to maintain a slightly disquieting tone in his story, he dispenses the irreducibility of the change most carefully, as in those fantastic tales in which, behind the inexplicable, the author allows us to suspect a whole causal order which will restore rationality in the universe. Thus, for the novelist who is a product of this stabilized society change is a non-being, as it is for Parmenides, as Evil is for Claudel. Moreover, even should it exist, it would never be anything else but an individual calamity in a maladjusted soul.

It is not a question of studying the relative movements of partial systems within a system in motion—society, the universe—but of considering from the viewpoint of absolute rest, the absolute movement of a relatively isolated partial system. That is, one sets up absolute landmarks in order to determine it, and consequently one knows it in its absolute truth. In an ordered society which meditates upon its eternity and celebrates it with rites, a man evokes the phantom of a past disorder, makes it glitter, embellishes it with old-fashioned graces, and at the moment when he is about to cause uneasiness, dispels it with a wave of his magic wand and substitutes for it the eternal hierarchy of causes and laws. In this magician who frees himself from history and life by understanding them and who is raised above his audience by his knowledge and experience we recognize the lofty aristocrat whom we spoke about earlier. [18]

If we have spoken at some length about Maupassant's narrative procedure it is because it constituted the basic technique for all the French novelists of his own generation, of the succeeding one, and of all the generations since. The internal narrator is always present. He may reduce himself to an abstraction; often he is not even explicitly designated; but, at any rate, it is through his subjectivity that we perceive the event. When he does not appear at all, it is not that he has been suppressed like a useless device; it is that he has become the *alter ego* of the author. The latter, with his blank sheet of paper in front of him, sees his imagination transmuted into experiences. He no longer writes in his own name but at the dictation of a mature and sober man who has witnessed the circumstances which are being related.

Daudet, for example, obviously had the mind of a

drawing-room raconteur who infuses into his style the twists and friendly casualness of worldly conversation, who exclaims, grows ironical, questions, and challenges his audience: 'Ah! how disappointed Tartarin was! And do you know why? You won't guess in a million years!' Even realistic writers who wished to be the objective historians of their time preserved the abstract scheme of the method; that is, in all their novels there is a common milieu, a common plot, which is not the individual and historical subjectivity of the novelist but the ideal and universal one of the man of experience. First of all, the tale is laid in the past: the ceremonial past, in order to put some distance between the events and the audience; the subjective past, equivalent to the memory of the story-teller; the social past, since the plot does not belong to that history without conclusion which is in the making but to history already made.

If it is true, as Janet claims, that memory is distinguished from the somnambulistic resurrection of the past in that the latter reproduces the event, whereas the former, indefinitely compressible, can be told in a phrase or a volume, according to need, it can well be said that novels of this kind, with their abrupt contractions of time followed by long expansions, are precisely memories. Sometimes the novelist lingers to describe a decisive moment; at other times he leaps across several years: 'Three years flowed by, three years of gloomy suffering . . .' He permits himself to shed light on his characters' present by means of their future: 'They did not think at the time that this brief encounter was to have fatal consequences . . .' And from his point of view he is not wrong, since this present and future are both past, since the time of memory has lost its irreversibility and one can cross it backwards and forwards.

Besides, the memories which he gives us, already worked upon, thought over, and appraised, offer us an immediately assimilable teaching; the feelings and actions are often presented to us as typical examples of the laws of the heart: 'Daniel, like all young people . . .', 'Eve was quite feminine in that she . . .', 'Mercier had the nasty habit, common among civil-service clerks . . .' And as these laws cannot be deduced *a priori* nor grasped by intuition nor founded on experiments which are scientific and capable of being universally reproduced, they refer the reader back to a subjectivity which has produced these recipes from the circumstances of an active life. In this sense it can be said that most of the French novels of the Third Republic aspired, whatever the age of their real author and much more so if the author was very young, to the honour of having been written by quinquagenarians.

During this whole period, which extends over several generations, the plot is related from the point of view of the absolute, that is, of order. It is a local change in a system at rest; neither the author nor the reader runs any risk; there is no surprise to be feared; the event is a thing of the past; it has been catalogued and understood. In a stable society which is not yet conscious of the dangers which threaten it, which has a morality at its disposal, a scale of values, and a system of explanations to integrate its local changes, which is convinced that it is beyond history and that nothing important will ever happen any more, in a bourgeois France tilled to the last acre, laid out like a chessboard by its secular walls, congealed in its industrial methods, and resting on the glory of its Revolution, no other fictional technique could be possible. New methods that some writers attempted to introduce were successful only as curiosities or were not followed up. Neither writers, readers, the structure of the collectivity, nor its myths had any need of them.[19]

Thus, whereas literature ordinarily represents an integrating and militant function in society, bourgeois society at the end of the nineteenth century offers the unprecedented spectacle of an industrious society, grouped round the banner of production, from which there issues a literature which, far from reflecting it, never speaks to it about what interests it, runs counter to its ideology, identifies the beautiful with the unproductive, refuses to allow itself to be integrated, and does not even wish to be read.

The authors are not to be blamed; they did what they could; among them are some of our greatest and purest writers. And besides, as every kind of human behaviour discloses to us an aspect of the universe, their attitude has enriched us despite themselves by revealing gratuitousness as one of the infinite dimensions of the world and as a possible goal of human activity. And as they were artists, their work covered up a desperate appeal to the freedom of the reader they pretended to despise. It pushed challenge to the limit, even to the point of challenging itself; it gives us a glimpse of a black silence beyond the massacre of words, and, beyond the spirit of seriousness, the bare and empty sky of equivalences; it invites us to emerge into nothingness by destruction of all myths and all scales of value; it discloses to us in man a close and secret relationship with the nothing, instead of the intimate relationship with the divine transcendence. It is the literature of adolescence, of that age when the young man, useless and without responsibility, still supported and fed by his parents, wastes his family's money, passes judgement on his father, and takes part in the demolition of the serious universe which protected his childhood. If one bears in mind that the festival, as Caillois has well shown, is one of those negative moments when the collectivity consumes the goods it has accumulated, violates the laws of its moral code, spends for the pleasure of spending, and destroys for the pleasure of destroying, it will be seen that literature in the nineteenth century was, on the margin of the industrious society which had the *mystique* of saving, a great sumptuous and funereal festival, an invitation to burn in a splendid immorality, in the fire of the passions, even unto death. When I come to say later on that it found its belated fulfilment and its end in Trotskyizing surrealism, one will better understand the function it assumes in a too closed society: it was a safety valve. After all, it's not so far from the perpetual holiday to the permanent revolution.

However, the nineteenth century was the time of the writer's transgression and fall. Had he accepted declassing from below and had he given his art a content, he would have carried on with other means and on another plane the undertaking of his predecessors. He might have helped literature pass from negativity and abstraction to concrete construction; without losing the autonomy which the eighteenth century had won for it and which there was no longer any question of taking away from it, it might have again integrated itself into society; by clarifying and supporting the claims of the proletariat, he would have attained the essence of the art of writing and would have understood that there is a coincidence not only between formal freedom of thought and political democracy, but also between the material obligation of choosing man as a perpetual subject of meditation and social democracy. His style would have regained an inner tension because he would have been addressing a split public. By trying to awaken the consciousness of the working class while giving evidence to the bourgeois of their own iniquity, his works would have reflected the entire world. He would have learned to distinguish generosity, the original source of the work of art, the unconditioned appeal to the reader, from prodigality, its caricature; he would have abandoned the analytical and psychological interpretation of 'human nature' for the synthetic appreciation of *conditions*. Doubtless it was difficult, perhaps impossible; but he went about it the wrong way. It was not necessary for him to get on his high horse in a vain effort to escape all class determination, nor to 'brood over' the proletariat, but on the contrary to think of himself as a bourgeois who had broken loose from his class and who was united with the oppressed masses by a solidarity of interest.

The sumptuousness of the means of expression which he discovered should not make us forget that he betrayed literature. But his responsibility goes even further; if the authors had found an audience in the oppressed classes, perhaps the divergence of their points of view and the diversity of their writings would have helped to produce in the masses what someone has very happily called a *movement* of ideas, that is, an open, contradictory, and dialectical ideology.

Without doubt, Marxism would have triumphed, but it would have been coloured with a thousand nuances; it would have had to absorb rival doctrines, digest them, and remain open. We know what happened; two revolutionary ideologies instead of a hundred: before 1870, the Prudhonians in the majority in the International, then crushed by the defeat of the Commune; Marxism triumphing over its adversary not by the power of the Hegelian negation which preserves while it surpasses, but because external forces pure and simple suppressed one of the forms of the antinomy. It would take a long time to tell all that this triumph without glory has cost Marxism; for want of contradiction, it has lost life. Had it been the better, constantly combated, transforming itself in order to win, stealing its enemies' arms, it might have been identified with mind; alone, it became the Church, while the gentlemen-writers, a thousand miles away, made themselves guardians of an abstract spirituality.

Will anyone doubt that I am aware how incomplete and debatable these analyses are? Exceptions abound, and I know them, but it would take a big book to go into them. I have touched only the high spots. But above all, one should understand the spirit in which I have undertaken this work. If one were to see in it an attempt, even superficial, at sociological explanation, it would lose all significance. Just as for Spinoza, the idea of a line segment rotating about one of its extremities remains abstract and false if one considers it outside the synthetic, concrete, and bounded idea of circumference which contains, completes, and justifies it, likewise here, the considerations remain arbitrary if they are not replaced in the perspective of a work of art, that is, of a free and unconditioned appeal to a freedom. One cannot write without a public and without a myth—without a *certain* public which historical circumstances have made, without a *certain* myth of literature which depends to a very great extent upon the demand of this public. In a word, the author is in a situation, like all other men. But his writings, like every human project, simultaneously enclose, specify, and surpass this situation, even explain it and set it up, just as the idea of a circle explains and sets up that of the rotation of a segment.

Being situated is an essential and necessary characteristic of freedom. To describe the situation is not to cast aspersions on freedom. The Jansenist ideology, the law of the three unities, and the rules of French prosody are not art; in regard to art they are even pure nothingness, since they can by no means produce, by a simple combination, a good tragedy, a good scene, or even a good line. But the art of Racine had to be invented *on the basis* of these; not by conforming to them, as has been rather foolishly said, and by deriving exquisite difficulties and necessary constraints from them, but rather by re-inventing them, by conferring a new and peculiarly Racinian function upon the division into acts, the caesura, rhyme, and the ethics of Port Royale, so that it is impossible to decide whether he poured his subject into a mould which his age imposed upon him or whether he really elected this *technique* because his subject required it. To understand what *Phèdre* could not be, it is necessary to appeal to all anthropology. To understand what it *is*, it is necessary only to read or listen, that is, to make oneself a pure freedom and to give one's confidence generously to a generosity. The examples we have chosen have served only to *situate* the freedom of the writer in different ages, to illuminate by the limits of the demands made upon him the limits of his appeal, to show by the idea of his rôle which the public fashions for itself the necessary boundaries of the idea which he invents of literature. And if it is true that the essence of the literary work is freedom totally disclosing and willing itself as an appeal to the freedom of other men, it is also true that the different forms of oppression, by hiding from men the fact that they were free, have screened all or part of this essence from authors. Thus, the opinions which they have formed about their profession are necessarily truncated. There is always some truth tucked away in them, but this partial and isolated truth becomes an error if one stops there, and the social movement permits us to conceive the fluctuations of the literary idea, although each particular work surpasses, in a certain way, all conceptions which one can have of art, because it is always, in a certain sense, unconditioned, because it comes out of nothingness and holds the world in suspense in nothingness. In addition, as our descriptions have permitted us to catch a glimpse of a sort of dialectic of the idea of literature, we can, without in the least pretending to give a history of belles-lettres, restore the movement of this dialectic in the last few centuries in order to discover at the end, be it as an ideal, the pure essence of the literary work and, conjointly, the type of public—that is, of society— which it requires.

I say that the literature of a given age is alienated when it has not arrived at the explicit consciousness of its autonomy and when it submits to temporal powers or to an ideology, in short, when it considers itself as a means and not as an unconditioned end. There is no doubt that literary works, in their particularity, surpass this servitude and that each one contains an unconditioned exigence, but only by implication. I say that a literature is abstract when it has not yet acquired the full view of its essence, when it has merely set up the principle of its formal autonomy and when it considers the subject of the work as indifferent. From this point of view the twelfth century offers us the image of a concrete and alienated literature. Concrete, because content and form are blended; one learns to write only to write about God; the book is the mirror of the world in so far as the world is His work; it is an inessential creation on the margin of a major Creation; it is praise, psalm, offering, a pure reflection. By the same token literature falls into alienation; that is, since it is, in any case, the reflectiveness of the social body, since it remains in the state of non-reflective reflectiveness, it mediates the Catholic universe; but, for the clerk, it remains the immediate; it retrieves the world, but by losing itself. But as the reflective idea must necessarily reflect *itself* on pain of annihilating itself with the whole reflected universe, the three examples which we have studied showed a movement of the retrieving of literature by itself, that is, its transition from the state of unreflective and immediate reflection to that of reflective mediation. At first concrete and alienated, it liberates itself by negativity and passes to abstraction; more exactly, it passes in the eighteenth century to abstract negativity before becoming in the late nineteenth and early twentieth century absolute negation. At the end of this evolution it has cut all its bonds with society; it no longer even has a public. 'Every one knows', writes Paulhan, 'that there are two literatures in our time, the bad, which is really unreadable (it is widely read) and the good, which is not read.'

But even that is an advance; at the end of this lofty isolation, at the end of this scornful rejection of all efficacity there is the destruction of literature by itself; at first, the terrible 'it's *only* literature'; then, that literary phenomenon which the same Paulhan calls terrorism, which is born at about the same time as the idea of parasitic gratuitousness, and as its antithesis, and which runs all through the nineteenth century, contracting as it goes a thousand irrational marriages, and finally bursts forth shortly before the First World War. Terrorism, or rather the terrorist complex, for it is a tangle of vipers. One might distinguish, first, so deep a disgust with the sign as such that it leads in all cases to preferring the thing signified to the word, the act to the statement, the word conceived as object to the word-meaning, that is, in the last analysis, poetry to prose, spontaneous disorder to composition; second, an effort to make literature one expression among others of life, instead of sacrificing life to literature; and third, a crisis of the writer's moral conscience, that is, the sad collapse of parasitism. Thus, without for a moment conceiving the idea of losing its formal autonomy, literature makes itself a negation of formalism and comes to raise the question of its essential content. Today we are beyond terrorism and we can make use of its experience and the preceding analyses to set down the essential traits of a concrete and liberated literature.

We have said that, as a rule, the writer addressed all men. But immediately afterwards we noted that he was read only by a few. As a result of the divergence between the real public and the ideal public, there arose the idea of abstract universality. That is, the author postulates the constant repetition in an indefinite future of the handful of readers which he has at present. Literary glory peculiarly resembles Nietzsche's eternal recurrence; it is a struggle against history; here, as there, recourse to the infinity of time seeks to compensate for the failure in space (for the author of the seventeenth century, a recurrence *ad infinitum* of the gentleman; for the one of the nineteenth century, an extension *ad infinitum* of the club of writers and the public of specialists). But as it is self-evident that the effect of the projection into the future of the real and present public is to perpetuate, at least in the representation of the writer, the exclusion of the majority of men, as, in addition, this imagining of an infinity of unborn readers is tantamount to extending the actual public by a public made up of merely possible men, the universality which glory aims at is partial and abstract. And as the choice of the public conditions, to a certain extent, the choice of subject, the literature which has set up glory as its goal and its governing idea must also remain abstract.

The term 'concrete universality' must be understood, on the contrary, as the sum total of men living in a given society. If the writer's public could ever be extended to the point of embracing this total, the result would not be that he would necessarily have to limit the reverberations of his work to the present time, but rather he would oppose to the abstract eternity of glory, which is an impossible and hollow dream of the absolute, a concrete and finite duration which he would determine by the very choice of his subjects, and which, far from uprooting him from history, would define his situation in social time. As a matter of fact, every human project outlines a certain future by its very motto: if I'm going to sow, I'm putting a whole year of waiting before me; if I get married, my venture suddenly causes my whole life to rise up before me; if I launch out into politics, I'm mortgaging a future which will extend beyond my death. The same with writing. Already, under the pretence of belaurelled immortality, one discerns more modest and more concrete pretensions. The aim of *The Silence of the Sea* was to lead the French to reject the enemy's efforts to get them to collaborate. Its effectiveness and consequently its actual public could not extend beyond the time of the occupation. The books of Richard Wright will remain alive as long as the negro question is raised in the United States. Thus, there is no question as to the writer's renouncing the idea of survival; quite the contrary, he is the one who decides it; he will survive so long as he acts. Afterwards, it's honorary membership, retirement. Today, for having wanted to escape from history, he begins his honorary membership the day after his death, sometimes even while he is alive.

Thus, the concrete public would be a tremendous feminine questioning, the waiting of a whole society which the writer would have to seduce and satisfy. But for that the public would have to be free to ask and the writer to answer. That means that in no case must the questions of one group or class cover up those of other milieus; otherwise, we would relapse into the abstract. In short, *actual* literature can only realize its full *essence* in a classless society. Only in this society could the writer be aware that there is no difference of any kind between his *subject* and his *public*. For the subject of literature has always been man in the world. However, as long as the virtual public remained like a dark sea round the sunny little beach of the real public, the writer risked confusing the interests and cares of man with those of a small and favoured group. But, if the public were identified with the concrete universal, the writer would really have to write about the human totality. Not about the abstract man of all the ages and for a timeless reader, but about the whole man of his age and for his contemporaries. As a result, the literary antinomy of lyrical subjectivity and objective testimony would be left behind. Involved in the same adventure as his readers and situated like them in a society without cleavages, the writer, in speaking about them, would be speaking about himself, and in speaking about himself would be speaking about them. As no aristocratic pride would any longer force him to deny that he is in a situation, he would no longer seek to soar above his times and bear witness to it before eternity, but, as his situation would be universal, he would express the hopes and anger of all men, and would thereby express himself completely, that is, not as a metaphysical creature like the medieval clerk, nor as a psychological animal like our classical writers, nor even as a social entity, but as a totality emerging into the world from the void and containing within it all those structures in the indissoluble unity of the human condition; literature would really be anthropological, in the full sense of the term.

It is quite evident that in such a society there would be nothing which would even remotely recall the separation of the temporal and the spiritual. Indeed, we have seen that this division necessarily corresponds to an alienation of man and, therefore, of literature; our analyses have shown us that it always tends to oppose a public of professionals or, at least, of enlightened amateurs, to the undifferentiated masses. Whether he identifies himself with the Good and with divine Perfection, with the Beautiful or the True, a clerk is always on the side of the oppressors. A watchdog or a jester: it is up to him to choose. M. Benda has chosen the cap and bells and M. Marcel the kennel; they have the right to do so, but if literature is one day to be able to enjoy its essence, the writer, without class, without colleges, without salons, without excess of honours, and without indignity, will be thrown into the world, among men, and the very notion of clerkship will appear inconceivable. The spiritual, moreover, always rests upon an ideology, and ideologies are freedom when they make themselves and oppression when they are made. The writer who has attained full self-consciousness will therefore not make himself the guardian of any spiritual hero; he will no longer know the centrifugal movement whereby certain of his predecessors turned their eyes away from the world to contemplate the heaven of established values; he will know that his job is not adoration of the spiritual, but rather spiritualization.

Spiritualization, that is, *renewal*. And there is nothing else to spiritualize, nothing else to renew but this multicoloured and concrete world with its weight, its opaqueness, its zones of generalization, and its swarm of anecdotes, and that invincible Evil which gnaws at it without ever being able to destroy it. The writer will renew it as it is, the raw, sweaty, smelly, everyday world, in order to submit it to freedoms on the foundation of a freedom. Literature in this classless society would thus be the world aware of itself, suspended in a free act, and offering itself to the free judgement of all men, the reflective self-awareness of a classless society. It is by means of the book that the members of this society would be able to get their bearings, to see themselves and see their situation. But as the portrait compromises the model, as the simple presentation is already the beginning of change, as the work of art, taken as the sum of its exigencies, is not a simple description of the present but a judgement of this present in the name of a future, finally, as every book contains an appeal, this awareness of self is a surpassing of self. The universe is not challenged in the name of simple consumption, but in the name of the hopes and sufferings of those who inhabit it. Thus, concrete literature will be a synthesis of Negativity, as a power of uprooting from the given, and a Project, as an outline of a future order; it will be the Festival, the flaming mirror which burns everything reflected in it, and generosity, that is, a free invention, a gift. But if it is to be able to ally these two complementary aspects of freedom, it is not enough to accord the writer freedom to say everything; he must write for a public which has the freedom of changing everything; which means, besides suppression of classes, abolition of all dictatorship, constant renewal of frameworks, and the continuous overthrowing of order once it tends to congeal. In short, literature is, in essence, the subjectivity of a society in permanent revolution. In such a society it would go beyond the antinomy of word and action. Certainly in no case would it be regarded as an act; it is false to say that the author *acts* upon his readers; he merely makes an appeal to their freedom, and in order for his works to have any effect, it is necessary for the public to adopt them on their own account by an unconditioned decision. But in a collectivity which constantly corrects, judges, and metamorphoses itself, the written work can be an essential condition of action, that is, the moment of reflective consciousness.

Thus, in a society without classes, without dictatorship, and without stability, literature would end by becoming conscious of itself; it would understand that form and content, public and subject, are identical, that the formal freedom of saying and the material freedom of doing complete each other, and that one should be used to demand the other, that it best manifests the subjectivity of the person when it translates most deeply collective needs and, reciprocally, that its function is to express the concrete universal to the concrete universal and that its end is to appeal to the freedom of men so that they may realize and maintain the reign of human freedom. To be sure, this is utopian. It is possible to conceive this society, but we have no practical means at our disposal of realizing it. It has allowed us to perceive the conditions under which literature might manifest itself in its fullness and purity. Doubtless, these conditions are not fulfilled today; and it is today that we must write. But if the dialectic of literature has been pushed to the point where we have been able to perceive the essence of prose and of writing, perhaps we may at this time attempt to answer the only question which is urgent for us: what is the situation of the writer in 1947; what is his public; what are his myths; what does he want to write about; what can he and what ought he write about?

Situation of the Writer in 1947

I AM speaking about the French writer, the only one who has remained a bourgeois, the only one who has to adjust himself to a language which a hundred and fifty years of bourgeois domination have broken, vulgarized, slackened, and stuffed with 'bourgeoisisms', each of which seems a little sigh of ease and abandon. The American writer has often practised manual occupations before writing his books; he goes back to them. Between two novels, his vocation seems to be on the ranch, in the shop, in the city streets; he does not see in literature a means of proclaiming his solitude, but an opportunity of escaping it. He writes blindly, out of an absurd need to rid himself of his fears and anger, somewhat as the Mid-West farmer writes to the New York radio commentators to pour out his heart to them. He muses less about glory than he dreams of fraternity. He does not invent his manner against tradition, but for want of one, and in certain ways his most extreme audacities are *naïvetés*. The world is new in his eyes, everything is yet to be said, no one before him has spoken of the skies or the crops. He rarely appears in New York, and if he goes there, it is only on the way through, or, like Steinbeck, he locks himself up for three months to write and he's quits for the year, a year which he will pass on the highways, in the work-yards, or in the bars. It is true that he belongs to 'guilds' and Associations, but that is purely to defend his material interests. He has no solidarity with other writers; he is often separated from them by the length or breadth of the continent;[20] nothing is more remote from him than the idea of college or clerkship; for a while he is fêted and then is lost and forgotten; he reappears with a new book to take a new plunge.[21]

Thus, at the mercy of twenty ephemeral glories and

twenty disappearances, he drifts continually between the working-class world, where he goes to seek adventures, and his middle-class readers (I don't dare call them bourgeois; I very much doubt whether there is a bourgeoisie in the United States), hard, brutal, young, and lost, who tomorrow will take the same plunge as he.

In England, the intellectuals are less integrated into the collectivity than we; they form an eccentric and slightly cantankerous caste which does not have much contact with the rest of the population. The reason is, first of all, that they have not had our luck; because remote predecessors whom we hardly deserve prepared the Revolution, the class in power, after a century and a half, still does us the honour of fearing us a little (very little); it treats us tactfully. Our confrères in London, who do not have these glorious memories, do not frighten anyone; they are considered quite harmless; and then, club life is less suitable for spreading their influence than salon life has been in spreading ours. Among themselves, the men speak about business, politics, women, or horses, never about literature, whereas our matrons, who practised literature as an accomplishment, helped, by their receptions, to bring together politicians, financiers, generals, and men of letters. The English writers make a virtue of necessity and by aggrandizing the oddness of their ways attempt to claim as a free choice the isolation which has been imposed upon them by the structure of their society. Even in Italy, where the bourgeoisie, without ever having counted for much, has been ruined by fascism and defeat, the condition of the writer, needy, badly paid, lodged in dilapidated palaces too vast and grandiose to be heated or even furnished, at grips with a princely language too pompous to be supple, is far removed from ours.

Thus, we are the most bourgeois writers in the world. Well housed, decently dressed, not so well fed, perhaps; but even that is significant: the bourgeois spends less on his food, proportionally, than the workman; much more for his clothes and lodging. All of us, moreover, are steeped in bourgeois culture; in France, where the school leaving-certificate is a hallmark of the bourgeoisie, it is not permissible to plan to write without it. In other countries, the possessed, with dreamy eyes, twist and squirm under the sway of an idea which has seized them from behind and which they never manage to look in the face. After having tried everything, they end by trying to pour their obsession on paper and to let it dry there with the ink. But as for us, we were used to literature long before beginning our first novel. To us it seemed natural for books to grow in a civilized society, like trees in a garden. It is because we loved Racine and Verlaine too much that when we were fourteen years old, we discovered, during the evening study period or in the great court of the *lycée*, our vocation as a writer. Even before having found ourselves at grips with a work of our own—that monster, so drab, so smeared with our own sticky juices, such a gamble—we had been brought up on literature already made, and we naïvely thought that our future writings would issue from our mind in the finished state in which we found those of others, with the seal of collective recognition and the pomp which comes from secular consecration, in short, like national resources. For us, the ultimate transformation of a poem, its last toilette for eternity, was, after having appeared in magnificent illustrated editions, that it should end by appearing in small type in a hard-covered book bound in green canvas, whose clean smell of ink and pulp seemed to us the very perfume of the Muses, and that it should move the dreamy, inky-fingered sons of the future bourgeoisie. Breton himself, who wanted to set fire to culture, got his first literary shock in class one day when his teacher was reading Mallarmé to him. In short, for a long time we thought that the final destination of our work was to furnish literary texts for the French *explication* classes of 1980. Later on, five years would be just about long enough after our first book for us to be shaking hands with all our confrères. Centralization has grouped us all in Paris. With a bit of luck, a busy American might meet us all in twenty-four hours, to know, in twenty-four hours, our opinions about U.N.R.R.A., the U.N., U.N.E.S.C.O., the Henry Miller affair, and the atomic bomb; in twenty-four hours, a trained cyclist might circulate —from Aragon to Mauriac, from Vercors to Cocteau, stopping off to see Breton in Montmartre, Queneau in Neuilly, and Billy at Fontainebleau—a report of the scruples and moral crises which are part of our professional obligations, one of those manifestoes, one of those petitions or protests to Tito for or against the return of Trieste, the annexation of the Saar, or the use of V3's in future warfare, by which we like to show that we belong to our century; in twenty-four hours, without a cyclist, a piece of gossip goes all about our college and returns, embroidered, to the one who launched it. We all—or almost all—can be seen together in certain cafés, at the Pléiade concerts, and, in certain strictly literary circumstances, at the British Embassy. From time to time, one of us who has been overworking has it announced that he's leaving for the country; we all go to see him; we advise him that it's all for the best, that one can't write in Paris, and we see him off with our envy and our best wishes; as for us, an aged mother, a young mistress, or an urgent job keeps us in town. He leaves with the reporters of *Samedi-Soir* who are going along to photograph his retreat. He gets bored; he comes back. 'After all,' he says, 'there's only Paris.' It is Paris to which writers from the provinces, if they are well-off, come to practise regionalism; it is Paris where the qualified representatives of North African literature have chosen to express their nostalgia for Algiers. Our path is cut out for us; for the haunted Chicago Irishman who suddenly decides to write as a last recourse, the new life which he is tackling is a fearful thing with no point of comparison. It is a block of dark marble which will take him a long time to hew into shape; but we knew, from the time we were adolescent, the memorable and edifying features of great lives; even if our father did not disapprove of our vocation, we knew from the time we were fourteen, in the fourth grade of the *lycée*, how one replies to recalcitrant parents, how much time the author of genius has to remain unknown, at what age it is normal for glory to crown him, how many women he should have and how many unhappy loves, whether it is desirable that he mix in politics, and when; everything is written down in books; it is enough to bear it well in mind. Romain Rolland had proved at the beginning of the century in *Jean Christophe* that one can achieve a rather good likeness by combining the features of a few famous musicians. But one can devise other schemes; it's not bad to start one's life like Rimbaud, to begin a Goethean return to order in one's thirties, to throw oneself at fifty, like Zola, into a public debate. After that, you can choose the death of Nerval, Byron, or Shelley. Naturally, it will not be a matter of realizing each episode in all its violence, but rather of *indicating* it, as a serious tailor indicates the fashion without servility. I know several among us, and not the least, who have thus taken the precaution of giving their lives a turn and an allure both typical and exemplary, so that if their genius remains doubtful in their books, it might at least shine forth in their behaviour. Thanks to these models and recipes, from our childhood on the career of a writer seemed to us magnificent, though without surprises; one is promoted partly by merit, partly by seniority. That's what we are. In other respects, saints, heroes, mystics, adventurers, angels, enchanters, executioners, victims, as you like. But, first of all, bourgeois. There's no shame in admitting it. And different from one another only in the way we each assume this common situation.

In fact, if one wanted to make a sketch of contemporary literature, it wouldn't be a bad idea to distinguish three generations. The first is that of the authors who began to produce before the war of 1914. By now they have finished their career, and their future books, even though they may be masterpieces, will hardly be able to add to their fame; but they are still alive, they think and judge, and their presence determines minor literary currents which must be taken into account. The main thing, it seems to me, is that in their persons and by their works, they opened the way to a reconciliation between literature and the bourgeois public. It should first be noted that they drew the greater part of their resources from something quite other than their writings. Gide and Mauriac have property, Proust had independent means, Maurois comes from a family of manufacturers; others came to literature from the liberal professions: Duhamel was a doctor, Romains, a teacher, Claudel and Giraudoux were in the diplomatic service. The reason was that, except for successful tripe, one could not support oneself by literature in the period when they began writing. Like politics under the Third Republic, it could only be a 'marginal' occupation, even if it ended by becoming the principal concern of the one who practised it. Thus, literary personnel were drawn by and large from the same milieu as political personnel; Jaurès and Péguy came from the same school; Blum and Proust wrote in the same reviews. Barrès carried on his literary campaigns and his electoral campaigns on the same front. As a result, the writer could no longer consider himself as a pure consumer; he directed the production or supervised the distribution of goods or he was a civil-servant; he had duties towards the State; in short, a whole part of him was integrated into the bourgeoisie; his behaviour, his professional relationships, his obligations, and his concerns were bourgeois; he bought, sold, ordered, and obeyed; he entered the charmed circle of courtesy and ceremony. Certain writers of this period have a well-founded reputation for greed which is belied by the appeals which they have launched in their writings. I don't know whether this reputation is justified. It proves, all the same, that they know the value of money; the divorce we pointed out between the author and his public is now in the author's very soul. Twenty years after symbolism he had not forgotten about the absolute gratuitousness of art, but at the same time he was involved in the utilitarian cycle of means-ends and ends-means. A producer and destroyer at the same time. Divided between the spirit of seriousness that he has to observe at Cuverville, Frontenac, Elbeuf, and, when he has to represent

France, at the White House, and the holiday spirit of contentiousness that he finds as soon as he sits down before a
blank sheet of paper; incapable of embracing bourgeois
ideology without reserve as well as of condemning without
recourse the class to which he belongs. What saves him in
this embarrassment is that the bourgeoisie itself has
changed; it is no longer that fierce rising class whose sole
concern was thrift and the possession of goods. The sons
and grandsons of successful peasants and shopkeepers are
born into money; they have learned the art of spending.
The utilitarian ideology, without at all disappearing, is relegated to the background. A hundred years of uninterrupted
reign have created traditions; bourgeois childhoods in the
great country house or in the château bought from a ruined
noble have acquired a poetic depth; the 'men of property'
have less recourse in their prosperity to the spirit of analysis;
they, in turn, ask the spirit of synthesis to establish their
right to govern; a synthetic—thus poetic—bond is established between the proprietor and the thing possessed.

Barrès was the first to invent it; the bourgeois is one with
his property. If he remains in his province and on his
estate, something passes into him from the gentle foot-hills
of his region, from the silvery trembling of the poplars,
from the mysterious and slow fecundity of the soil, from
the rapid and capricious changes of mood in the skies; in
assimilating the world, he assimilates its depth; henceforth,
his soul has substrata, mines, gold-lodes, veins, underground
sheets of oil. Henceforth the *rallié** writer has his path cut
out for him; to save himself he will save the bourgeoisie
depthwise.

Of course, he will not serve utilitarian ideology. He will
even be, if necessary, its severe critic, but he will disclose
all the gratuity in the exquisite hothouse of the bourgeois
soul, all the spirituality which he needs to practise his art
with a good conscience. Instead of reserving this symbolic
aristocracy, which he won in the nineteenth century, for

* *Les ralliés*: 'Royalists and imperialists who have accepted the
Republic.' This term will appear hereafter in the text.—*Translator*.

himself and his confrères alone, he will extend it to the whole bourgeoisie. In about 1850 an American writer showed, in a novel, an old colonel sitting in a Mississippi steamboat; for a moment he was tempted to ponder the innermost recesses of the souls of the passengers about him. He soon dismissed this preoccupation, saying to himself, or approximately, 'It is not good for man to penetrate too far into himself.' That was the reaction of the first bourgeois generation.

About 1900 the machine was reversed in France: it was understood that one would find the seal of God in the human heart, provided one sounded it deeply enough. Estaunié speaks about secret lives. The postal-clerk, the blacksmith, the engineer, the departmental treasurer, all have their nocturnal and solitary fêtes. Consuming passions and wild conflagrations dwell deeply within them. In the wake of this author, and a hundred others, we were to learn to recognize in stamp and coin collecting all the nostalgia for the beyond, all the Baudelairean dissatisfaction. For I ask you, why would one spend one's time and money acquiring medallions, were it not that one was past caring for the friendship of men and the love of women and power? And what is more gratuitous than a stamp collection? Not everybody can be a Leonardo or a Michelangelo, but those useless stamps pasted on the pink pages of an album are a touching homage to all the nine muses; it is the very essence of destructive consumption.

Others saw in bourgeois love a desperate appeal mounting towards God. What is more disinterested, what is more poignant than an adultery? And that taste of ashes in one's mouth after coitus, is it not negativity itself and the contentiousness of all pleasures? Others went even further. They discovered a divine grain of madness not in the weaknesses of the bourgeoisie but in its very virtues. We were shown that the oppressed and hopeless life of the mother of a family was so absurd and so lofty in its obstinacy that all the extravagances of the surrealists appeared as common sense in comparison. A young author who underwent the influence of these teachers without belonging to their generation and who has since changed his mind, if I may judge by his behaviour, once said to me, 'Is there any madder wager than conjugal fidelity? Isn't it braving the Devil and even God? Show me a madder and more magnificent blasphemy.' You can see the trick; it's a matter of beating the great destroyers on their own ground. You name Don Juan and I answer by Orgon; there's more generosity, more cynicism, and more despair in raising a family than in seducing a thousand and one women. You offer Rimbaud, I come back with Chrysale; there's more pride and Satanism in assuming that the chair that one sees is a chair than in practising the systematic deranging of the senses. And so that there will be no doubt about it, the chair which is given to our perception is only probable; to assert that it is a chair, one must take a leap to the infinite and suppose an infinity of concordant representations. Doubtless, the vow of conjugal love also involves a virgin future; the sophism begins when one presents these necessary and, so to speak, natural inductions that man makes against time and to insure his tranquillity as the most audacious defiances, the most desperate challenges.

Be that as it may, that is how the writers I am talking about established their reputation. They addressed a new generation and explained to it that there was a strict equivalence between production and consumption and between construction and destruction; they demonstrated that order was a perpetual festival and disorder the most boring monotony. They discovered the poetry of daily life, made virtue enticing, even disturbing, and painted the bourgeois epic in long novels full of mysterious and perturbing smiles. That was all their readers asked for; when one is honest out of self-interest, virtuous out of pusillanimity, and faithful out of habit, it is agreeable to hear it said that one surpasses a professional seducer or a highwayman in boldness. In about 1924, I knew a young man of good family who was infatuated with literature, particularly contemporary authors. He fooled about when it was the thing to do, gorged himself on the poetry of the bars when it was *à la mode*, flashily paraded a mistress, and then, when his father died, prudently took over the family factory and followed the straight and narrow. He has since married an heiress; he doesn't deceive her, or, if he does, it's only on the sly, when he takes a trip. In short, the most faithful of husbands. Just about the time he got married, he drew from his reading the formula that was to justify his life: 'One should do what everyone else does', he wrote to me one day, 'and be like no one else.' You can guess that I regard that as the most abject garbage and the justification of all sorts of dishonesty. But it sums up rather well, I think, the ethics which our authors sold their public. They justified themselves with it first of all: you've got to do what everyone else does, that is, sell Elbeuf cloth or Bordeaux wine according to the conventional rules, take a wife with a dowry, visit your parents regularly, and your in-laws and the friends of your in-laws: you've got to be like no one else, that is, save your soul and your family's by fine writings which are both destructive and respectful. I shall call all these works an alibi literature. They rapidly supplanted those of the hireling writers. Since before the First World War, the governing classes needed alibis more than incense. The marvellous of Fournier was an alibi; a whole line of bourgeois fairies sprang from him; in each case it was a matter of leading each reader approximately to that obscure spot of the most bourgeois soul where all dreams meet and melt in a desperate desire for the impossible, where all the events of the most human everyday existence are lived as symbols, where the real is devoured by the imaginary, where the whole man is no longer anything but a divine absence. People are sometimes astonished that Arland was the author of both *Terres Etrangères* and *L'Ordre*; but they shouldn't be. The so noble dissatisfaction of his first heroes has meaning only if one experiences it at the heart of a strict order; it is not at all a matter of revolting against marriage, the professions, and the social disciplines, but of delicately going beyond them by means of a nostalgia which nothing can satisfy because at bottom it is not a desire for anything.

Thus, order is there only to be transcended, but it must be there. There you have it, justified and solidly re-established. It's certainly better to challenge it by a dreamy melancholy than to overthrow it by arms. I shall say as much about the restlessness of Gide, which later became confusion, and the sin of Mauriac, the place from which God is absent. It is always a matter of putting daily life in parentheses and living it scrupulously but without soiling one's hands; it is always a matter of proving that man is worth more than his life, that love is much more than love and the bourgeois much more than the bourgeois. In the greater writers there is, of course, something else. In Gide, in Claudel, in Proust, one finds the real experience of a man, and a thousand directions. But I have not wanted to draw a picture of a period but rather to show a climate and isolate a myth.[22]

The second generation came of age after 1918. Of course, this is a very rough classification since we are including Cocteau, who started before the war, whereas Marcel Arland, whose first book, to my knowledge, does not antedate the armistice, has definite affinities with the writers whom we have just spoken about. The obvious absurdity of a war whose true causes it took us thirty years to know leads back the spirit of Negativity. I am not going to enlarge upon this period of 'decompression', as Thibaudet has so well named it. It was all fireworks; now that it has fallen, so much has been written about it that we seem to know it thoroughly. All we need note is that its most magnificent rocket, surrealism, ties in with the destructive tradition of the writer-consumer. These turbulent young bourgeois wanted to ruin culture because they were cultivated; their chief enemy was Heine's philistine, Monnier's Prudhomme, and Flaubert's bourgeois, in short, their papa. But the violence of the preceding years had brought them to radicalism. Whereas their predecessors had confined themselves to combating the utilitarian ideology of the bourgeoisie by *consumption*, they more deeply identified the quest of the useful with the human project, that is, with the conscious and voluntary life. Consciousness is bourgeois, the

self is bourgeois. Negativity should devote itself, in the first
place, to that nature which, as Pascal says, is only a first
layer of custom. The first thing to be done is to eliminate
the conventional distinctions between conscious and unconscious life, between dream and waking. This means that
subjectivity is dissolved. There is, in effect, the subjective
when we recognize, the moment they appear, that our
thoughts, our emotions, and our will come from us, and
when we believe both that it is certain that they belong to us
and only probable that the external world is guided by them.

The surrealist took a hearty dislike to that humble certainty on which the stoic based his ethics. It displeased him
both by the limits it assigns us and the responsibilities it
places upon us. Any means were good for escaping consciousness of self and consequently of one's situation in
the world. He adopted psycho-analysis because it presented
consciousness as being invaded by parasitical outgrowths
whose origin is elsewhere; he rejected 'the bourgeois idea'
of work because work implies conjectures, hypotheses, and
projects, thus, a perpetual recourse to the subjective. Automatic writing was, above all, destruction of subjectivity.
When we try our hand at it, rushes of blood spasmodically
tear through us; we are ignorant of their origin; we do
not know them before they have taken their place in the
world of objects and we must then perceive them with
foreign eyes. Thus, it was not a matter, as has too often been
said, of substituting their unconscious subjectivity for consciousness, but rather of showing the subject as a flimsy
illusion at the heart of an objective universe. But the
surrealist's second step was to destroy objectivity in turn. It
was a matter of exploding the world, and as dynamite was
not enough, as, on the other hand, a *real* destruction of all
that exists was impossible, because it would simply cause
everything to pass from one *real* state to another *real* state,
one had to do one's best rather to disintegrate particular
objects, that is, to do away with the very structure of
objectivity in these witness-objects. Evidently this operation
cannot be tried out on things that *really* exist, which are

already given with their indeformable essence. Hence, one will produce imaginary objects, so constructed that their objectivity does away with itself. We are given a first draft of this procedure in the false pieces of sugar which Duchamp actually cut in marble and which suddenly revealed themselves as having an unexpected weight. The visitor who weighed them in his hand was supposed to feel, in a blazing and instantaneous illumination, the self-destruction of the objective essence of sugar. It was necessary to let him know the deception of all being, the malaise, the off-balance feeling we get, for example, from trick gadgets, when the spoon abruptly melts in the tea-cup, when the sugar (an inverse hoax to the one Duchamp constructed) rises to the surface and floats. It was hoped that by means of his intuition the whole world would be exposed as a radical contradiction. Surrealist painting and sculpture had no other aim than to multiply these local and imaginary explosions, which were like holes through which the entire universe would be drained out. The paranoiacally critical method of Dali was only a perfecting and complication of the procedure. It also professed to be an effort 'to contribute to the total discredit of the world of reality'. Literature also did its best to make language go through the same kind of thing and to destroy it by telescoping words. Thus, the sugar refers to the marble and the marble to the sugar; the limp watch challenges itself by its limpness; the objective destroys itself and suddenly refers to the subjective, since one disqualifies reality and is pleased to 'consider the very images of the external world as unstable and transitory' and to 'put them into the service of the reality of our mind'. But the subjective then breaks down in its turn and allows a mysterious objectivity to appear behind it.

All this without even starting a single real destruction. Quite the contrary; by means of the symbolic annulment of the self by sleep and automatic writing, by the symbolic annulment of objects by producing evanescent objectivities, by the symbolic annulment of language by producing aberrant meanings, by the destruction of painting by painting and of literature by literature, surrealism pursues this curious enterprise of realizing nothingness by too much fullness of being. It is always by *creating*, that is, by adding paintings to already existing paintings and books to already published books, that it destroys. Whence, the ambivalence of its works: each of them can pass for the barbaric and magnificent invention of a form, of an unknown being, of an extraordinary phrase, and, as such, can become a voluntary contribution to culture; and as each of them is a project for annihilating all the rest by annihilating itself along with it, Nothingness glitters on its surface, a Nothingness which is only the endless fluttering of contradictions. And the *esprit* which the surrealists wish to attain on the ruins of subjectivity, this *esprit* of which it is not possible to have an inkling otherwise than by the accumulation of self-destructive objects, also sparkles and flickers in the reciprocal and congealed annihilation of things. It is neither Hegelian Negativity, nor hypostasized Negation, nor even Nothingness, though it bears a likeness to it; it would be more correct to call it the *Impossible* or, if you like, the imaginary point where dream and waking, the real and the fictitious, the objective and the subjective, merge. Confusion and not synthesis, for synthesis would appear as an articulated existence, dominating and governing its internal contradictions. But surrealism does not desire the appearance of this novelty which it would again have to contest. It wants to maintain itself in the enervating tension which is produced by an unrealizable intuition. At least Rimbaud wanted to see a drawing-room in a lake; the surrealist wants to be perpetually on the point of seeing lake and drawing-room; if, by chance, he encounters them, he gets disgusted or he gets scared and gets into bed with the blinds drawn. He ends up by doing a lot of painting and writing but he never actually destroys anything. Moreover, Breton recognized this in 1925 when he wrote: 'The immediate reality of the surrealist revolution is not so much to change anything whatever in the physical and apparent order of things as to criticize a movement in the mind.' The destruction of the universe is the object of a subjective enterprise very like what has always been called philosophical conversion. This world, perpetually annihilated without one's touching a grain of wheat or sand or a feather of a bird, is quite simply *put in parentheses.* It has not been sufficiently noted that the constructions, paintings and poem-objects of surrealism were the manual realization of the sterilities by which the sceptics of the third century B.C. justified their perpetual *epochē.* After which, Carneades and Philo, sure of not compromising themselves by an imprudent adherence, lived like everybody else. In the same way, the surrealists, once the world is destroyed and miraculously preserved by its destruction, can shamelessly give full play to their immense love of the world. This world, the world of every day, with its trees and roofs, its women, its sea-shells, and its flowers, but haunted by the impossible and by nothingness, is what is called the marvellous in surrealism. I cannot keep myself from thinking of that other parenthesis by which the *rallié* writers of the preceding generation destroyed bourgeois life and preserved it with all its nuances. Isn't the marvellous in surrealism that of *Le Grand Meaulnes,* but *radicalized?* Certainly its passion is sincere, as are its hatred of and disgust with the bourgeois class. But the situation has not changed: one must save oneself without breaking anything —or by a symbolic breaking—wash oneself of the original contamination without giving up the advantages of one's position.

The root of the matter is that once again one has to find an eagle's nest. The surrealists, more ambitious than their fathers, count on the radical and metaphysical destruction which they are initiating to confer upon them a dignity a thousand times superior to that of the parasitic aristocracy. It is no longer a matter of escaping from the bourgeois class; one must leap out of the human condition. It is the family patrimony that these sons want to squander, it is the world. They have come back to parasitism as to a lesser evil, abandoning everything, studies and professions, by common consent; but they have never been satisfied with being parasites on the bourgeoisie; their ambition has been to be parasites on the human race. Metaphysical as it may be, it is clear that they have been unclassed from above and that their preoccupations have strictly forbidden them from finding a public in the working class. Breton once wrote: 'Marx said, "Transform the world." Rimbaud said, "Change life." For us, these two orders are one and the same.' That would be enough to reveal the bourgeois intellectual. For it is a question of knowing which change precedes which. For the militant Marxist there is no doubt that social transformation alone can permit radical transformations of thought and feeling. If Breton thinks that he can pursue his inner experiences on the margin of revolutionary activity and parallel to it, he is condemned in advance, for that would amount to saying that a freedom of spirit is conceivable in chains, at least for certain people, and, consequently, to making revolution less urgent. This is the very betrayal of which revolutionaries have always accused Epictetus and of which Politzer not long ago accused Bergson. And if it is maintained that Breton intended in this text to announce a progressive and interlinked metamorphosis of the social state and the intimate life, I answer by citing this other passage: 'Everything leads us to believe that there is a certain point in the mind from which life and death, the real and the imaginary, the past and the future, the communicable and the incommunicable, the high and the low, cease to be regarded as contradictory. . . . One would be wasting one's time looking for any other motive in surrealist activity than the hope of determining this point.' Is this not a proclamation of divorce from a working-class public more than from a bourgeois public? For the proletariat, engaged in struggle, must at every moment, in order to bring its undertaking to a successful conclusion, distinguish the past from the future, the real from the imaginary, and life from death. It is not by accident that Breton has cited these contraries; they are all categories of action; revolutionary activity, more than any other, needs them. And just as surrealism has radicalized the negation of the useful in order to transform it into a rejection of the project and the conscious life, it radicalizes the old literary claim of gratuitousness in order to make of it a rejection of action by destroying its categories. There is a surrealist quietism. Quietism and permanent violence; two complementary aspects of the same position. As the surrealist has deprived himself of the means of planning an enterprise, his activity is reduced to impulsions in the immediate. We find here a heavier and duller version of Gide's moment. That's not surprising; there is quietism in all parasitism and the favourite *tempo* of consumption is the moment.

Yet, surrealism declares itself revolutionary and offers its hand to the Communist Party. It is the first time since the Restoration that a literary school explicitly claims kinship with an organized revolutionary movement. The reasons are clear: these writers, who are also young people, want, above all, to destroy their family, their uncle the general, their cousin the curé, as Baudelaire in 1848 saw in the February revolution an opportunity to set fire to the house of General Aupick; if they were born poor, they have also certain complexes to liquidate, envy and fear; and then they are also rebelling against external constraints: the recently ended war, with its censorship, military service, taxes, army-ridden legislature, and all the general eye-wash; they are all anti-clerical, neither more nor less than Combes and the pre-war radicals, and they are nobly disgusted with colonialism and the war in Morocco. This indignation and hatred can be expressed abstractly by a conception of radical Negation which, *a fortiori*, will bring about, without there being any need of making it the object of a particular act of will, the negation of the bourgeois class. And youth being the metaphysical age *par excellence*, as Auguste Comte well noted, this metaphysical and abstract expression of their revolt is evidently the one they are choosing by preference. However, it is also the one which leaves the world strictly intact. It is true that they also add a few sporadic acts of violence, but at most, these scattered acts of violence succeed in provoking scandal. The best they can hope for is to set themselves up as a primitive and secret society on the model of the Ku Klux Klan. Thus, they get so far as to want others to take upon themselves, on the margin of their spiritual experiences, the forceful execution of acts of concrete destruction. In short, they would like to be the clerks of an ideal society whose temporal function would be the permanent practice of violence.[23] In this way, after praising the suicides of Vaché and Rigaut as exemplary acts, after presenting gratuitous massacre ('firing into the crowd') as the simplest surrealistic act, they summon to their aid the yellow peril. They do not see the profound contradiction which opposes these brutal and partial destructions to the poetic process of annihilation which they have undertaken. Indeed, every time a destruction is partial, it is a *means* for attaining a positive and more general end. Surrealism stops at this means; it makes it an absolute end; it refuses to go further. On the contrary, the total abolition it dreams of does not harm anybody precisely because it is total. It is an absolute located outside history, a poetic fiction. And it brings into the picture, among the realities to abolish, the end which, in the eyes of Asiatics or revolutionaries, justifies the violent means to which they are forced to have recourse.

As for the Communist Party, hounded by the bourgeois police, very inferior in number to the Socialist Party, with no hope of taking power except in the distant future, new, uncertain in its tactics, it is still in the negative phase. Its job is to win over the masses, bore from within among the socialists, and incorporate the elements that it will be able to detach from the collectivity which repulses it; its intellectual arm is criticism. Thus, it is not disinclined to see in surrealism a temporary ally which it is getting ready to reject when it will no longer need it; for negation, the essence of surrealism, is only a stage for the C.P. The latter is not willing even for a moment to consider automatic writing, induced sleep, and objective chance, except in so far as they may contribute to the disintegration of the bourgeois class. Thus, it seems that we have re-encountered that community of interests between the intellectuals and the oppressed classes which was the good fortune of the authors of the eighteenth century. But this is only superficial. The deep source of the misunderstanding lies in the fact that the surrealist is very little concerned with the dictatorship of the proletariat and sees in the Revolution, as pure violence, the absolute end, whereas the end that communism proposes to itself is the taking of power, and by means of that end it justifies the blood it will shed. And then the bond between surrealism and the proletariat is indirect and abstract. The strength of a writer lies in his direct action upon the public, in the anger, the enthusiasm, and the reflections which he stirs up by his writings. Diderot, Rousseau, and Voltaire were in constant contact with the bourgeoisie because it read them. But the surrealists have no readers in the proletariat; there is just a bare chance of their communicating with the party from the outside, or rather with its intellectuals. Their public is elsewhere, among the cultivated bourgeoisie; the C.P. knows this and uses them simply to stir up trouble in ruling-class circles. Thus, their revolutionary doctrines remain purely theoretical (since they change nothing by their attitude), do not help them gain a single reader, and find no echo among the workers; they remain the parasites of the class they insult; their revolt remains on the margin of the revolution. Breton finally recognizes this himself and returns to his independence as a clerk. He writes to Naville: 'There is not one of us who does not wish for the passing of power from the hands of the bourgeoisie to those of the proletariat. In the meantime, it is none the less necessary that the experiences of the inner life continue and, of course, with no external control, even Marxist. . . . The two problems are essentially distinct.'

The opposition will be accentuated when Soviet Russia and consequently the French Communist Party pass to the phase of constructive organization; surrealism, having remained *negative* in essence, will turn away from them. Breton will then draw near the Trotskyists precisely because the latter, a hounded minority, are still at the stage of critical negation. The Trotskyists, in their turn, will use the surrealists as an instrument of disintegration; a letter from Trotsky to Breton leaves no doubt about the matter. If the Fourth International too had been able to pass to the constructive phase, it is clear that it would have been the occasion of a break.

Thus, the bourgeois writer's first attempt to reconcile himself with the proletariat remains utopian and abstract because he is not seeking a public but an ally, because he preserves and reinforces the division of the temporal and spiritual and because he maintains himself within the limits of a clerkship. The agreement on principle between surrealism and the C.P. against the bourgeoisie does not go beyond formalism; it is the formal idea of negativity which unites them. In fact, the negativity of the Communist Party is temporary; it is a necessary, historical moment in its great enterprise of social reorganization; surrealist negativity, whatever one may say about it, remains outside history, in the moment and in the eternal simultaneously; it is the absolute end of life and art. Breton somewhere asserts the identity, or at least parallelism with reciprocal symbolization, of mind in its struggle against its bug-bears and the proletariat in its struggle against capitalism, which amounts to asserting the 'sacred mission' of the proletariat. But the fact is that this class, conceived as a legion of destroying angels, which the C.P. defends against the approaches of the surrealists like a wall, is really only a quasi-religious myth for the authors, one which plays, for the tranquillization of their conscience, a role analogous to that of the myth of the people in 1848 for the writers of goodwill.

The originality of the surrealist movement resides in its attempt to appropriate *everything* at the same time: unclassing from above, parasitism, aristocracy, the metaphysic of consumption, and alliance with revolutionary forces. The history of this attempt has shown that it was doomed to failure. But fifty years earlier it would not even have been conceivable; the only relation a bourgeois writer could have had at that time with the working class was to write for it and about it. The thing that permits dreaming, be it only for a moment, of concluding a temporary pact between an intellectual aristocracy and the oppressed classes is the appearance of a new factor: the party as a mediator between the middle classes and the proletariat.

I understand well enough that surrealism with its ambiguous aspect of literary chapel, spiritual college, church, and secret society[24] is only one of the post-war products. One would have to speak of Morand, Drieu la Rochelle, and a host of others. But if the works of Breton, Peret, and Desnos have seemed to us the most representative, the fact is that all the others implicitly contain the same traits. Morand is the consuming type, the traveller, the wayfarer. He nullifies national traditions by putting them into contact with each other according to the old procedure of the sceptics and Montaigne; he throws them into a basket like crabs, and, without commentary, leaves it to them to tear each other apart. It is a matter of achieving a certain *gamma* point, highly akin to the *gamma* point of the surrealists, whence differences of custom, language, and interests abolish each other in the total indistinctness. Here *speed* plays the rôle of the paranoiac-critical method. *Gallant Europe* is the nullification of countries by the railroad; *Nothing but the Earth*, the nullification of continents by the aeroplane. Morand has Asiatics go about in London, Americans in Syria, and Turks in Norway; he shows our customs as seen through these eyes, as Montesquieu did by those of Persians, which is the surest way of removing their *raison d'être.* But at the same time he arranges it so that these visitors have lost much of their pristine purity and are already thorough traitors to their customs without having completely adopted ours; at this particular moment of their transformation each of them is a battlefield where the exotic and picturesque and our rationalistic mechanism are being destroyed by each other. His books, full of tinsel and trinkets and strange, lovely names, nevertheless, ring the knell of exoticism; they are at the origin of a whole literature which aims at doing away with local colour, either by showing that the distant cities we dreamed of in our childhood are as hopelessly familiar and commonplace to the eyes of their inhabitants as the Saint Lazare Station and the Eiffel Tower are to ours, or by letting us perceive the comedy, trickery, and absence of faith behind ceremonies which travellers of past centuries described for us with the utmost respect, or by revealing to us through the worn-out screen of oriental or African picturesqueness the universality of capitalist mechanism and rationalism. In the end nothing else is left but the world, similar and monotonous everywhere. I have never felt the deeper meaning of this procedure so keenly as I did one day in the summer of 1938, between Mogador and Sufi, when I was in a bus which passed a veiled Mohammedan woman who was riding a bicycle. A Mohammedan woman on a bike! There you have a self-destructive object which the surrealists or Morand can equally well lay claim to. The precise mechanism of the bicycle challenges the idle harem dreams which one ascribes to this veiled creature as she passes by but at the same moment what remains of the voluptuous and magical darkness between the painted eyebrows and behind the low forehead challenges, in turn, mechanism; it gives us a feeling that behind capitalist standardization, there is something beyond, which, though chained and conquered, is yet virulent and bewitching. Phantom exoticism, the surrealist impossible, and bourgeois dissatisfaction: in all three cases the real breaks down; behind it one tries to maintain the irritating tension of the contradictory. In the case of the travel writers the ruse is obvious: they suppress exoticism because one is always exotic in relation to someone, and they don't want to be; they destroy history and traditions in order to escape from their historical *situation*; they want to forget that the most lucid consciousness is always grafted on to something; they want to effect a fictitious liberation by means of an abstract internationalism and to achieve, by means of universality, an aristocratic detachment.

Drieu, like Morand, sometimes makes use of self-destruction by exoticism; in one of his novels, the Alhambra becomes an arid provincial park under a monotonous sky. But through the literary destruction of the object, of love, over twenty years of follies and bitterness, he was pursuing the destruction of himself; he was the empty valise, the opium smoker, and in the end, the vertigo of death drew him into National Socialism. *Gilles*, the squalid and glib novel about his life, shows clearly that he was the enemy brother of the surrealists. His Nazism, which also was only an appetite for universal conflagration, proved, in practice, to be as ineffectual as the communism of Breton. Both of them are clerks. Both of them, innocently and without ulterior motives, ally themselves with the temporal. But the surrealists are healthier; their myth of destruction covers up an enormous and magnificent appetite; they want to destroy everything but themselves, as is shown by their horror of disease, vice, and drugs. Drieu, gloomy and more genuine, meditated upon his death; it was because of self-hatred that he hated his country and mankind. They all were after the absolute, and as they were hemmed in everywhere by the relative, they identified the absolute with the *impossible*. They all hesitated between two rôles: that of proclaimers of a new world and that of gravediggers of the old. But as it was easier to discern signs of decadence in post-war Europe than those of renewal, they chose to be grave-diggers. And to soothe their conscience they restored to a place of honour the old Heraclitean myth according to which life is born from death. They were all haunted by that imaginary *gamma* point, the only steadfast thing in a world in movement, when destruction, because it is utterly and hopelessly destruction, is identified with absolute construction. They were all fascinated by violence, wherever it might come from; it was by violence that they wanted to free man from his human condition. That is why they joined hands with extreme parties by gratuitously ascribing to them apocalyptic aims. They were all duped: the Revolution has not come off and Nazism has been beaten. They lived in a comfortable and lavish period when despair was still a luxury. They condemned their country because they were still insolent with victory; they denounced war because they thought the peace would be a long one. They were all victims of the disaster of 1940: the reason is that the moment for action had come and that none of them were armed for it. Some killed themselves, others are in exile; those who have returned are exiled among us. They were the proclaimers of catastrophe in the time of the fat cows; in the time of the lean cows they have nothing more to say.[25]

On the margin of the prodigal children of the *ralliés* who found more unexpectedness and madness in their father's house than on the mountain footpaths and the trails of the desert, on the margin of the great tenors of despair, of the prodigal youths for whom the hour for returning to the fold had not yet struck, there flourished a discrete humanism. Prévost, Pierre Bost, Chamson, Aveline, and Beucler were about the same age as Breton and Drieu. Their débuts were brilliant; Bost was still a *lycée* boy when Copeau performed his *L'Imbécile*; Prévost, at the École Normale, was already notorious. But they remained modest in their budding glory; they had no taste for playing the Ariels of capitalism. They did not pretend to be either damned or prophetic. When Prévost was asked why he wrote, he answered, 'To earn my living.' The phrase shocked me at the time because the last remnant of the great literary myths of the nineteenth century were still trailing in my head. Nevertheless he was wrong. One does not write to earn one's living. But what I took for facile cynicism was actually a will to think toughly, lucidly, and, if need be, disagreeably. These authors, in complete reaction against satanism and angelism, wanted to be neither saints nor beasts, only men. Perhaps they were the first writers since romanticism who did not think of themselves as aristocrats of consumption but rather as workmen in a room, like bookbinders or lacemakers. They did not consider literature as a trade in order to give themselves licence to sell their wares to the highest bidder, but, on the contrary, to re-establish themselves, without humility or pride, in an industrious society. One learns a trade, and then he who practises it has no right to scorn his clientèle. So they too launched a reconciliation with the public. Much too honest to believe they had genius and to demand its rights, they trusted much more to hard work than to inspiration. They lacked perhaps that absurd confidence in their destiny, that iniquitous and blind pride which characterises great men.[26] They all had that strong self-seeking culture which the Third Republic gave to its future civil-servants. Thus, almost all of them became civil-servants, administrative officers in the Senate and Chamber, teachers, and curators of museums. But, as they came for the most part from modest backgrounds they were not concerned with using their ability to defend bourgeois traditions. They never enjoyed that culture as a *historic* property; they saw in it only a precious instrument for becoming men. Besides, they had in Alain a master and thinker who detested history. Convinced, like him, that the moral problem is the same in all ages, they saw society in an instantaneous cross-section.

Hostile to psychology as well as to the historical sciences, sensitive to social injustice but too Cartesian to believe in the class struggle, their only concern was to practise their trade, against passions and impassioned errors and against myths, by using—without weakness—will and reason. They liked the common people, the Parisian workmen, the craftsmen, the petty bourgeois, the clerks, the tramps, and the care they took in telling the stories of these individual destinies sometimes led them into flirting with populism. But this sequel to naturalism was different in that they never admitted that social and psychological determinism formed the web and woof of these humble existences. And, differing from the point of view of socialist realism, they did not want to see their heroes as hopeless victims of social oppression. In each case, these moralists applied themselves to showing the rôle of will, patience, and effort, presenting deficiencies as faults and success as merit. They rarely took an interest in exceptional careers, but they wanted to make people see that it is possible to be a man even in adversity.

Today several of them are dead; others are silent or produce only at long intervals. By and large it can be said that the writers whose débuts were so brilliant and who in about 1927 were able to form a 'club of those under thirty' have almost all fallen by the wayside. To be sure, individual accidents must be taken into account, but the fact is so striking that it requires a more general explanation. Indeed, they lacked neither talent nor inspiration, and from the point of view which concerns us, they must be regarded as precursors: they renounced the proud solitude of the writer; they liked their public; they did not attempt to justify the privileges which they acquired; they did not meditate upon death or upon the impossible; rather they wanted to give us rules for living. They were widely read, certainly much more than the surrealists. Yet, if one wishes to mark the chief literary tendencies between the two wars with a name, it is of surrealism that one will think. What is the reason for their failure?

I believe it is explained, paradoxical as it may seem, by the public which they chose for themselves. About 1900, on the occasion of its triumph in the Dreyfus affair, an industrious and liberal petty bourgeoisie became conscious of itself. It was anti-clerical and republican, anti-racialist, individualistic, rationalistic and progressive. Proud of its institutions, it was ready to modify them but not to overthrow them. It did not scorn the proletariat, but it felt itself too close to it to be conscious of oppressing it. It lived moderately, sometimes uneasily, but it aspired not so much to wealth, or to inaccessible greatness, as it did to improve its way of life within very narrow limits. Above all, it wanted to live. To live: by that it meant to choose a trade, to practise it conscientiously and even passionately, to maintain a certain initiative in its work, to control effectively its political representatives, to express itself freely in state matters, and to raise its children with dignity. It was Cartesian in that it distrusted improve-

ments which were too abrupt and in that, contrary to the
romantics who have always hoped that happiness would
burst upon them like a catastrophe, it dreamed rather of
mastering itself than of changing the course of the world.
This class, which has been happily baptized 'average',
teaches its sons that there is no need for too much and that
the best is the enemy of the good. It is well disposed towards the demands of the working-class provided that these
remain on a strictly professional level. It has no history and
no historical sense, since, unlike the upper bourgeoisie, it
has neither a past nor traditions, nor, unlike the working
class, does it have immense hope for the future. As it does
not believe in God, but needs very strict imperatives to give
meaning to the privations which it endures, one of its intellectual concerns has been to establish a lay morality. The
university, which belongs completely to this average class,
strove for twenty years without success to achieve this
through the writings of Durkheim, Brunschvicg, and Alain.
Now, these professors were, directly or indirectly, the
masters of the writers we are now considering. These young
people, born of the petty bourgeoisie, taught by petty-
bourgeois professors, prepared at the Sorbonne or in the
great schools for petty-bourgeois professions, returned to
their class when they began to write. Better still, they never
left it. They carried over this morality—but improved and
refined—into their novels and short stories, a morality
which everybody was familiar with but whose principles
no one has ever discovered. They dwelt upon the beauties
and the risks, upon the austere grandeur of the profession;
they sang not of mad love but rather of conjugal friendship
and that enterprise in common which is marriage. They
founded their humanism upon profession, friendship, social
solidarity, and sport. Thus, the petty bourgeoisie which
already had its political party, Radical Socialism, its mutual
aid society, the League for Human Rights, its secret society,
Freemasonry, and its daily paper, *L'Œuvre*, had writers, and
even a literary weekly, which was called symbolically,
Marianne. Chamson, Bost, Prévost, and their friends wrote

for a public of civil-servants, university people, higher clerks, doctors, and so on. They made literature Radical Socialist. Now Radicalism has been the great victim of this war. By 1910 it had realized its programme. For thirty years it has lived on its momentum. By the time it found its writers it was already living on its past. Today it has definitely disappeared. When the reform of the administrative personnel and the separation of church and state had been accomplished, Radical Socialist politics could become only a matter of opportunism; in order to maintain itself for a single moment it presupposed social and international peace. Two wars in twenty-five years and the aggravation of the class struggle have been too much for it; the party has not resisted, but even more than the party it is the Radical Socialist spirit which has been the victim of circumstances.

These writers, who did not fight in the first war and who did not see the second one coming, who did not want to believe in the exploitation of man by man, and who rather bet on the possibility of living honestly and modestly in capitalist society, whom their class of origin—which had become their public—deprived of the feeling for history without giving them, in compensation, a metaphysical absolute, did not have a sense of the tragic in one of the most tragic of all eras, not of death when death threatened all Europe, nor of Evil when so brief a moment separated them from the most cynical attempt to debase them. They limited themselves, in all honesty, to stories of lives which were ordinary and without greatness, while circumstances were forging careers which were exceptional in Evil as well as in Good. On the eve of a poetic springtime— more apparent, to be sure, than real—their lucidity dispelled within them that double-dealing which is one of the sources of poetry; their morality, which could support the soul in daily life, which perhaps had supported it during the First World War, was revealed as inadequate for great catastrophes. In such times man turns towards Epicureanism or Stoicism—and these authors were neither Stoics nor Epicureans[27]—or he asks for help from irrational forces, and they had chosen to see no farther than the boundary of their reason. Thus, history stole their public from them as it stole voters from the Radical Socialist party. They remained silent, I imagine, out of disgust, lacking power to adopt their wisdom to the follies of Europe. After twenty years of plying their craft and finding nothing to tell us in the time of misfortune, they have wasted their labour.

So there remains the third generation, our own, which began to write after the defeat or shortly before the war. I do not want to talk about it before saying something about the climate in which it appeared. First, the literary climate: *ralliés*, extremists, and radicals peopled our sky. Each of these stars exerted, in its way, its own influence upon our world, and all these influences, combining, managed to form about us the strangest, most irrational, and most contradictory idea of what literature is. We breathed in this idea, which I shall call objective, with the air of our time. Whatever the effort these writers did actually make to distinguish themselves from one another, their works were reciprocally contaminated in the minds of the readers where they co-existed. Moreover, if the differences are sharp and deep, their works have common traits. It is striking, at first, that neither the radicals nor the extremists were concerned with history, although one side aligned itself with the progressive left and the other with the revolutionary left. The first were on the level of Kierkegaardian repetition; the second were on that of the moment; that is, the aberrant synthesis of eternity and the infinitesimal present. In an age when we were being crushed by the pressure of history the literature of the *ralliés* alone offered some taste for history and some historical sense. But as it was a question of justifying privileges they envisaged only the action of the past on the present in the development of societies. Today, we know the reasons for these refusals, and that they are social: the surrealists are clerks, the petty bourgeoisie has neither traditions nor future, the upper bourgeoisie has done with conquest and aims at maintaining itself. But these diverse attitudes were compounded to produce an objective myth according to which literature had to choose eternal subjects or at the very least those which were not of the moment. And then our elders had only one fictional technique at their disposal, the one inherited from the French nineteenth century. Now, there is none more hostile to a historical view of society.

Thus, *ralliés* and radicals have used the traditional technique; the latter because they were moralists and intellectuals and wanted to understand matters by their causes, the former because it served their purpose. By its systematic denial of change it was better able to bring out the perenniality of bourgeois virtues. Behind the vain, forgotten turmoils it let us catch a glimpse of that fixed and mysterious order, that motionless poetry that they wished to reveal in their works. Thanks to this technique, these new Eleatics wrote against the age, against change; they discouraged agitators and revolutionaries by making them see their enterprises in the past even before they had begun.

We learned it by reading their books, and at first it was our only means of expression. About the time we were beginning to write, good minds were calculating the 'optimum time' at the end of which a historical event might be the object of a novel. Fifty years—that, it appeared, was too much; one no longer enters into the thing. Ten—that wasn't enough; one does not have enough perspective. Thus, we were gently led to see in literature the kingdom of untimely considerations.

Moreover, these hostile groups made alliances among themselves; sometimes the radicals became reconciled with the *ralliés*. After all, they had in common the ambition of reconciling themselves with the reader and of honestly serving his needs. Doubtless their publics differed appreciably, but one passed continually from one to the other, and the left wing of the public of the *ralliés* formed the right wing of the radical public. On the other hand, if the radical writers sometimes went along for a way with traditional politics, if, when the Radical Socialist party joined the

Popular Front, they all decided together to collaborate in *Vendredi,* they never concluded an alliance with the extreme literary left, that is, with the surrealists.

The extremists, on the contrary, have this in common, though reluctantly, with the *ralliés,* that they both hold that the object of literature is a certain ineffable beyondness which can only be suggested and that it is essentially the imaginary realization of the unrealizable. This is particularly obvious when we are dealing with poetry. Whereas the radicals banished it, so to speak, from literature, the novels of the *ralliés* were steeped in it. This fact, one of the most important in contemporary literary history, has often been noted; the reason for it has not been given. What the bourgeois writers really wanted to prove was that there is no life so bourgeois or so humdrum that it has not its poetic *beyondness.* They considered themselves catalysts of bourgeois poetry.

At the same time the extremists identified all forms of artistic activity with poetry, that is, with the inconceivable beyondness of destruction. Objectively, this tendency was expressed at the moment we were beginning to write by the confusion of genres and the mistaken notion of what the novel is essentially. And it is not rare, even today, for critics to accuse a work of prose of lacking poetry.

This whole literature is literature with a thesis, since these writers, though they vigorously protest to the contrary, all defend ideologies. Extremists and *ralliés* profess to despise metaphysics. But how shall we name those endlessly repeated declarations that man is too large for himself and, by a whole dimension of his being, escapes psychological and social determinations?

As to the radicals, while proclaiming that literature is not made with fine feelings, their chief concern was moralizing. In the objective mind, all this is translated by tremendous oscillations of the concept of literature: it is pure gratuitousness—it is teaching; it exists only by denying itself and being reborn from its ashes; it is the exquisite, the impossible, the ineffable beyond language—it is an austere profession which addresses a specific public, tries to clarify its needs, and strives to satisfy them. It is terror, it is rhetoric. The critics then come along and try, for their convenience, to unify these opposite concepts; they invent the notion of the *message*, which we spoke of earlier.

Everything, to be sure, is a message. There is a message in Gide, in Chamson, in Breton, and of course, it is what they were unwilling to say, what criticism made them say in spite of themselves. Whence a new theory is added to the preceding ones; in these delicate and self-destroying works where the word is only a hesitant guide which stops half-way and lets the reader continue on his way alone and whose truth is quite beyond language, in an undifferentiated silence, it is always the unintentional contribution of the writer which has chief importance.

A work is never beautiful unless it in some way escapes its author. If he paints himself without planning to, if his characters escape his control and impose their whims upon him, if the words maintain a certain independence under his pen, then he does his best work. Boileau would be completely dumbfounded if he read this kind of statement, which one frequently finds in the articles of our critics: 'the author knows too well what he wants to say; he is too lucid; the words come too easily; he does whatever he wants with his pen; he is not dominated by his subject'.

Unfortunately, everybody is in agreement on this point. For the *ralliés*, the essence of the work is the poetry, and therefore the beyond which, by an imperceptible gliding, becomes what escapes the author himself—the Devil's share. For the surrealist the only valid mode of writing is automatism. Even the radicals, following Alain, insist that a work of art is never finished until it has become a collective representation and that it then contains, by virtue of all that generations of readers have put into it, infinitely more than at the moment of its conception.

This idea, which, moreover, is correct, amounts to making evident the reader's rôle in the constitution of the work; but at the time it helped to increase the confusion.

In short, the objective myth inspired by these contradictions is that every lasting work has its secret.

Well and good, if it were a secret of fabrication; but no, it starts at the point where technique and will leave off. Something from above is reflected in the work of art and breaks like sunlight on the waves. To put it briefly, from pure poetry to automatic writing the literary climate is Platonism. In this mystical epoch which is without faith, or rather dishonestly mystical, a major literary current leads the writer to surrender before his work as a political current leads him to surrender before the party. It is said that Fra Angelico painted on his knees; if that is true, many writers resemble him, but go much further than he; they think that it is enough to write on one's knees to write well.

When we were still schoolboys on the *lycée* benches or in the Sorbonne amphitheatres, the leafy shadow of the beyond spread itself over literature. We knew the bitter and deceptive taste of the impossible, of purity, of impossible purity. We felt ourselves to be in turn the unsatisfied and the Ariels of accomplishment. We believed that one could save one's life by art, and then, the following term, that one never saved anything and that art was the lucid and desperate balance sheet of our perdition. We swung between terror and rhetoric, between literature-as-martyrdom and litera-ture-as-profession. If someone were to amuse himself by carefully reading our writings he would doubtless find there, like scars, the traces of these varying temptations—but he would have to have time to waste.

That is all very far away from us now. However, since it is by writing that the author forges his ideas on the art of writing, the collectivity lives on the literary conceptions of the preceding generation, and the critics who have under-stood them twenty years late are quite happy to use them as touchstones to judge contemporary works.

The literature of the period between the wars has a hard time of it these days. Georges Bataille's reflections on the impossible do not have the value of the slightest surrealistic

tract. His theory of expense is a feeble echo of great days
which are past. Lettrism is a substitute product, a flat and
conscientious imitation of Dadaist exuberance. One's heart
is no longer in it; one feels the application and the haste to
succeed. Neither André Dhotel nor Marius Groult are
worth Alain Fournier. Many former surrealists have joined
the Communist Party like the Saint Simonians who, in about
1880, turned up on boards of directors of big business.
Neither Cocteau nor Mauriac nor Green has any challengers;
Giraudoux has a hundred, but all mediocre. Most of the
radicals are silent. The reason is that the gap has been revealed not between the author and his public—which, after
all, would be in the great literary tradition—but between
the literary myth and the historical reality.

We started feeling this gap about 1930, quite a while
before publishing our first books.[28] It was about this time
that most Frenchmen were stupefied on discovering their
historical character. They had, of course, learned at school
that man plays and wins or loses in the womb of universal
history, but they did not apply it to their own case. They
thought in a vague sort of way that it was all right for the
dead to be historical. The striking thing about lives of the
past is that they always unfold *on the eve* of the great events
which exceed forecasts, disappoint expectations, upset plans,
and bring new light to bear on the years that have gone by.
We have here a case of trickery, a perpetual juggling, as if
men were all like Charles Bovary who, discovering after his
wife's death the letters she had received from her lovers, all
at once saw twenty years of conjugal happiness which *had
already been lived* slipping away.

In the century of the aeroplane and electricity we did not
think that we were exposed to these surprises. It didn't seem
to us that we were *on the eve* of anything. On the contrary,
we had the vague pride of feeling that it was *the day after* the
last disruption of history. Even if we were at times disturbed by German rearmament, we thought that we were
moving on a long, straight road and we felt certain that our
lifetime would be uniquely woven of individual circum-

stances and marked by scientific discoveries and happy reforms.

From 1930 on, the world depression, the coming of Nazism, and the events in China opened our eyes. It seemed as if the ground were going to fall from under us, and suddenly, *for us too*, the great historical juggling began. The first years of the great world Peace suddenly had to be regarded as the years between wars. Each sign of promise which we had greeted had to be seen as a threat. Each day we had lived revealed its true face; we had abandoned ourselves to it trustingly and it was leading us to a new war with secret rapidity, with a rigour hidden beneath its nonchalant airs. And our life as an individual which had seemed to depend upon our efforts, our virtues, and our faults, on our good and bad luck, on the good and bad will of a very small number of people, seemed governed down to its minutest details by obscure and collective forces, and its most private circumstances seemed to reflect the state of the whole world. All at once we felt ourselves abruptly *situated*.

The detachment which our predecessors were so fond of practising had become impossible. There was a collective adventure which was taking form in the future and which would be *our* adventure. That was what would later permit our generation, with its Ariels and its Calibans, to be dated. Something was awaiting us in the future shadow, something which would reveal us to ourselves, perhaps in the illumination of a last moment, before annihilating us. The secret of our gestures and our most intimate designs lay ahead of us in the catastrophe to which our names would be attached.

History flowed in upon us; in everything we touched, in the air we breathed, in the page we read, in the one we wrote; in love itself we discovered, like a taste of history, so to speak, a bitter and ambiguous mixture of the absolute and the transitory. What need had we patiently to construct self-destructive objects since each of the moments of our life was subtly whisked away from us at the very time that we were enjoying it, since each *present* that we lived with gusto, like an absolute, was struck with a secret death, seemed to us to have its meaning outside itself, for other eyes which had not yet seen the light, and, in a way, to be *already past* in its very presence? Besides, what did surrealist destruction, which leaves everything in place, matter to us, when a destruction by sword and fire threatened everything, surrealism included?

It was, I believe, Miró who painted a *Destruction of Painting*. But incendiary bombs could destroy the painting and its destruction together. We would no longer have dreamed of crying up the exquisite virtues of the bourgeoisie. To do that we would have had to believe that they were eternal, but did we know whether the French bourgeoisie would exist tomorrow? Nor of teaching, as the radicals had done, the means of leading in peace-time the life of an honest man, when our greatest care was to know whether one could remain a man in war-time.

The pressure of history suddenly revealed to us the interdependence of nations. An incident in Shanghai was a snip of the scissors in our destiny, but at the same time it replaced us, in spite of ourselves, in the national collectivity. We very soon had to realize that the travelling of our elders, their sumptuous voyages abroad, and the whole ceremonial of travel on the grand scale, was an illusion. Everywhere they went they carried France with them. They travelled because France had won the war and the exchange was favourable. They followed the franc. Like the franc, they had more access to Seville and Palermo than to Zurich and Amsterdam.

As for us, when we were old enough to make our world tour, autarchy had killed off the novels about the grand tour, and then, we no longer had the heart to travel. With a perverse taste for standardizing the world, they amused themselves with finding the imprint of capitalism everywhere. We would have found, without any difficulty, a much more obvious uniformity—cannons everywhere. And then, whether travellers or not, in the face of the conflict which threatened our country, we had understood that we were not citizens of the world since we could not make ourselves be Swiss, Swedish, or Portuguese. The destiny of our works themselves was bound to that of a France in danger. Our elders wrote for idle souls, but for the public which we, in our turn, were going to address the holiday was over. It was composed of men of our sort who, like us, were expecting war and death. For these readers without leisure, occupied without respite with a single concern, there was only one fitting subject. It was about their war and their death that we had to write. Brutally reintegrated into history, we had no choice but to produce a literature of a historical character.

But what makes our position original, I believe, is that the war and the occupation, by turning us into a world in a state of fusion, perforce made us rediscover the absolute at the heart of relativity itself. For our predecessors the rule of the game was to save everybody, because suffering is atoned for, because nobody is bad voluntarily, because man's heart is unfathomable, because divine grace is shared equally. That meant that literature—apart from the Surrealist extreme left which simply spread mischief—tended to establish a sort of moral relativism. Christians no longer believed in hell. Sin was the place devoid of God; carnal love was love of God gone astray.

As democracy tolerated all opinions, even those which aimed expressly at destroying it, republican humanism, which was taught in the schools, made tolerance the primary virtue. Everything would be tolerated, even intolerance. Hidden truths had to be recognized in the silliest ideas, in the vilest feelings. For Léon Brunschvicg, the philosopher of the régime, who all his life assimilated, unified, and integrated, and who shaped three generations, evil and error were only false shows, fruits of separation, limitation, and finiteness. They were annihilated as soon as one overthrew the barriers which compartmentalized systems and collectivities.

The radicals followed Auguste Comte in this, that they held progress to be the development of order; thus, order was already there, *in posse*, like the hunter's cap in the illustrated puzzles. It was only a matter of discovering it. That was how they passed their time; it was their spiritual exercise. They thereby justified everything—starting with themselves.

The Marxists at least recognized the reality of oppression and capitalist imperialism, of the class struggle and misery. But the effect of dialectical materialism, as I have shown elsewhere, is to make Good and Evil vanish conjointly. There remains only the historical process, and then Stalinist communism does not attribute so much importance to the individual that his sufferings and even his death cannot be redeemed if they help to hasten the day when power is seized.

The notion of Evil, which had been abandoned, had fallen into the hands of some Manichaeans—Anti-Semites, fascists, anarchists of the right—who used it to justify their bitterness, their envy, and their lack of understanding of history. That was enough to discredit it. For political realism as for philosophical idealism Evil was not a very serious matter.

We have been taught to take it seriously. It is neither our fault nor our merit if we lived in a time when torture was a daily fact. Châteaubriand, Oradour, the Rue des Saussaies, Tulle, Dachau, and Auschwitz have all demonstrated to us that Evil is not an appearance, that knowing its cause does not dispel it, that it is not opposed to Good as a confused idea is to a clear one, that it is not the effects of passions which might be cured, of a fear which might be overcome, of a passing aberration which might be excused, of an ignorance which might be enlightened, that it can in no way be diverted, brought back, reduced, and incorporated into idealistic humanism, like that shade of which Leibnitz has written that it is necessary for the glare of daylight.

Satan, Maritain once said, is pure. Pure, that is, without mixture and without remission. We have learned to know this horrible, this irreducible purity. It blazes forth in the close and almost sexual relation between the executioner and his victim. For torture is first of all a matter of debasement.

Whatever the sufferings which have been endured, it is the victim who decides, as a last resort, what the moment is when they are unbearable and when he must talk. The supreme irony of torture is that the sufferer, if he breaks down and talks, applies his will as a man to denying that he is a man, makes himself the accomplice of his executioners and, by his own movement, throws himself into abjection. The executioner is aware of this; he watches for this weakness, not only because he will obtain the information he desires, but because it will prove to him once again that he is right in using torture and that man is an animal who must be led with a whip. Thus, he attempts to destroy the humanity in his fellow-creature. Also, as a consequence, in himself; he knows that the groaning, sweating, filthy creature who begs for mercy and abandons himself in a swooning consent with the moanings of an amorous woman, and who yields everything and is even so carried away that he improves upon his betrayals because the consciousness that he has done evil is like a stone round his neck dragging him still farther down, exists also in his own image and that he—the executioner—is bearing down upon himself as much as upon his victim. If he wishes, on his own account, to escape this total degradation, he has no other recourse than to affirm his blind faith in an iron order which like a corset confines our repulsive weaknesses—in short, to commit man's destiny to the hands of inhuman powers.

A moment comes when torturer and tortured are in accord, the former because he has, in a single victim, symbolically gratified his hatred of all mankind, the latter because he can bear his failing only by pushing it to the limit, and because the only way he can endure his self-hatred is by hating all other men along with himself. Later, perhaps, the executioner will be hanged. Perhaps the victim, if he recovers, will be redeemed. But what will blot out this Mass in which two freedoms have communed in the destruction of the human? We knew that, to a certain extent, it was being celebrated everywhere in Paris while we were eating, sleeping, and making love. We heard whole streets screaming and we understood that Evil, fruit of a free and sovereign will, is, like Good, absolute.

Perhaps a day will come when a happy age, looking back at the past, will see in this suffering and shame one of the paths which led to peace. But we were not on the side of history already made. We were, as I have said, *situated* in such a way that every lived minute seemed to us like something irreducible. Therefore, in spite of ourselves, we came to this conclusion, which will seem shocking to lofty souls: Evil cannot be redeemed.

But, on the other hand, most of the resisters, though beaten, burned, blinded, and broken, did not speak. They broke the circle of Evil and reaffirmed the human—for themselves, for us, and for their very torturers. They did it without witness, without help, without hope, often even without faith. For them it was not a matter of believing in man but of wanting to. Everything conspired to discourage them: so many indications everywhere about them, those faces bent over them, that misery within them. Everything concurred in making them believe that they were only insects, that man is the impossible dream of spies and squealers, and that they would awaken as vermin like everybody else.

This man had to be invented with their martyrized flesh, with their hunted thoughts which were already betraying them—invented on the basis of nothing, for nothing, in absolute gratuitousness. For it is within the human that one can distinguish means and ends, values and preferences, but they were still at the creation of the world and they had only to decide in sovereign fashion whether there would be anything more than the reign of the animal within it. They remained silent and man was born of their silence. We knew that every moment of the day, in the four corners of Paris, man was a hundred times destroyed and reaffirmed.

Obsessed as we were by these tortures, a week did not go by that we did not ask ourselves: 'Suppose I were tortured, what would I do?' And this question alone carried us to the very frontiers of ourselves and of the human. We oscillated between the no-man's-land where mankind denies itself and the barren desert from which it surges and creates itself. Those who had immediately preceded us in the world, who had bequeathed us their culture, their wisdom, their customs, and their proverbs, who had built the houses that we lived in and who had marked the roads with the statues of their great men, practised modest virtues and remained in the moderate regions. Their faults never caused them to fall so low that they did not find others beneath them who were more guilty, nor did their merits cause them to rise so high that they did not see other souls above them whose merit was greater. Their gaze encountered men farther than the eye can reach. The very sayings they made use of and which we had learned from them—'a fool always finds a bigger fool to admire him,' 'we always need someone smaller than ourselves'—their very manner of consoling themselves in affliction by telling themselves that, whatever their unhappiness, there were others worse off, all goes to show that they considered mankind as a natural and infinite milieu that one could never leave and whose limits could not be touched. They died with a good conscience and without ever having explored their condition.

Because of this, their writers gave them a literature of *average situations*. But we could no longer find it *natural* to be men when our best friends, if they were taken, could choose only between abjection and heroism, that is, between the two extremes of the human condition, beyond which there is no longer anything. If they were cowards and traitors, all men were above them; if heroic, all men were below them. In the latter case, which was the more frequent, they no longer felt humanity as a limitless milieu. It was a thin flame within them which they alone kept alive. It kept itself going in the silence which they opposed to their executioners. About them was nothing but the great polar night of the inhuman and of unknowingness, which they did not even *see*, which they guessed in the glacial cold which pierced them.

Our fathers always had witnesses and examples available.

For these tortured men, there was no longer any. It was Saint-Exupéry who said in the course of a dangerous mission, 'I am my own witness.' The same for all of them; anguish and forlornness and the sweating of blood begin for a man when he can no longer have any other witness than himself. It is then that he drains the cup, that he experiences his human condition to the bitter end. Of course, we are quite far from having all felt this anguish, but it haunted us like a threat and a promise.

Five years. We lived entranced and as we did not take our profession of writer lightly, this state of trance is still reflected in our writings. We have undertaken to create a literature of extreme situations. I am not at all claiming that in this we are superior to our elders. Quite the contrary. Bloch-Michel, who has earned the right to talk, has said that fewer virtues are needed in great circumstances than in small. It is not for me to decide whether he is right or whether it is better to be a Jansenist than a Jesuit. I rather think that there must be something of everything and that the same man cannot be one and the other at the same time.

Therefore, we are Jansenists because the age has made us such, and in so far as it has made us touch our limits I shall say that we are all metaphysical writers. I think that many among us would deny this designation or would not accept it without reservations, but this is the result of a misunderstanding. For metaphysics is not a sterile discussion about abstract notions which have nothing to do with experience. It is a living effort to embrace from within the human condition in its totality.

Forced by circumstances to discover the pressure of history, as Torricelli discovered atmospheric pressure, and tossed by the cruelty of the time into that forlornness from where we can see our condition as man to the very limit, to the absurd, to the night of unknowingness, we have a task for which we may not be strong enough (this is not the first time that an age, for want of talents, has lacked its art and its philosophy). It is to create a literature which unites and reconciles the metaphysical absolute and the relativity of the historical fact, and which I shall call, for want of a better name, the literature of great circumstances.[29] It is not a question for us of escaping into the eternal or of abdicating in the face of what the unspeakable Mr. Zaslavsky calls in *Pravda* the 'historical process'.

The questions which our age puts to us and which remain *our* questions are of another order. How can one make oneself a man in, by, and for history? Is there a possible synthesis between our unique and irreducible consciousness and our relativity; that is, between a dogmatic humanism and a perspectivism? What is the relationship between morality and politics? How, considering our deeper intentions, are we to take up the objective consequences of our acts? We can rigorously attack these problems in the abstract by philosophical reflection. But if we want to live them, to support our thoughts by those fictive and concrete experiences which are what novels are, we have at our disposal the technique which I have already analysed here and whose ends are rigorously opposed to our designs. Specially perfected to relate the events of an individual life within a stable society, it enabled the novelist to record, describe, and explain the weakening, the vections, the involutions, and the slow disorganization of a particular system in the middle of a universe at rest. But from 1940 on, we found ourselves in the midst of a cyclone. If we wished to orient ourselves in it we suddenly found ourselves at grips with a problem of a higher order of complexity, exactly as a quadratic equation is more complex than a linear. It was a matter of describing the relationship of different partial systems to the total system which contains them when both are in movement and the movements condition each other reciprocally.

In the stable world of the pre-war French novel, the author, placed at a gamma point which represented absolute rest, had fixed guide-marks at his disposal to determine the movements of his characters. But we, involved in a system in full evolution, could only know relative movements. Whereas our predecessors thought that they could keep themselves outside history and that they had soared to heights from which they could judge events as they really were, circumstances have plunged us into our time. But since we were in it, how could we see it as a whole? Since we were *situated*, the only novels we could dream of were novels of *situation*, without internal narrators or all-knowing witnesses. In short, if we wished to give an account of our age, we had to make the technique of the novel shift from Newtonian mechanics to generalized relativity; we had to people our books with minds that were half lucid and half overcast, some of which we might consider with more sympathy than others, but none of which would have a privileged point of view either upon the event or upon itself. We had to present creatures whose reality would be the tangled and contradictory tissue of each one's evaluations of all the other characters—himself included—and the evaluation by all the others of himself, and who could never decide from within whether the changes of their destinies came from their own efforts, from their own faults, or from the course of the universe.

Finally, we had to leave doubts, expectations, and the unachieved throughout our works, leaving it up to the reader to conjecture for himself by giving him the feeling, without giving him or letting him guess our feeling, that his view of the plot and the characters was merely one among many others.

But, on the other hand, as I have just pointed out, our very historicity reinstated us because from day to day we were living that absolute which it had seemed at first to take away from us. If our plans, our passions, and our acts were explicable and relative from the viewpoint of past history, they again took on in this forlornness the uncertainty and the risks of the present, their irreducible density.

We were not unaware of the fact that a time would come when historians would be able to survey from all angles this stretch of time which we lived feverishly minute by minute, when they would illuminate our past by our future and would decide upon the value of our undertakings by their outcome and upon the sincerity of our intentions by their success. But the irreversibility of our age belonged only to us. We had to save or lose ourselves gropingly in this irreversible time. These events pounced upon us like thieves and we had to do our job in the face of the incomprehensible and the untenable, to bet, to conjecture without evidence, to undertake in uncertainty and persevere without hope. Our age would be explained, but no one could keep it from having been inexplicable to us. No one could remove the bitter taste, the taste it will have had for us alone and which will disappear with us.

The novels of our elders related the event as having taken place in the past. Chronological order permitted the reader to see the logical and universal relationship, the eternal verities. The slightest change was already understood. A past was delivered to us which had already been thought through. Perhaps two centuries from now an author who may decide to write a historical novel about the war of 1940 may find this a suitable technique. But if it occurred to us to meditate on our future writings, we were convinced that no art could really be ours if it did not restore to the event its brutal freshness, its ambiguity, its unforeseeability, if it did not restore to time its actual course, to the world its rich and threatening opacity, and to man his long patience.

We did not want to delight our public with its superiority to a dead world—we wanted to take it by the throat. Let every character be a trap, let the reader be caught in it, and let him be tossed from one consciousness to another as from one absolute and irremediable universe to another similarly absolute; let him be uncertain of the very uncertainty of the heroes, disturbed by their disturbance, flooded with their present, docile beneath the weight of their future, invested with their perceptions and feelings as by high insurmountable cliffs. In short, let him feel that every one of their moods and every movement of their minds encloses all mankind and is, in its time and place, in the womb of history and, despite the perpetual juggling of the present by the future, a descent without recourse towards Evil or an ascent towards Good which no future will be able to contest. This is what explains the success we have accorded Kafka's works and those of the American novelists. As for Kafka, everything has been said: that he wanted to paint a picture of bureaucracy, the progress of disease, the condition of the Jews in eastern Europe, the quest for inaccessible transcendence, and the world of grace when grace is lacking. This is all true. Let me say that he wanted to describe the human condition. But what we were particularly sensitive to was that this trial perpetually in session, which ends abruptly and evilly, whose judges are unknown and out of reach, in the vain efforts of the accused to know the leaders of the prosecution, in this defence patiently assembled which turns against the defender and figures in the evidence for the prosecution, in this absurd present which the characters live with great earnestness and whose keys are elsewhere, we recognize history and ourselves in history.

We were far from Flaubert and Mauriac. There was in Kafka, at the very least, a new way of presenting destinies which were tricked and undermined at their foundation, which were lived minutely, ingeniously, and modestly, of rendering the irreducible truth of appearances and of making felt beyond them another truth which will always be denied us. One does not imitate Kafka. One does not rewrite him. One had to extract a precious encouragement from his books and look elsewhere.

As for the Americans, it was not their cruelty or pessimism which moved us. We recognized in them men who had been swamped, lost in too large a continent as we were in history and who tried, without traditions, with the means available, to render their stupor and forlornness in the midst of incomprehensible events. The success of Faulkner, Hemingway, and Dos Passos was not the effect of snobbery, or at least, not at first. It was the defence reflex of a literature which, feeling itself threatened because its techniques and its myths were no longer going to allow it to cope with the historical situation, grafted foreign methods upon itself in order to be able to fulfil its function in new situations.

Thus, at the very moment that we were facing the public, circumstances forced us to break with our predecessors. They had chosen literary idealism and had presented us with events through a privileged subjectivity. For us, historical relativism, by positing the *a priori* equivalent of all subjectivities,[30] restored to the living event all its value and led us back, in literature, to dogmatic realism by way of absolute subjectivism. They thought that they were justifying, at least apparently, the foolish business of storytelling by ceaselessly bringing to the reader's attention, explicitly or by allusion, the existence of an author. We hope that our books remain in the air all by themselves and that their words, instead of pointing backwards towards the one who has designed them, will be toboggans, forgotten, unnoticed, and solitary, which will hurl the reader into the midst of a universe where there are no witnesses; in short, that our books may exist in the manner of things, of plants, of events, and not at first like products of man. We want to drive providence from our works as we have driven it from our world. We should, I believe, no longer define beauty by the form nor even by the matter, but by the density of being.[31]

I have shown how 'retrospective' literature denotes the taking of a position from which one surveys the whole of society and how those who choose to narrate from the viewpoint of past history seek to deny their body, their historicity, and the irreversibility of time. This leap into the eternal is the direct effect of the divorce which I have pointed out between the writer and his public. Vice versa, it will be understood without difficulty that our decision to re-integrate the absolute into history is accompanied by an effort to confirm this reconciliation of author and reader which the radicals and the *ralliés* had already undertaken.

When the writer thinks that he has pathways to the eternal, he is beyond comparison. He has the benefit of an illumination which he cannot communicate to the vulgar throng which crawls beneath him. But if it has occurred to him to think that one does not escape one's class by fine

sentiments, that there is no privileged consciousness anywhere, that belles-lettres are not *lettres de noblesse*, that the
best way to be bowled over by one's age is to turn one's
back on it or to pretend to be above it, and that one does
not transcend it by running away from it but by taking hold
of it in order to change it, that is, by going beyond it
towards the immediate future, then he is writing for everybody and with everybody because the problem which he is
trying to solve by means of his own talents is everybody's
problem. Besides, those among us who collaborated in the
underground newspapers addressed themselves in their
articles to the whole community. We were not prepared for
this kind of thing and we turned out to be not very clever;
the literature of resistance did not produce anything to get
excited about. But this experience made us feel what a
literature of the concrete universal might be.

In these anonymous articles we practised, in general, only
pure negativity. In the face of a manifest opposition and the
myth it was shaping from day to day to sustain itself,
spirituality was dissent. Most of the time our job was to
criticize a political action, to denounce an arbitrary measure,
to warn against a man or against propaganda, and when we
happened to glorify someone who had been deported or
shot, it was for having had the courage to say no. Against
the vague and synthetic notions which were crammed into
us day and night, Europe, Race, the Jew, the anti-bolshevik
crusade, we had to reawaken the old spirit of analysis which
alone was capable of tearing them to pieces. Thus, our
function seemed a humble echo of the one which the
eighteenth-century writers had so brilliantly fulfilled. But as
we could not address the oppressor, as Diderot and Voltaire
could, except by literary fiction, be it only to have made him
ashamed of his oppression, as we never had relations with
him, we did not have the illusion of these authors that we
were escaping our oppressed condition by practising our
profession.

On the contrary, from within oppression itself we depicted
to the oppressed community of which we were part its anger

and its hopes. With more luck, more skill, more talent, more cohesion, and more drive, we might have been able to write the interior monologue of occupied France. Moreover, even if we might have managed it, there would have been no reason for glorifying us inordinately. The National Front grouped its members by profession. Those among us who worked for the Resistance in their specialized jobs could not ignore the fact that the doctors, the engineers, and the railway workers were, in their specialized jobs, doing work of far greater importance.

Whatever the case may be there was the risk that after the liberation this attitude, which was easy for us because of the great tradition of literary negativity, might turn into systematic negation and might once again bring about the divorce of writer and public; because we were at war, we glorified all forms of destruction; desertions, refusals to obey, derailing of trains, setting harvests on fire, and criminal attacks.

The war was over. By persisting in this attitude, we might have joined the surrealist group and all those who make of art a permanent and radical form of destruction. But 1945 does not resemble 1918. It was fine to invoke the flood upon a victorious and smug France which thought that it would dominate Europe. The flood has come. What remains to be destroyed? The great metaphysical destruction of the other post-war period was carried on joyously, in a spirit of unleashed explosion. Today, there is the threat of war, famine, and dictatorship. We are again super-charged. 1918 was holiday-time. A bonfire might be built of twenty centuries of culture and accumulations. Today the fire would go out by itself or would refuse to catch. It will be a long time before the holiday season comes round again.

In this age of lean cows, literature refuses to link its destiny to that of consumption, which is too precarious. In a rich oppressive society art can still be taken for the supreme luxury because luxury seems the mark of civilization. But today luxury has lost its sacred character. The black market has turned it into a phenomenon of social disintegration. It has lost the aspect of 'conspicuous con-sumption' which made up half its charm. One hides oneself in order to consume; one isolates oneself; one is no longer at the top of the social hierarchy, but on the margin. An art of pure consumption would be neither here nor there. It would no longer be supported by solid luxury, whether culinary or sartorial. It might just barely provide a handful of privileged souls with solitary escapes, onanistic pleasures, and the opportunity to miss the old sweetness of living.

When the whole of Europe is preoccupied before every-thing else with reconstruction, when nations deprive them-selves of necessities in order to export, literature (which, like the Church, adapts itself to all situations and saves itself, come what may), reveals its other face. Writing is not living. Neither is it running away from life in order to contemplate Platonic essences and the archetype of beauty in a world at rest. Nor is it letting oneself be slashed, as by swords, by words which, unfamiliar and not understood, come up to us from behind. It is the practising of a profession, a pro-fession which requires an apprenticeship, sustained work, professional consciousness, and the sense of responsibility.

It is not we who have discovered these responsibilities. Quite the contrary. For a hundred years the writer has been dreaming of giving himself to his art in a sort of innocence, beyond Good and Evil, and, so to speak, before the fall. It is society which has just laid our burdens and our duties on our shoulders. It must think that we are quite formidable since it condemned to death a hundred of us who collabor-ated with the enemy while it left manufacturers who were guilty of the same crime at liberty. It is said nowadays that it was better to build the Atlantic wall than to talk about it. I don't find that particularly scandalizing.

To be sure, it is because we are pure consumers that the collectivity proves to be pitiless towards us. An author shot is one mouth less to feed. The least important producer would be a greater loss to the nation.[32] And I am not saying that this is just. On the contrary, it opens the way to all sorts of abuses, to censorship, to persecution. But we ought to rejoice that our profession involves some dangers. When we wrote clandestinely, the risks for us were minimal, but for the printers they were considerable. It often made me feel ashamed. At least it taught us to practise a sort of verbal deflation. When each word might cost a life, you ought not take time off to play the 'cello. You go as fast as possible. You make it snappy. The war of 1914 precipitated the crisis of language. I would readily say that the war of 1940 has revalorized it. But it is to be hoped that in taking up our names again, we were taking risks on our own account. After all; a steeple-jack will always be running a great many more.

In a society which insists upon production and restricts consumption to what is strictly necessary, the work of literature is evidently gratuitous. Even if the writer strongly stresses the work that he puts into it, even if he points out, and rightfully, that this work, considered in itself, involves the same faculties as that of an engineer or doctor, the fact remains that the created object is not to be compared with *goods*. This gratuitousness, far from grieving us, is our pride, and we know that it is the image of freedom.

The work of art is gratuitous because it is an absolute end and because it presents itself to the spectator as a categorical imperative. In addition, although it neither can nor wants to be production by itself, it wants to represent the free consciousness of a productive society, that is, to reflect production upon the producer in terms of freedom, as Hesiod did in the past. It is not, to be sure, a matter of picking up the thread of that boring literature of work of which Pierre Hamp was the most solemn and soporific representative. But as this type of reflection is both a summons and a surpassing, it is necessary to manifest to the men of this age the principles, aims, and inner constitution of their productive activity, at the same time that we show them their works and days.

If negativity is one aspect of freedom, constructiveness is the other. Now, the paradox of our age is that constructive freedom has never been so close to becoming conscious of itself and never has it been so profoundly alienated. Never has work more powerfully manifested its productivity, and never have workers been more swindled out of its products and its significance. Never has *homo faber* better understood that he has *made* history and never has he felt so powerless before history.

Our job is cut out for us. In so far as literature is negative it will challenge the alienation of work; in so far as it is a creation and an act of surpassing, it will present man as *creative action*. It will go along with him in his effort to pass beyond his present alienation towards a better situation. If it is true that to have, to make, and to be are the prime categories of human reality, it might be said that the literature of consumption has limited itself to the study of the relations which unite *being* to *having*. The sensation is presented as enjoyment, which is philosophically false, and the one who knows best how to enjoy himself is the one who exists most. From *The Culture of the Self* to *The Possession of the World*, including *Fruits of the Earth* and *Barnabooth's Journal*, to be is to appropriate.

The work of art, an outcome of similar pleasures, itself pretends to be enjoyment or promise of enjoyment. So the circle is completed. We, on the contrary, have been led by circumstances to bring to light the relationship between *being* and *doing* in the perspective of our historical situation. *Is* one what one *does*? What one makes of *oneself*? In present-day society, where work is alienated? *What* should one do, what end should one choose *today*? And *how* is it to be done, by what means? What are the relationships between ends and means in a society based on violence?

The works deriving from such preoccupations cannot aim first to please. They irritate and disturb. They offer themselves as tasks to be discharged. They urge the reader on to quests without conclusions. They present us with experiences whose outcomes are uncertain. The fruits of torments and questions, they cannot be enjoyment for the reader, but rather questions and torments. If our results turn out successful, they will not be diversions, but rather obsessions. They will give not a world 'to see' but to change.

On the other hand, this old, used, sore, snivelling world will lose nothing thereby. Since Schopenhauer it has been assumed that objects are revealed in their full dignity when man silences in his heart the wish for power. It is to the idle consumer that they yield their secrets. It is permitted to *write* about them only in moments when one has nothing to *do* about them. The fastidious descriptions of the last century were a rejection of utility. One did not touch the universe; one took it in raw, with the eyes. The writer, in opposition to bourgeois ideology, chose to speak to us of things at the privileged moment when all the concrete relations which united him with the objects were broken, save the slender thread of his gaze, and when they gently undid themselves to his eyes, untied sheaves of exquisite sensations.

It was the age of impressions, impressions of Italy, of Spain, of the Orient. The man of letters described these landscapes, which he absorbed consciously, at the indefinable moment between the end of the taking-in and the beginning of the digestion, when subjectivity had come to impregnate the object but before its acids had begun to eat into it, when fields and woods are still fields and woods and already a state of soul. A glazed and polished world inhabited bourgeois books, a world for sojourns in the country, which tinges us with a decent gaiety or a well-bred melancholy. We see it from our windows; we are not in it. When the novelist peoples it with peasants, they are in contrast with the vacant shadow of the mountains and the silvery sheen of the rivers. While they are hard at work digging their spades into the earth, we are made to see them dressed up in their Sunday clothes. These workers, lost in this seventh-day universe, resemble the academician of Jean Eiffel whom Prévost introduced into one of his caricatures and who excused himself by saying, 'I'm in the wrong cartoon.' Or, perhaps they too have been transformed into objects—into objects and states of soul.

For us, *doing* reveals *being*. Each gesture traces out new forms on the earth. Each technique, each tool, is a way that opens upon the world; things have as many aspects as there are ways of using them. We are no longer with those who want to possess the world, but with those who want to change it, and it is to the very plan of changing it that it reveals the secrets of its being. One knows the hammer best, says Heidegger, when one uses it to hammer. And the nail, when one drives it into the wall, and the wall when one drives the nail into it.

Saint-Exupéry has opened the way for us. He has shown that, for the pilot, the aeroplane is an organ of perception.[33] A chain of mountains at three hundred and seventy-five miles an hour and in the new perspective of flight is a tangle of snakes. They settle down, grow dark, thrust their hard, scorched heads against the sky, trying to do damage, to strike. Speed with its astringent power gathers the folds of the earthly gown and hems them in. At fourteen thousand feet above, the obscure attraction which draws San Antonio towards New York shines like rails.

After him, after Hemingway, how could we dream of describing? We must plunge things into action. Their density of being will be measured for the reader by the multiplicity of practical relations which they maintain with the characters. Have the mountain climbed by the smuggler, the customs-officer, and the guerilla, have it flown over by the aviator[34] and the mountain will suddenly surge from these connected actions and jump out of your book like a jack-in-the-box. Thus, the world and man reveal themselves by *undertakings*. And all the undertakings we might speak of reduce themselves to a single one, that of *making history*. So here we are, led by the hand to the moment when the literature of *exis* must be abandoned to inaugurate that of *praxis*.

Praxis as action in history and on history; that is, as a synthesis of historical relativity and moral and metaphysical absolute, with this hostile and friendly, terrible and derisive world which it reveals to us. There is our subject. I do not say that we have chosen these austere paths. There are surely some among us who are carrying within them some charming and heart-breaking love story which will never see the light of day. What can we do about it? It is not a matter of choosing one's age but of choosing oneself within it.

The literature of production which is being proclaimed will not make us forget the literature of consumption, its antithesis; it should not pretend to surpass it, and maybe it will never equal it. No one is dreaming of claiming that because of it we shall get to the very bottom and realize the essence of the art of writing. Maybe it will even disappear soon. The generation which is following us seems hesitant; many of its novels are about sad and stolen holidays, like those parties during the occupation when young people danced between two alerts while drinking cheap wine to the sound of pre-war gramophone records. In that case, it will be a revolution that didn't come off. And even if this literature does manage to establish itself, it will pass like the other, and the other will return, and perhaps the history of the next few decades will record the alternating from one to the other. That will mean that men will have definitely botched up another Revolution of infinitely greater importance. The fact is that only in a socialist collectivity would literature, having finally understood its essence and having made the synthesis of *praxis* and *exis*, of negativity and construction, of doing, having, and being, deserve the name of *total literature*. While waiting, let us cultivate our garden. We have our work cut out for us.

Indeed, to recognize literature as a freedom, to replace spending by giving, to renounce the old aristocratic lie of our elders, and to want to launch, through all our works, a democratic appeal to the whole of the collectivity is not the whole story. We still have to know who reads us and whether the present state of affairs does not make our desire of writing for the 'concrete universal' utopian. If our desires could be realized, the twentieth-century writer would occupy between the oppressed and the oppressors an analogous position to that of eighteenth-century authors between the bourgeois and the aristocracy, to that of Richard Wright between the blacks and the whites, read by both the oppressed and the oppressor, furnishing the oppressor with his image, both inner and outer, being conscious with and for the oppressed of the oppression, contributing to the formation of a constructive and revolutionary ideology. Unfortunately, these are anachronistic hopes; what was possible in the time of Proudhon and Marx is so no longer. So let us take up the question from the beginning, and without any preconceived conclusions let us take an inventory of our public.

From this point of view, the situation of the writer has never been so paradoxical. It seems to be made up of the most contradictory characteristics. On the credit side, brilliant appearances, vast possibilities; on the whole, an enviable way of life. On the debit side, only this: that literature is dying. Not that talent or good will is lacking, but it has no longer anything to do in contemporary society. At the very moment that we are discovering the importance of *praxis*, at the moment that we are beginning to have some notion of what a *total* literature might be, our public collapses and disappears. We no longer know—literally—for whom to write.

At first glance, to be sure, it would seem as if writers of the past ought to envy our lot.[35] Malraux once said, 'We are profiting from the suffering of Baudelaire.' I don't think that that's quite true, but it is true that Baudelaire died without a public and that we, without having proved our merit, without even knowing whether we ever will prove it, have readers all over the world. One might be tempted to blush at this, but, after all, it is not our fault; it's all the result of circumstances. The pre-war autarchies and the war deprived national publics of their annual contingent of foreign works. Today people are catching up. They're gobbling up double mouthfuls. On this point alone there is decompression. The states are in on it. I have shown elsewhere that in the conquered or ruined countries literature has recently begun to be considered as an article for export. This literary market was expanded and regularized when the collectivities got busy with it. We find there the usual procedures: dumping (for example, the American *Overseas* editions), protectionism (in Canada, in certain countries of Central Europe), international agreements. The countries flood each other reciprocally with 'Digests', that is, as the name indicates, of literature already digested, of literary pap. In short, belles-lettres, like the movies, are in the process of becoming an industrialized art. To be sure, we benefit: the plays of Cocteau, of Salacrou, and of Anouilh are being performed everywhere. I could cite any number of works which have been translated into six or seven languages less than three months after their publication. Yet, all this is brilliant only on the surface. Perhaps we are read in New York or Tel Aviv, but the shortage of paper has limited our editions in Paris. Thus the public has been dispersed more than it has increased. Perhaps ten thousand people read us in four or five foreign countries and another ten thousand in our own. Twenty thousand readers—a minor pre-war success. These worldwide reputations are far less well established than the national reputations of our elders. I know, paper is coming back. But at the same moment, European publishing is entering a crisis; the volume of sales remains constant.

Even though we might have a certain amount of celebrity outside France, there would be no reason for rejoicing; it would be an ineffectual glory. Nations today are separated by differences of economic and military potential more surely than by seas or mountains. An idea can *descend* from a country with a high potential towards a country with a low potential—for example, from America to France—it cannot *rise*. To be sure, there are so many newspapers, so many international contacts, that Americans finally get to hear about the literary or social theories that are circulating in Europe, but these doctrines are exhausted in their ascent; virulent in a country with a weak potential, they are in a languid state when they reach the summit. We know that intellectuals in the United States gather European ideas into a bouquet, inhale them for a moment, and then toss them away because the bouquets wither more quickly there than in other climates. As for Russia, she gleans and takes what she can easily convert into her own substance. Europe is conquered and ruined; she is no longer master of her destiny; and that is the reason why her ideas can no longer make their way. The only concrete circuit for the exchange of ideas passes through England, France, the Northern countries, and Italy.

It is true that our reputations are far more widespread than our books. We make contact with people, without even wanting to do so, by new means, with new angles of incidence. Of course, the book is still the heavy infantry which clears and occupies the terrain. But literature has its aeroplanes, its V1's and V2's which go a great distance, upsetting and harassing, without bringing about the actual decision. First, the newspaper. An author used to write for ten thousand readers. He is given the critic's column in a weekly and he has three hundred thousand even if his articles are worthless. Then the radio. *In Camera*, one of my plays, banned in England by the theatre censors, was broadcast four times by the B.B.C. On a London stage it would not have found, even making the improbable assumption that it would be a success, more than twenty to thirty thousand spectators. The drama broadcast of the B.B.C. automatically provided me with a half-million. Finally, the cinema. Four million people frequent the French cinemas. If we recall that at the beginning of the century Paul Souday reproached Gide for publishing his works in limited editions, the success of *The Pastoral Symphony* will enable us to measure the distance that we have covered.

However, of the columnist's three hundred thousand readers, he'll be lucky if a few thousand have the curiosity to buy his works, into which he has put the best of his talent. The others will learn his name from having read it a hundred times on the second page of the magazine, like that of the physic which they've seen a hundred times on the twelfth. The Englishmen who would have gone to see *In Camera* in the theatre would have done so with a knowledge of why they were going, on the basis of the reviews and mouth to mouth criticism, and with the intention of judging the work. When my B.B.C. listeners were turning on their radios they were unaware of the existence of the play or of me. They wanted to hear, as usual, the Thursday drama broadcast. As soon as it was over, they forgot it, as they did the preceding ones.

In the cinemas, the public is attracted by the names of the stars, then by the name of the director, and last of all by that of the writer. The name of Gide recently entered certain heads by invasion, but I am sure that it is curiously married there with the beautiful face of Michèle Morgan. It is true that the film has caused a few thousand copies of the work to be sold, but in the eyes of its new readers the latter appears as a more or less faithful commentary on the former. The wider the public that the author reaches, the less deeply does he affect it, the less he recognizes himself in the influence he has; his thoughts escape him; they become distorted and vulgarized. They are received with more indifference and scepticism by bored and weary souls who, because the author cannot speak to them in their 'native language', still consider literature as a diversion. What remains is formulas attached to names. And since our reputations extend much farther than our books, that is, than our merits, whether great or small, we need not see in these passing favours which are granted us the sign of a first awakening of the concrete universal but quite simply that of a literary inflation.

That would be nothing; it would be enough, in short, to be on guard; after all, it depends on us for literature not to be industrialized. But there is worse; we have readers but no public.[36] In 1780 the oppressing class alone had an ideology and political organizations. The bourgeoisie had neither party nor political self-consciousness. The writer worked for it directly by criticizing the old myths of monarchy and religion, and by giving it a few elementary notions whose content was chiefly negative, such as those of liberty, political equality, and habeas corpus. In 1850 the proletariat, in the presence of a conscious bourgeoisie which was provided with a systematic ideology, remained formless and obscure to itself, pervaded by vain and hopeless anger. The First International had only scratched its surface. Everything remained to be done. The writer could have addressed the workers directly. We have seen that he missed his chance. But at least he served the interests of the oppressed class unintentionally and even unknowingly by practicing his negativity on bourgeois values. Thus, in either case, circumstances permitted him to testify for the oppressed before the oppressor and to help the oppressed become conscious of themselves. The essence of literature found itself in accord with the exigencies of the historical situation. But today everything is reversed. The oppressing class has lost its ideology; its self-consciousness vacillates; its limits are no longer clearly definable; it opens up and it calls the writer to the rescue. The oppressed class, cramped in a party and tied down by a rigorous ideology, becomes a closed society. One can no longer communicate with it without an intermediary. The fate of the bourgeoisie was tied up with European supremacy and colonialism. It is losing its colonies at a time when Europe is ceasing to govern its destiny. It is no longer a matter of little kings carrying on wars for Rumanian oil or the Bagdad railroad; the next conflict will necessitate an industrial equipment that the entire Old World is incapable of furnishing. Two world powers, neither of which is bourgeois and neither of which is European, are disputing the possession of the universe. The triumph of one means the advent of state control and international bureaucracy; of the other, the coming of abstract capitalism. Everybody a civil servant? Everybody an employee? The bourgeoisie will be lucky if it can keep the illusion of the sauce with which it will be eaten. It knows today that it represented a moment in the history of Europe, a stage in the development of techniques and tools and that it has never been the measuring rod of the world. Besides, the feeling it had of its essence and its mission has been dimmed. It has been shaken, undermined, and eroded by economic crises with consequent internal fissures, displacements, and landslides. In certain countries it stands like the façade of a building which has been gutted; in others, great sections of it have collapsed into the proletariat. It can no longer be defined by the possession of goods, of which it has less and less each day, nor by political power, which it shares almost everywhere with new men who have sprung directly from the proletariat. At present it is the bourgeoisie which has taken on the amorphous and gelatinous aspect which characterizes oppressed classes before they have become conscious of their state. In France we discover that it is fifty years behind in equipment and in the organization of heavy industry. Whence, the crisis in our birth-rate, an undeniable sign of regression. Besides, the black market and the occupation have caused forty per cent. of its wealth to pass into the hands of a new bourgeoisie which has neither the morals, the principles, nor the goals of the old one. Ruined, but still oppressive, the European bourgeoisie barely manages to keep governing, and with modest means. In Italy, it keeps the workers in check because it is supported by the coalition of the Church and misery. Elsewhere, it makes itself indispensable because it supplies the technical staffs and administrative personnel. Elsewhere again, it rules by dividing. And then, above all, the era of national revolutions is closed. The revolutionary parties do not want to overturn this worm-eaten carcase. They even do what they can to prevent its collapsing. At the first sound of cracking there would be foreign intervention and perhaps the world-wide conflict for which Russia is not yet ready. An object of everybody's solicitude, doped by the U.S.A., by the Church, and even by the U.S.S.R., at the mercy of the changing fortunes of the diplomatic game, the bourgeoisie can neither preserve nor lose its power without the concurrence of foreign powers. It is the 'sick man' of contemporary Europe. Its agony may last a long time.

As a result, its ideology is collapsing. It justified property by work and also by that slow osmosis which diffuses into the soul of the possessors the virtues of the things possessed. The possession of property was, in its eyes, a merit and the finest self-culture. But, property is becoming symbolic and collective. One no longer possesses things but their signs or the signs of their signs. The arguments of 'work-merit' and 'enjoyment-culture' have turned flat. Out of hatred of the trusts and the bad conscience which abstract property induces, many turned towards fascism. Summoned by their wishes, it came, replaced the trusts by a system of directorship, then disappeared, and the system remained. The bourgeois gained nothing. If they still possess, they do so harshly and joylessly. They considered wealth as an unjustifiable state of fact; they have lost faith. Neither do they retain much confidence in that democratic régime which was their pride and which collapsed at the first push. But as national socialism in turn collapsed just when they were about to rally to it, they no longer believe either in Republic or Dictatorship. Nor in Progress; it was fine when their class was on the way up; now that it is declining, they are no longer concerned with the notion; it would be heart-breaking for them to think that other men and other classes will ensure it. Their work brings them into no more direct contact with actual matter than before, but two wars have made them discover fatigue, blood and tears, violence, and evil. The bombs have not only destroyed their factories but have caused fissures to appear in their idealism as well. Utilitarianism was the philosophy of saving; it loses all meaning when the savings are compromised by inflation and threats of bankruptcy. To quote Heidegger roughly, 'The world is revealed at the horizon of instruments which are out of order.' When you use a tool, you do so to produce a certain modification which is itself the means of bringing about another, and so on. Thus, you are engaged in a chain of means and ends whose scope escapes you, and you are too absorbed in the details of your action to question its final ends. But if the tool should break, the action is suspended and you see the whole chain. So with the bourgeois; his instruments are out of order; he sees the chain and knows the gratuitousness of his ends. As long as he believed in them without seeing them, and as long as he was working over the nearest links with his head down, they justified him; now that they hit him right between the eyes, he discovers that he is unjustifiable. The whole world is disclosed and likewise his forlornness in the world. Anguish is born.[37] And shame too. Even for those who judge it in the name of its own principles, it is manifest that the bourgeoisie has been guilty of three betrayals: at Munich, in May '40, and under the Vichy government. Of course, it corrected itself; many Vichyites of the first hour were in the resistance in '42. They realized that they had to fight against the occupier in the name of bourgeois nationalism. And it is true that the Communist Party hesitated more than a year; it is true that the Church hesitated until the Liberation. But both of them have enough strength, unity, and discipline to demand of their initiates that they forget their past faults. The bourgeoisie has forgotten nothing. It still carries about the wounds inflicted upon it by one of its sons, the one it was most proud of. By condemning Pétain to life imprisonment, it feels that it has put itself behind bars. It might apply to itself the words of Paul Chack, an officer, a Catholic, and a bourgeois, who, because he blindly followed the orders of a Catholic and bourgeois marshal of France, was accused before a bourgeois tribunal under the government of a Catholic and bourgeois general, and who, stupefied by this sleight-of-hand, kept mumbling throughout the trial, 'I don't understand.' Harassed, without a future, without guarantees, without justification, the bourgeoisie, which objectively had become the *sick man*, has subjectively entered the phase of the guilty conscience. Many of its members are bewildered; they shuttle between anger and fear, which are two kinds of flight. The best of them still try to defend, if not their goods, which in a good many cases have gone up in smoke, at least the real bourgeois conquests: the universality of laws, freedom of expression, habeas corpus. It is they who form our public. Our *only* public. They understood, in reading the old books, that literature, by its nature, is ranged on the side of democratic freedom. They turn to it; they beg it to give them reasons for living and hoping, a new ideology. Perhaps never since the eighteenth century has so much been expected of the writer.

We have nothing to tell them. In spite of themselves, they belong to an oppressing class. Victims, doubtless, and innocent, but, still tyrants and guilty. All we can do is reflect their unhappy conscience in our mirrors, that is, advance a bit further the decomposition of their principles. We have the thankless job of reproaching them for their faults when they have become a curse. Ourselves bourgeois, we have known bourgeois anguish. We have had that harassed soul. But since the characteristic of an unhappy conscience is to want to tear itself away from the state of unhappiness, we cannot remain tranquilly in the bosom of our class, and since it is no longer possible for us to leave it with a flap of our wings by giving ourselves the appearance of a parasitic aristocracy, we must be its gravediggers, even if we run the risk of burying ourselves along with it.

We turn towards the working class which today, like the bourgeoisie in 1780, might constitute for the writer a revolutionary public. It is still a virtual public, but it is singularly present. The worker of 1947 has a social and professional culture. He reads technical, union, and political journals. He has become conscious of himself and his position in the world and he has much to teach us. He has lived all the adventures of our time, in Moscow in 1917, in Budapest, in Munich, in Madrid, in Stalingrad, and in the Maquis. At the time that we are discovering in the art of writing freedom in its two aspects of negation and the creative transcendence of negation, he is trying to free himself and, by the same token, to free all men from oppression for ever. As a member of the oppressed, he may see the object of his anger reflected by literature in its aspect of negation; as a producer and revolutionary, he is, *par excellence*, the subject of a literature of *praxis*. We share with him the duty of contesting and destroying; he demands the right to make history at the moment when we are discovering that we are part of history. We are not yet familiar with his language; neither is he with ours; but we already know the means of reaching him. We also know that in Russia he engages in discussion with the writer himself and that a new relationship between the public and the writer has appeared there which is neither a passive and female waiting nor the specialized criticism of the intellectual. I do not believe in the 'Mission' of the proletariat, nor that it is endowed with a state of grace; it is made up of men, just and unjust, who can make mistakes and who are often mystified. But it must be said without hesitation that the fate of literature is bound up with that of the working class.

Unhappily, these men, to whom we *must* speak, are separated from us by an iron curtain in our own country; they will not hear a word that we shall say to them. The majority of the proletariat, strait-jacketed by a single party, encircled by a propaganda which isolates it, forms a closed society without doors or windows. There is only one way of access, a very narrow one, the Communist Party. Is it desirable for the writer to engage himself in it? If he does it out of conviction as a citizen and out of disgust with literature, very well, he has chosen. But can he become a communist and remain a writer?

The C.P. aligns its politics with that of Soviet Russia because this is the only country in which one finds the rough draught of a socialist organization. But if it is true that Russia began the social revolution, it is also true that she has not ended it. The retardation of her industry, her shortage of supervisory personnel, and the masses' lack of culture have prevented her from realizing socialism by herself and even from imposing it upon other countries by the contagion of her example. If the revolutionary movement which started from Moscow could have spread to other nations, it would have continued to evolve in Russia itself in proportion to the ground it gained outside. Contained within the Soviet frontiers, it congealed into a defensive and conservative nationalism because it had to save, at any cost, the results it had achieved. At the very moment when it was becoming the Mecca of the working classes, Russia saw that it was impossible, on one hand, for her to assume her historical mission and, on the other, to deny it. She was forced to withdraw into herself, to apply herself to creating supervisors, to catch up on her equipment, and to perpetuate herself by an authoritarian régime in the form of a revolution at a standstill. As the European parties which derived from her, and which were preparing for the coming of the proletariat, were nowhere strong enough to take the offensive, she had to use them as the advance bastions of her defence. But as they could serve her, in regard to the masses, only by fostering revolutionary politics, and as she has never lost hope of becoming the leader of the European proletariat if circumstances should some day show themselves more favourable, she has left them their red flag and their faith. Thus the forces of the World Revolution have been diverted to the maintenance of a revolution in a state of hibernation. Still, it must be acknowledged that, in so far as it has honestly believed in the possibility, even though remote, of seizing power by insurrection, and in so far as it has made it its business to weaken the bourgeoisie and to bore from within the Socialist Party, the C.P. has practised a negative criticism of capitalistic institutions and régimes which has maintained the outer appearances of freedom. Before 1939 it made use of everything: pamphlets, satires, bitter novels, Surrealistic violence, overwhelming evidence regarding our colonial methods. Since 1944 things have become aggravated; a collapsing Europe has simplified the situation. Two powers remain standing, the U.S.S.R. and the U.S.A.; each one frightens the other. From fear, as we know, comes anger, and from anger, blows.

Now, the U.S.S.R. is the less strong. Hardly out of a war which she had feared for twenty years, she still has to temporize, to catch up in the armament race, to retighten the dictatorship internally, and, externally, to assure herself of allies, vassals, and positions.

The revolutionary tactic is changed into diplomacy. It must have Europe on its side. Thus, it must appease the bourgeoisie, lull it to sleep with fables, and at any cost keep it from throwing itself into the Anglo-Saxon camp out of fright. The time has quite passed when *L'Humanité* could write: 'Every bourgeois who meets a workman ought to be scared.' Never have the Communists been so powerful in Europe, and yet never have the chances of a revolution been slighter. If the Party should somewhere consider the possibility of seizing power, this attempt would be nipped in the bud. The Anglo-Saxons have at their disposal a hundred ways of annihilating it, even without having recourse to arms, and for that matter the Soviets would not look upon it very favourably. If, by chance, the insurrection succeeded, it would simply vegetate without spreading. If by some miracle it finally became contagious, it would risk being the occasion of a third world war. Thus, it is no longer for the coming of the proletariat that the Communists are preparing in their respective nations, but for war, plain and simple war. If victorious, the U.S.S.R. will spread its régime to Europe; the nations will fall like ripe fruit; if beaten, it's all up with her and the Communist parties. To reassure the bourgeoisie without losing the confidence of the masses, to permit it to govern while appearing to keep up the offensive, and to occupy positions of command without letting itself be compromised—that's the politics of the C.P. Between 1939 and 1940 we were the witnesses and victims of the decay of a war; today we are present at the decaying of a revolutionary situation.

If it should be asked whether the writer, in order to reach the masses, should offer his services to the Communist Party, I answer no. The politics of Stalinist Communism is incompatible in France with the honest practice of the literary craft. A party which is planning revolution should have nothing to lose. For the C.P. there is something to lose and something to handle circumspectly. As its immediate goal can no longer be the establishment of a dictatorship of the proletariat by force, but rather that of safeguarding a Russia which is in danger, it now presents an ambiguous appearance. Progressive and revolutionary in its doctrine and in its avowed ends, it has become conservative in its means. Even before it has seized power, it has adopted the

turn of mind, the reasoning, and the artifices of those who
have long since attained it, those who feel that it is escaping
them and who want to maintain themselves. There is something in common, and it is not talent, between Joseph de
Maistre and M. Garaudy. And generally it is enough to skim
through a piece of Communist writing to pick out at random
a hundred conservative practices: persuasion by repetition,
by intimidation, by veiled threats, by forceful and scornful
assertion, by cryptic allusions to demonstrations that are not
forthcoming, by exhibiting so complete and superb a conviction that, from the very start, it places itself above all
debate, casts its spell, and ends by becoming contagious; the
opponent is never answered; he is discredited; he belongs to
the police, to the Intelligence Service; he's a fascist. As for
proofs, they are never given, because they are terrible and
implicate too many people. If you insist upon knowing
them, you are told to stop where you are and to take
someone's word for the accusation. 'Don't force us to bring
them out; you'll be sorry if you do.' In short, the Communist intellectual adopts the attitude of the staff which
condemned Dreyfus on secret evidence. He also reverts, to
be sure, to the Manichaeism of the reactionaries, though he
divides the world according to other principles. For the
Stalinist a Trotskyist is an incarnation of evil, like the Jew
for Maurras. Everything that comes from him is necessarily
bad. On the other hand, the possession of certain titles
serves as a seal of approval. Compare this sentence of Joseph
de Maistre, 'The married woman is necessarily chaste,' with
this one of a correspondent of *Action*, 'The communist is
the *permanent* hero of our time.' That there are heroes in the
Communist Party—let me be the first to admit it. So what?
Has no married woman ever been weak? No, since she is
married before God. And is it enough to enter the Party to
become a hero? Yes, since the C.P. is the party of heroes.
But what if someone cited the name of a Communist who
sometimes was not all he should be? It's because he wasn't
a *real* Communist.

In the nineteenth century one had to give all sorts of

guarantees and lead an exemplary life in order to cleanse oneself in the eyes of the bourgeois of the sin of writing, for literature is, in essence, heresy. The situation has not changed except that it is now the Communists, that is, the qualified representatives of the proletariat, who as a matter of principle regard the writer as suspect. Even though he may be irreproachable in his morals, a Communist intellectual bears within him this original defect: that he entered the party *freely*; he was led to this decision by a thoughtful reading of *Capital*, a critical examination of the historical situation, an acute sense of justice and generosity, and a taste for solidarity; all this is proof of an independence which doesn't smell so very good. He entered the party by free choice; therefore, he can leave it.[38] He entered because he had criticized the politics of his class of origin; therefore, he will be able to criticize that of the representatives of his class of adoption. But in the very action by which he inaugurates a new life, there is a curse which will weigh upon him all through this life. From the moment of ordination there begins for him a long trial, similar to the one Kafka has described for us, in which the judges are unknown and the dossiers secret, where the only final sentences are condemnations. It is not up to his invisible accusers to give proof of his crime, as is customary in justice; it is for him to prove his innocence. As everything he writes can be held against him and as he knows it, each of his works presents the ambiguous character of being both a public appeal in the name of the C.P. and a secret plea for his own cause. Everything that, from the outside, for the readers, seems a chain of peremptory assertions, appears within the Party, in the eyes of the judges, as a humble and clumsy attempt at self-justification. When to *us* he appears most brilliant and most effective, he is perhaps then most guilty. Sometimes it seems to us—and perhaps he too believes it—that he has been raised into the hierarchy of the Party and that he has become its spokesman, but he is being tested or tricked; the rungs of the ladder are faked; when he thinks he's high up, he's far down. You can read his writings a hundred times but you'll never be able to decide their real importance. When Nizan, who was in charge of foreign politics for *Ce soir*, was in all honesty trying his utmost to prove that our only chance for salvation lay in a Franco-Russian pact, his secret judges, who let him talk on, already knew about Ribbentrop's conversations with Molotov. If he thinks that he can get out of it by a corpselike obedience, he is mistaken. He is expected to have wit, pungency, lucidity, and inventiveness. But at the same time that they are required of him, he is penalized for these virtues, for they are, in themselves, tendencies towards crime. How is he to practise the critical spirit? The flaw is in him like the worm in a piece of fruit. He can please neither his readers, his judges, nor himself. In the eyes of everyone and even of himself he is only a guilty subjectivity which deforms Knowledge by reflecting it in his troubled waters. This deformation can be useful; as his readers make no distinction between what comes from the author and what from the 'historical process', it is always possible to disclaim him. It is taken for granted that he dirties his hands in his job, and as his mission is to express C.P. politics from day to day, his articles still remain when the line has long since changed, and these are what the opponents of Stalinism refer to when they want to show its contradictions or versatility. Thus, the writer is not only *presumed guilty in advance;* he is charged with all past faults, since his name remains attached to the errors of the Party, and he is the scapegoat of all the political purges.

Nevertheless, it is not impossible that he may hold out for a long time if he learns to keep his qualities in leash when they run the risk of pulling him too far. Yet he must not use cynicism. Cynicism is as serious a vice as good will. Let him know how to keep his eyes shut; let him see what need not be seen, and let him forget sufficiently what he has seen in order never to write about it, yet let him remember it sufficiently so that in the future he may avoid looking at it; let him carry his criticism far enough to determine the point where it should be brought to a halt, that is, let him

go beyond this point in order to be able in the future to
avoid the temptation of going beyond it, but let him know
how to detach himself from this prospective criticism, to
put it in parentheses, and to regard it as null and void; in
short, let him at all times be aware that the mind is finite,
bounded everywhere by magic frontiers, by mists, like the
primitives who can count up to twenty and are mysteriously
denied the power of going any further. This artificial fog
which he must be always ready to spread between himself
and risky evidence, we shall call, very simply, dishonesty.
But we're not finished yet: let him avoid speaking too often
about dogmas; it's not good to show them in broad daylight; the works of Marx, like the Bible of the Catholics,
are dangerous to anyone who approaches them without a
director of conscience; there is one in each cell; if doubts or
scruples arise it is to him that one must go and talk. Nor
should you put too many Communists in your novels or on
the stage; if they have faults, they run the risk of displeas-
ing; if they are too perfect, they bore. Stalinist politics has
no desire to find its image in literature because it knows that
a portrait is already a challenge. One can get out of it by
painting the 'permanent hero' *en profil perdu*—by making
him appear at the end of the story to draw conclusions, or by
everywhere suggesting his presence but without showing it,
as Daudet with the Arlésienne. As far as possible, avoid
bringing up the revolution; that's rather dated. The European proletariat no more governs its destiny than does the
bourgeoisie; history is written elsewhere. It must be slowly
weaned of its old dreams, and the perspective of insurrection must be gently replaced by that of war. If the writer
conforms to all these prescriptions, he will not be in greater
favour on that account. He's a useless mouth; he doesn't
work with his hands. He knows it; he suffers from an inferiority complex; he is almost ashamed of his craft and puts
as much zeal into bowing before the workers as Jules
Lamaître put into bowing before the generals round about
1900.

During this period, the Marxist doctrine—which is quite

intact—has been withering away; for want of internal controversy, it has been degraded to a stupid determinism. Marx, Lenin, and Engels said any number of times that explanation by causes had to yield to the dialectical process. But the dialectic does not admit of being put into the formulas of a catechism. An elementary scientism is being spread. History is accounted for by juxtapositions of causal and linear series. Shortly before the war, Politzer, the last of the great minds of French Communism, was forced to teach that 'the brain secretes thought' as an endocrine gland secretes hormones; when the Communist intellectual today wants to interpret history or human behaviour, he borrows from bourgeois ideology a deterministic psychology based on mechanism and the law of interest.

But there is worse. The conservation of the C.P. is today accompanied by an opportunism which contradicts it. It is not only a matter of safeguarding the U.S.S.R., but it is also necessary to deal tactfully with the bourgeoisie. Thus, they talk its language: family, country, religion, morality. And as they have not thereby given up the idea of weakening it, they try to fight it on its own ground by improving upon its principles. The result of this tactic is to superimpose two contradictory conservatisms, materialist scholasticism and Christian moralism. The truth is that once you abandon all logic, it is not so difficult to pass from one to the other because both suppose the same sentimental attitude; it is a matter of holding fast to positions which are threatened, of refusing to discuss, and of masking fear behind anger. But the point is that the intellectual, by definition, must *also* use logic. Therefore, he is asked to cover up the contradictions by sleight-of-hand. He must do his best to reconcile the irreconcilable, to unite by force ideas which repel each other, and to cover up the soldering by glittering layers of fine style—to say nothing of the task which has fallen to him only recently, that is, to steal the history of France from the bourgeoisie, to annex the great Ferré, little Bara, Saint Vincent de Paul, and Descartes. Poor Communist intellectuals. They have fled the ideology of their class of origin only to find it again in the class they have chosen. This time, there is no more laughing; work, family, country—these are the words they must sing. I imagine that they must often rather want to let loose, but they are chained. They are allowed to roar at phantoms or against some writers who have remained free and who represent nothing.

They'll start naming illustrious writers. To be sure, I recognize the fact that they had talent. Is it an accident if they no longer have any? I have shown above that the work of art, which is an absolute end, is opposed in essence to bourgeois utilitarianism. Do they think that it can accommodate itself to Communist utilitarianism? In a genuinely revolutionary party it would find the propitious climate for its blossoming because the freedom of man and the coming of the classless society are likewise absolute goals, unconditioned exigencies which literature can reflect in its own exigency. But the C.P. today has entered the infernal circle of means. It must take and keep key positions, that is, means of acquiring means. When ends withdraw, when means are swarming like gnats as far as the eye can see, the work of art in turn becomes a means. It enters the chain. Its ends and its principles become external to it. It is governed from the outside. It takes man by the belly or the short hairs. The writer maintains the appearance of talent, that is, the art of finding words which gleam, but something is dead within. Literature has changed into propaganda.[39] Yet it is someone like M. Garaudy, a Communist and a propagandist, who accuses me of being a gravedigger. I could return the insult, but I prefer to plead guilty; if I could do so, I would bury literature with my own hands rather than make it serve ends which utilize it. But why the excitement? Grave-diggers are honest people, certainly unionized, perhaps Communists. I'd rather be a grave-digger than a lackey.

Since we are still free, we won't join the C.P. watchdogs. The fact that we have talent does not depend upon us, but as we have chosen the profession of writing, each of us is responsible for literature, and whether or not it becomes alienated does depend upon us. It is sometimes claimed that our books reflect the hesitations of the petty bourgeoisie which decides for neither the proletariat nor for capitalism. That's false; we've made up our minds. We are then told that our choice is ineffectual and abstract, that it is an intellectual game if it is not accompanied by our adhesion to a revolutionary party. It is true that today in France one can hardly reach the working classes if not through the Party. But only loose thinking can identify their cause with the C.P.'s. Even if, as citizens, we can in strictly specific circumstances support its politics with our votes, that does not mean that we should serve it with our pens. If the two alternatives are really the bourgeoisie and the C.P., then the choice is impossible. For we do not have the right to write for the oppressing class *alone*, nor to join forces with a party which asks us to work dishonestly and with a bad conscience. In so far as the Communist Party canalizes, almost in spite of itself, the aspirations of an entire oppressed class which irresistibly leads it to demand, for fear of being 'outflanked on the left', such measures as peace with the Viet Nam or the increase of salaries—which its whole political line is inclined to avoid—we are with this party against the bourgeoisie; in so far as certain well-intentioned bourgeois circles recognize that spirituality must be simultaneously a free negativity and a free construction, we are with these bourgeois against the C.P. In so far as a scurvy, opportunistic, conservative, and deterministic ideology is in contradiction with the very essence of literature we are against both the C.P. and the bourgeoisie. That means clearly that we are writing against everybody, that we have readers but no public. Bourgeois who have broken with our class but who have remained bourgeois in our morals, separated from the proletariat by the Communist screen, we remain up in the air; our good will serves no one, not even us; we are in the age of the undiscoverable public. Worse still, we are writing against the current.

The authors of the eighteenth century helped to make history because the historical perspective of the moment was revolution and because a writer can and ought to align himself on the side of revolution if it is proved that there is no other means of bringing an end to oppression. But the writer today can in no case approve of a war, because the social structure of war is dictatorship, because its results are always a matter of chance, and because, whatever happens, its costs are infinitely greater than the gains, and finally because war alienates literature by making it serve the propagandist hullabaloo.

Since our historical perspective is war, since we are asked to choose between the Anglo-Saxon and the Soviet blocs, and since we refuse to prepare for war with either one or the other, we have fallen outside history and are speaking in the desert. We are not even left with the illusion of winning our case by means of an appeal; there will be no appeal, and we know that the posthumous fate of our works will depend neither upon our talents nor our efforts, but upon the results of future conflicts. In the event of a Soviet victory, we will be passed over in silence until we die a second time; in the event of an American victory, the best of us will be put into the jars of literary history and won't be taken out again.

A clear-sighted view of the darkest possible situation is in itself already an optimistic act. It implies, in effect, that the situation can be *thought about*, that is, that we are not lost in a dark forest and that, on the contrary, we can break away from it, at least in spirit, that we can examine it and thus already go beyond it and take up our resolutions in the face of it, even if these resolutions are hopeless. Our engagement must begin the moment we are repulsed and excommunicated by the Churches, when the art of writing, wedged in between different propagandas, seems to have lost its characteristic effectiveness. It is not a question of adding to the exigencies of literature, but simply of serving them all together, even without hope.

(1) First, let us list our *virtual* readers, that is, the social

categories which do not read us, but which might. I do not think that we have made much headway among teachers, which is a pity. They have already served as intermediaries between literature and the masses.[40] By now, most of them have already chosen. They dispense the Christian or the Stalinist ideology to their pupils, according to the side they have taken. However, there are still some who are hesitating. These are the ones who must be reached. A great deal has been written about the petty bourgeoisie, distrustful and always mystified, so ready, in its bewilderment, to follow fascist agitators. I do not think that much has been written *for it*[41] except propaganda tracts. Yet it is accessible through certain of its elements. Finally, more remote, difficult to distinguish, and still more difficult to touch are those popular factions which have not joined up with communism or which detach themselves from it and risk falling into resigned indifference or formless discontent. Outside that, nothing. The peasants hardly read—though slightly more than they did in 1914. The working class is locked up. Such are the data of the problem; they are not encouraging, but we must adapt ourselves to them.

(2) How shall we incorporate some of our potential readers into our actual public? Books are inert. They act upon those who open them, but they cannot open by themselves. There can be no question of popularizing; we would be literary morons, and in order to keep literature from falling into the pitfalls of propaganda we would be throwing it right in ourselves. So we must have recourse to new means. They already exist; the Americans have already adorned them with the name of 'mass media'; these are the real resources at our disposal for conquering the virtual public—the newspaper, the radio, and the cinema. Naturally, we have to quieten our scruples. To be sure, the book is the noblest, the most ancient of forms; to be sure, we will always have to return to it. But there is a *literary* art of radio, film, editorial work, and reporting. There is no need to popularize. The film, by its very nature, speaks to crowds; it speaks to them about crowds and about their destiny.

The radio surprises people at the table or in bed, at the moment when they are most defenceless, in the almost organic abandon of solitude. At the present time, it makes use of its opportunity in order to fool them, but it is also the moment when one might better appeal to their good faith; they have not yet put on or have laid aside the personality with which they face the world. We've got one foot inside the door. We must learn to speak in images, to transpose the ideas of our books into these new languages.

It is by no means a matter of letting our works be adapted for the screen or the broadcasts of the French Radio. We must write directly for the cinema and the wireless. The difficulties which I have mentioned above arise from the fact that radio and cinema are machines. Since considerable capital is at stake, it is inevitable that they are today in the hands of the state or of conservative corporations. They apply to the writer under a sort of misapprehension; he believes that they are asking him for his work, which they are not concerned with, whereas all they want of him is his signature, which pays. And since in this respect he is so lacking in practical sense that, in general, they can't persuade him to sell one without the other, at least they try to get him to please and to assure the stockholders of their profits or to be persuasive and serve the politics of the state. In both cases, they demonstrate to him statistically that bad productions have more success than good ones, and when they explain to him about the bad taste of the public, he is requested to be so good as to submit to it. When the work is finished, in order to be sure that it's bad enough they hand it over to mediocrities who cut out what's beyond them.

But this is exactly the point that we have to fight about. It is improper for us to stoop in order to please; on the contrary, our job is to reveal to the public its own needs and, little by little, to form it so that it *needs to read*. We must appear to be giving in and yet must make ourselves indispensable and consolidate our positions, if possible, by facile successes; then, we must take advantage of the disorder in the governmental services and the incompetence of certain producers to turn these arms against them. Then the writer will launch out into the unknown; he will speak in the dark to people he does not know, to whom no one has ever spoken except to lie. He will lend his voice to their anger and their worries. Through him, men whom no mirror has ever reflected, who have learned to smile and weep like blind men, without seeing themselves, will suddenly find themselves before their image. Who could dare claim that literature will lose thereby? I think that on the contrary it will gain. All the numbers and fractions which formerly were the whole of arithmetic, today represent only a small sector of the science of numbers. The same with literature: 'total literature', if ever it sees the day, will have its algebra, its irrational and imaginary numbers. Let it not be said that these industries have nothing to do with art. After all, printing is also an industry, and the authors of former times conquered it for us. I do not think that we shall ever have the full use of the 'mass media', but it would be a fine thing to begin conquering it for our successors. In any case, what is certain is that if we do not make use of it, we must resign ourselves to be forever writing for nobody but the bourgeois.

(3) Bourgeois, intellectuals, teachers, non-communist workers; granted we touch all these disparate elements, how are we going to make a public out of them, that is, an organic unity of readers, listeners, and spectators?

Let us bear in mind that the man who reads strips himself in some way of his empirical personality and escapes from his resentments, his fears, and his lusts in order to put himself at the peak of his freedom. This freedom takes the literary work and, through it, mankind, for absolute ends. It sets itself up as an unconditioned exigence in relationship to itself, to the author, and to possible readers. It can therefore be identified with Kantian *good will* which, in every circumstance, treats man as an end and not as a means. Thus, by his very exigence, the reader attains that chorus of good wills which Kant has called the City of Ends, which thousands of readers all over the world who do not know each other are, at every moment, helping to maintain. But in order that this ideal chorus should become a concrete society, it must satisfy two conditions: first, that readers replace this theoretical acquaintance with each other, in so far as they are all particular examples of mankind, by an intuition or, at the very least, by a presentiment of their physical presence in the midst of this world; second, that, instead of remaining solitary and uttering appeals in the void, which, in regard to the human condition in general, affect no one, these abstract good wills establish real relations among themselves when actual events take place, or, in other words, that these non-temporal good wills *historicize* themselves while preserving their purity, and that they transform their exigences into material and timely demands. Lacking the wherewithal, the city of ends lasts for each of us only while we are reading; on passing from the imaginary life to real life we forget this abstract, implicit community which rests on nothing. Whence, there arise what I might call the two essential mystifications of reading.

When a young communist while reading *Aurélien*, or a Christian student while reading *The Hostage*, have a moment of aesthetic joy, their feeling envelops a universal exigence; the city of ends surrounds them with its phantom walls. But during this time the works are supported by a concrete collectivity—in one case, the Communist Party, in the other, the community of the faithful—which sanctions them and which manifests its presence between the lines: the priest has spoken of it from the pulpit, *L'Humanité* has recommended it. The student never feels alone when he reads. The book dons a sacred character. It is an accessory of the cult. Reading becomes a rite, more precisely, a communion. On the other hand if a Nathanaël should open *Fruits of the Earth*, as soon as he gets into the swing of the book he launches the same impotent appeal to the goodwill of men. The city of ends, magically evoked, does not refuse to appear. Yet, his enthusiasm remains essentially solitary. The reading in this case is *disjunctive*; he is turned against his family, against the society about him; he is cut off from the past and the future to be reduced to his naked presence in the moment; he is taught to descend within himself in order to recognize and take stock of his most particular desires. Our Nathanaël pays no heed to the possibility that somewhere else in the world, wherever it may be, there may be another Nathanaël plunged in the same reading and the same raptures. The message is addressed only to him. When all has been said and done, he is invited to reject the book, to break the pact of mutual exigences which unite him to the author; he has found nothing but himself, himself as a separate entity. As Durkheim might have put it, the solidarity of Claudel's readers is organic and that of Gide's mechanical.

In both cases, literature runs very serious risks. When the book is sacred, it does not draw its religious virtue from its intentions or its beauty, but rather receives it from without, like a seal, and as the essential moment of the reading in this case is the communion, that is, the symbolic integration into the community, the written work passes to the *inessential*, it really becomes an *accessory* of the ceremony. The example of Nizan shows this rather clearly: as a communist, he was read with fervour by the communists; now that he is an apostate, and dead, it would not occur to any Stalinist to pick up his books again; to these biased eyes they now offer nothing but the image of treason. But as in 1939 the reader of *The Trojan Horse* and *The Conspiracy* addressed an unconditioned universal appeal for the adherence of all free men, as, on the other hand, the sacred character of these works was, on the contrary, conditional and temporary and implied the possibility, in the event of the excommunication of their author, of rejecting them like sacrificial offerings that had been defiled, or simply of forgetting them if the C.P. changed its line, these two contradictory implications destroyed the very meaning of the reading.[42] There's nothing surprising in that, since we have seen the communist writer himself ruin the very meaning of writing; the circle is completed.

Must we therefore be satisfied with being read in secret,

almost by stealth? Must the work of art mature like a fine, ripe vice in the depths of solitary souls? Here again I think that I discern a contradiction: we have discovered in the work of art the presence of all mankind; reading is a commerce of the reader with the author and with other readers; how can it be, at the same time, an invitation to segregation?

We do not want our public, however numerous it may be, to be reduced to the juxtaposition of individual readers nor to have its unity conferred upon it by the transcendent action of a Party or a Church. Reading should not be mystical communion any more than it should be masturbation, but rather a companionship. On the other hand we recognize that the purely formal recourse to abstract good wills leaves each one in his original isolation. However, that is the point from which we must start; if one loses this conducting wire, one is suddenly lost in the wilds of propaganda or in the egotistical pleasures of a style which is a matter of 'purely personal taste'. It is therefore up to us to convert the city of ends into a concrete and open society— and this by the very content of our works.

If the city of ends remains a feeble abstraction, it is because it is not realizable without an objective modification of the historical situation. Kant, I believe, saw this very well, but sometimes he counted on a purely subjective transformation of the moral subject and at other times he despaired of ever meeting a goodwill on this earth. In fact, the contemplation of beauty might well arouse in us the purely formal intention of treating men as ends, but this intention would reveal itself to be utterly futile in practice since the fundamental structures of our society are still oppressive. Such is the present paradox of ethics; if I am absorbed in treating a few chosen persons as absolute ends, for example, my wife, my son, my friends, the needy person I happen to come across, if I am bent upon fulfilling all my duties towards them, I shall spend my life doing so; I shall be led *to pass over in silence* the injustices of the age, the class struggle, colonialism, Anti-Semitism, etc., and, finally, to *take advantage of oppression in order to do good*. Moreover, the former will be found in person-to-person relationships and, more subtly, in my very intentions. The good that I try to do will be vitiated at the roots. It will be turned into radical evil. But, vice versa, if I throw myself into the revolutionary enterprise I risk having no more leisure for personal relations—worse still, of being led by the logic of the action into treating most men, and even my friends, as means. But if we start with the moral exigence which the aesthetic feeling envelops without meaning to do so, we are starting on the right foot. We must *historicize* the reader's goodwill, that is, by the formal agency of our work, we must, if possible, provoke his intention of treating men, in every case, as an absolute end and, by the *subject* of our writing, direct his intention upon his neighbours, that is, upon the oppressed of the world. But we shall have accomplished nothing if, in addition, we do not show him—and in the very warp and weft of the work—that it is quite impossible to treat concrete men as ends in contemporary society. Thus, he will be led by the hand until he is made to see that, in effect, what he wants is to eliminate the exploitation of man by man and that the city of ends which, with one stroke, he has set up in the aesthetic intuition is an ideal which we shall approach only at the end of a long historical evolution. In other words, we must transform his formal goodwill into a concrete and material will to change *this world* by specific means in order to help the coming of the concrete society of ends. For goodwill is not possible in this age, or rather, it is and can be only the intention of making goodwill possible. Whence, a particular *tension* which must manifest itself in our works and which remotely recalls the one I mentioned in regard to Richard Wright. For a whole section of the public which we wish to win over still consumes its goodwill in person-to-person relationships, and another whole section, because it belongs to the oppressed classes, has given itself the job of obtaining, by all possible means, the material improvement of its lot. Thus, we must at the same time teach one group that the reign of ends cannot be realized without revolution and the other group that revolution is conceivable only if it prepares the reign of ends. It is this perpetual tension—if we can keep it up—which will realize the unity of our public. In short, we must militate, in our writings, in favour of the freedom of the person *and* the socialist revolution. It has often been claimed that they are not reconcilable. It is our job to show tirelessly that they imply each other.

We were born into the bourgeoisie, and this class has taught us the value of its conquests: political freedom, habeas corpus, etc. We remain bourgeois by our culture, our way of life, and our present public. But at the same time the historical situation drives us to join the proletariat in order to construct a classless society. No doubt that for the time being the latter is not very much concerned with freedom of thought; they've got other fish to fry. The bourgeoisie, on the other hand, pretends not even to understand what the words 'material freedom' mean. Thus, each class can, at least in this regard, preserve a good conscience, since it is unaware of one of the terms of the antinomy.

But we others, though we have nothing to mediate at present, are none the less in the position of mediators. Pulled from both sides, we are condemned to suffer this double exigence as a Passion. It is our personal problem as well as the drama of our age. It will, of course, be said that this antinomy which tortures us is merely due to our still dragging round the remains of bourgeois ideology which we have not been able to shake off; on the other hand, it will be said that we suffer from revolutionary snobbery and that we want to make literature serve ends for which it is not designed. That would not be too bad, but these voices find responsive echoes in some of us who have unhappy consciences. Therefore, it would be well for us to impress this truth upon our minds: it is, perhaps, tempting to abandon formal liberties in order to deny more completely our bourgeois origins, but that would be enough to discredit fundamentally the project of writing. It might be more simple for us to disinterest ourselves in material demands in order to produce 'pure literature' with a serene conscience, but we would thereby be giving up the idea of choosing our readers outside the oppressing class. Thus, opposition must also be overcome for ourselves and within ourselves. Let us first persuade ourselves that it can be overcome: literature in itself proves this, since it is the work of a total freedom addressing plenary freedoms and thus in its own way manifests the totality of the human condition as a free product of a creative activity. And if, on the other hand, a full solution is beyond the powers of most of us, it is our duty to overcome the opposition in a thousand detailed syntheses. Every day we must take sides: in our life as a writer, in our articles, in our books. Let it always be by preserving as our guiding principle the rights of total freedom as an effective synthesis of formal and material freedoms. Let this freedom manifest itself in our novels, our essays, and our plays. And if our characters do not yet enjoy it, if they live in our time, let us at least be able to show what it costs them not to have it. It is not enough to denounce abuses and injustices in a fine style, nor to make a brilliant and negative psychological study of the bourgeoisie, nor even to let our pens serve social parties in order to save literature. We must take up a position *in our literature*, because literature is in essence a taking of position. We must, in all domains, both reject solutions which are not rigorously inspired by socialist principles and, at the same time, stand off from all doctrines and movements which consider socialism as the absolute end. In our eyes it should not represent the final end, but rather the end of the beginning, or, if one prefers, the last means before the end which is to put the human person in possession of his freedom. Thus, our works should be presented to the public in a double aspect of negativity and construction.

First, negativity. We are familiar with the great tradition of critical literature which goes back to the end of the eighteenth century; it is concerned with separating by analysis that which specifically belongs to each notion from what tradition or the mystifications of the oppressor have added to it. Writers like Voltaire or the Encyclopedists considered the practice of this criticism as one of their essential tasks. Since the matter and the tool of the writer are language, it is normal for writers to think of cleaning their instrument. This negative function of literature was, to tell the truth, ignored in the following century, probably because the class in power made use of these concepts which had been established on their behalf by the great writers of the past, and because there was, at the beginning, a kind of equilibrium among its institutions, its aims, the kind of oppression it practised, and the meaning it gave to the words it used. For example, it is clear that in the nineteenth century the word 'freedom' never designated anything but political freedom and that the words 'disorder' or 'licence' were reserved for all other forms of freedom. Similarly, the word revolution necessarily referred to a great historical revolution, the one of '89. And as the bourgeoisie, by a very general convention, neglected the *economic* aspect of this revolution, as, in its history, it barely mentioned the name of Gracchus Baboeuf and the views of Robespierre and Marat so that it might give its official respect to Desmoulins and the Girondists, the result was that any political insurrection which succeeded could be designated a revolution, and that this denomination could be applied to the events of 1830 and 1848 which, at bottom, merely brought about a simple change of the directing personnel.

This narrowness of vocabulary caused the picture to lack certain aspects of the historical, psychological, and philosophical reality, but as these aspects were not manifest by themselves, as they corresponded to a dull malaise in the consciousness of the masses or the individual rather than to effective factors of social or personal life, one was struck by the dry property of the words and by the immutable clearness of their meanings rather than by their insufficiency. In the eighteenth century to write a Philosophical Dictionary was secretly to undermine the class in power. In the nineteenth, Littré and Larousse were positivist and conservative bourgeois; their dictionaries aimed solely at verifying and settling matters. The crisis of language which marked the literature between the two wars was the result of the fact that after ripening silently, neglected aspects of the historical and psychological reality passed abruptly to the first level. Yet, we have the same verbal apparatus at our disposal for naming them. Perhaps it may not be too serious because in most cases it is only a matter of deepening concepts and changing definitions. For example, when we have rejuvenated the meaning of the word 'Revolution' by pointing out that what should be designated by this word is a historical phenomenon involving the change of the régime of property, the change of political personnel, and the recourse to insurrection, we shall have proceeded, without great effort, to the rejuvenation of a sector of the French language, and the word, impregnated with a new life, will be off to a new start. It must be noted, however, that the fundamental job to be done on language is of a synthetic nature, whereas in Voltaire's century it was analytic; it is necessary to enlarge, to deepen, and to open the doors and to let the troop of new ideas enter while controlling them as they pass by. In other words, to be anti-academic.

Unfortunately, what complicates our job in the extreme is that we are living in a century of propaganda. In 1914 the two opposing camps were arguing only the question of God; it still wasn't too serious. Today, there are five or six enemy camps which want to wrest the key-notions from each other because these are what exert the most influence on the masses. It will be recalled how the Germans preserved the external aspect, the title, the arrangement of articles, and even the typographical character of the pre-war French newspapers and used them to diffuse ideas which were entirely opposed to those which we were accustomed to find in them. They thought that we would not notice the difference in the pills since the coating did not change. The same with words: each party shoves them forward like Trojan horses, and we let them enter because they make the nineteenth-century meaning of the words shine before us. Once they are in place, they open up, and strange, astounding meanings spread out within us like armies; the fortress

is taken before we are on guard. Thereafter, neither conversation nor argument is any longer possible. Brice Parain
saw this quite clearly; to quote him roughly, 'If you use the
word freedom in front of me, I start fuming, I approve, or
I contradict, but I don't understand what you mean by it.
So we're talking in the dark.' That's true, but it's a modern
evil. In the nineteenth century Littré's dictionary might
have brought us together; before this war we could have
had recourse to the vocabulary of Lalande. Today, there is
no longer an arbiter.

Nevertheless, we are all accomplices because these slippery
notions serve our dishonesty. That's not all; linguists have
often noted that in troubled periods words preserve the
traces of the great human migrations. A barbaric army
crosses Gaul, the soldiers amuse themselves with the native
language, and so it stays twisted for a long time. Our own
still bears the marks of the Nazi invasion. The word 'Jew'
formerly designated a certain type of man; perhaps French
anti-Semitism had given it a slight pejorative meaning, but
it was easy to brush it off. Today one fears to use it; it
sounds like a threat, an insult, or a provocation. The word
'Europe' formerly referred to the geographical, economic,
and political unity of the Old Continent. Today, it preserves
a musty smell of Germanism and servitude. Even the
innocent and abstract term 'collaboration' is in disrepute.
On the other hand, as Soviet Russia is now at a standstill the
words which the communists used before the war have also
stopped short. They stop in the middle of their meaning,
just as the Stalinist intellectuals do in the middle of their
thought, or else they get off on side-paths. The transformations of the word 'Revolution' are quite significant in this
respect. In an earlier chapter I quoted the saying of a
journalist who was a collaborator: 'Stand firm! That's the
motto of the Nationalist Revolution.' To which I now
add this one, which comes from a communist intellectual:
'Produce! That's the real Revolution!' Things have gone so
far that recently in France one could have read on the
election posters: 'To vote for the Communist Party is to

vote for the defence of property.'[43] Vice versa, who is not a socialist today? I remember a writers' congress—all of them leftists—which refused to use the word socialism in a manifesto 'because it was too discredited'. And the linguistic reality is today so complicated that I still do not know whether these authors rejected the word for the reason they gave or because it was so down at the heel that it scared them. Moreover, we know that in the United States the term *communist* designates any American citizen who does not vote for the Republicans, and in Europe the word *fascist* means any European citizen who does not vote for the communists. To confuse things still more, we must add that French conservatives state that the Soviet régime—which, however, subscribes neither to a theory of race, nor a theory of anti-Semitism, nor a theory of war—is one of national socialism, whereas on the left it is said that the United States—which is a capitalist democracy with a loose dictatorship of public opinion—borders on fascism.

The function of a writer is to call a spade a spade. If words are sick, it is up to us to cure them. Instead of that, many writers live off this sickness. In many cases modern literature is a cancer of words. It is perfectly all right to write 'horse of butter' but in a sense it amounts to doing the same thing as those who speak of a fascist United States or a Stalinist national socialism. There is nothing more deplorable than the literary practice which, I believe, is called poetic prose and which consists of using words for the obscure harmonics which resound about them and which are made up of vague meanings which are in contradiction with the clear meaning.

I know: the purpose of a number of writers was to destroy words as that of the surrealists was to destroy both the subject and the object; but it was the extreme point of the literature of consumption. But today, as I have shown, it is necessary to construct. If one starts deploring the inadequacy of language to reality, like Brice Parain, one makes oneself an accomplice of the enemy, that is, of propaganda. Our first duty as a writer is thus to re-establish language in its dignity. After all, we think with words. We would have to be quite vain to believe that we are concealing ineffable beauties which the word is unworthy of expressing. And then, I distrust the incommunicable; it is the source of all violence. When it seems impossible to get others to share the certainties which we enjoy, the only thing left is to fight, to burn, or to hang. No. We are no better than our life, and it is by our life that we must be judged; our thought is no better than our language, and it ought to be judged by the way it uses it. If we want to restore their virtue to words, we must carry on a double operation; on the one hand, an analytical cleaning which rids them of their adventitious meanings, and, on the other hand, a synthetic enlargement which adapts them to the historical situation. If an author wished to devote himself completely to this job, there would be more than enough for a whole lifetime. With all of us working on it together, we shall do a good job of it without too much trouble.

That is not all: we are living in the age of mystifications. Some are fundamental ones which are due to the structure of society; some are secondary. At any rate, the social order today rests upon the mystification of consciousness, as does disorder as well. Nazism was a mystification; Gaullism is another; Catholicism is a third. At the present there can be no doubt that French communism is a fourth. Obviously we could pay no attention to it and do our work honestly without aggressiveness. But as the writer addresses the freedom of his reader, and as each mystified consciousness, in so far as it is an accomplice of the mystification which enchains it, tends to persist in its state, we will be able to safeguard literature only if we undertake the job of demystifying our public. For the same reason the writer's duty is to take sides against all injustices, wherever they may come from. And as our writings would have no meaning if we did not set up as our goal the eventual coming of freedom by means of socialism, it is important in each case to stress the fact that there have been violations of formal and personal liberties or material oppression or both. From this point of view we must denounce British politics in

Palestine and American politics in Greece as well as the Soviet deportations. And if we are told that we are acting as if we were quite important and that it is quite childish of us to hope that we can change the course of the world, we shall reply that we have no illusions about it, but that nevertheless it is fitting that certain things be said, even though it be only to save face in the eyes of our children; and besides, we do not have the crazy ambition of influencing the State Department, but rather the slightly less crazy one of acting upon the opinion of our fellow citizens.

Yet, we must not let off great inkwell explosions carelessly and without discernment. In each case we must consider the aim in view. Former communists would like to make us see Soviet Russia as enemy number one because she has corrupted the very idea of socialism and has transformed the dictatorship of the proletariat into the dictatorship of the bureaucracy. Consequently, they would like us to devote all our time to stigmatizing its extortion and its violence; at the same time they point out to us that capitalist injustices are highly obvious and are not likely to deceive anyone; thus, we would be wasting our time exposing them. I am afraid that I surmise only too well the interests which this advice serves. Whatever the putative violence may be, still, before passing judgement upon it, it is advisable to consider the situation of the country which commits it and the perspectives in which it has committed it. It would first be necessary to prove, for example, that the present machinations of the Soviet government are not, in the last analysis, dictated by its desire to protect the revolution which has stalled and to 'hold on' until the moment when it will be possible to resume its march forward. Whereas American anti-Semitism and negrophobia, our own colonialism and the attitude of the powers in regard to Franco, often lead to injustices which are less spectacular but which aim none the less at perpetuating the present régime of the exploitation of man by man. It will be said that everybody knows this. That may be true, but if nobody *says* it, what good does it do us to know it? Our job as a writer is to represent the world and to bear witness to it. Besides, even if it were proven that the Soviet Union and the Communist Party are pursuing genuinely revolutionary ends, that would not exempt us from judging the *means*. If one regards freedom as the principle and the goal of all human activity, it is equally false that one must judge the means by the end and the end by the means. Rather, the end is the synthetic unity of the means employed. Thus, there are means which risk destroying the end which they intend to realize because by their mere presence they smash the synthetic unity which they wish to enter.

The attempt has been made to determine by quasi-mathematical formulas the conditions under which a means may be called legitimate; in these formulas are included the probability of the end, its proximity, and what its returns are in regard to the cost of the means employed. One might think that we were back at Bentham and the arithmetic of pleasure. I am not saying that a formula of this kind might not be applied in certain cases, for example, in the hypothesis, itself quantitative, in which a certain number of lives must be sacrificed to save others. But in the majority of cases the problem is quite different; the means employed introduce a *qualitative* alteration into the end and consequently are not measurable. Let us imagine that a revolutionary party systematically lies to its militants in order to protect them against uncertainties, cries of conscience, and adverse propaganda. The end pursued is the abolition of a régime of oppression; but the lie is itself oppression. May one perpetuate oppression with the pretext of putting an end to it? Is it necessary to enslave man in order the better to free him? It will be said that the means are transitory. Not if it helps to create a *lied-to* and *lying* mankind; for then the men who take power are no longer those who deserve to get hold of it; and the reasons one had for abolishing oppression are undermined by the way one goes about abolishing it. Thus, the politics of the Communist Party, which consists of lying to its own troops, of calumniating, of hiding its defeats and its faults, compromises the goal which it pursues. On the other hand, it is easy to reply that in war—and every revolutionary party is at war—one cannot tell soldiers the whole truth. Thus, we have here a question of measure. No ready-made formula will excuse us from an examination in each particular case. It is up to us to make this examination. Left to itself, politics always takes the path of least resistance, that is, it goes downhill. The masses, duped by propaganda, follow it. So who can *represent* to the government, the parties, and the citizens the means that are being employed, if not the writer? That does not mean that we must be systematically opposed to the use of violence. I recognize that violence, under whatever form it may show itself, is a setback. But it is an inevitable setback because we are in a universe of violence; and if it is true that recourse to violence against violence risks perpetuating it, it is also true that it is the only means of bringing an end to it. A certain newspaper in which someone wrote a rather brilliant article saying that it was necessary to refuse any complicity with violence wherever it came from had to announce the following day the first skirmishes of the Indo-Chinese war. I should like to ask the writer today how we can refuse to participate indirectly in all violence. If you say nothing, you are necessarily for the continuation of the war; one is always responsible for what one does not try to prevent. But if you got it to stop at once and at any price, you would be at the origin of a number of massacres and you would be doing violence to all Frenchmen who have interests over there. I am not, of course, speaking of compromises, since war is born of compromise. Violence for violence; one must make a choice, according to other principles. The politician will wonder whether the transport of troops is possible, whether by continuing the war he will alienate public opinion, what the international repercussions will be. It is incumbent upon the writer to judge the means not from the point of view of an abstract morality, but in the perspectives of a precise goal which is the realization of a socialist democracy. Thus, we must mediate upon the modern problem of ends and means not only in theory but in each concrete case.

Evidently, there is a big job to be done. But even if we consume our life in *criticism* who can reproach us? The task of criticism has become *total*; it engages the whole man. In the eighteenth century the tool was forged; the simple utilization of analytical reason was enough to clean the concepts; today when it is necessary both to clean and to complete, to push to their conclusions notions which have become false because they have stopped along the way, criticism is *also* synthetic. It brings into action all our faculties of invention; instead of limiting itself to making use of a reason already established by two centuries of mathematics, on the contrary, it is this criticism which will form modern reason so that, in the end, it has creative freedom as its foundation. Doubtless, it will not by itself bring about a positive solution. But what does today? I see all about us only absolute formulas, patchwork, dishonest compromises, outdated and hastily refurbished myths. Even if we did nothing but puncture all these inflated wind-bladders one by one, we would be well deserving of our readers.

However, at about 1750 criticism was a direct preparation for changing the régime since it contributed to the weakening of the oppressing class by dismantling its ideology. The case today is not the same since the concepts to be criticized belong to all ideologies and all camps. Thus, it is no longer negativity alone which can serve history even if it finally does become a positivity. The *individual* writer may limit himself to his critical task, but our literature as a whole must be, above all, constructive. That does not mean that we must make it our business, individually or as a group, to find a new ideology. In every age, as I have pointed out, it is literature in its entirety which is the ideology because it constitutes the synthetic and often contradictory[44] totality of everything which the age has been able to produce to enlighten itself, taking into account the historical situation and the talent. But since we have recognized that we have to produce a literature of *praxis*, we ought to stick to our purpose to the very end. We no longer have time to *describe* or *narrate*; neither can we limit ourselves to *explaining*. Description, even though it be psychological, is pure contemplative enjoyment; explanation is acceptance, it excuses everything. Both of them assume that the die is cast. But if perception itself is action, if, for us, to show the world is to disclose it in the perspectives of a possible change, then, in this age of fatalism, we must reveal to the reader his power, in each concrete case, of doing and undoing, in short, of acting. The present situation, revolutionary by virtue of the fact that it is unbearable, remains in a state of stagnation because men have dispossessed themselves of their own destiny; Europe is abdicating before the future conflict and seeks less to prevent it than to range itself in advance in the camp of the conquerors. Soviet Russia considers itself to be alone and cornered, like a wild boar surrounded by a fierce pack ready to tear it apart. The United States, which does not fear the other nations, is infatuated with its own weight; the richer it is, the heavier it is. Weighed down with fat and pride, it lets itself be rolled towards war with its eyes closed. As for us, we are writing for only a few men in our own country and a handful of others in Europe. But we must go and seek them where they are, lost in their age like needles in a haystack, and we must remind them of their power. Let us take them in their job, in their family, in their class, and in their country, and let us examine their servitude with them, but let it not be to push them deeper into it; let us show them that in the most mechanical gesture of the worker there is already the complete negation of oppression; let us never envisage their situation as factual data but as a problem; let us point out that it keeps its form and its boundaries of infinite possibilities, in a word, that it has no other shape than what they confer upon it by the way they have chosen to go beyond it; let us teach them both that they are victims and that they are responsible for everything, that they are at once the oppressed, the oppressors, and the accomplices of their own oppressors and that one can never draw a line between what a man submits to, what he accepts, and what he wants; let us show that the world they live in is never defined except in reference to the future which they project before them, and since reading reveals their freedom to them, let us take advantage of it to remind them that this future in which they place themselves in order to judge the present is none other than that in which man rejoins himself and finally reaches himself as a totality by the coming of the City of Ends, for it is only the presentiment of Justice which permits us to be shocked by particular injustices, that is, to put it precisely, to regard them as injustices; finally, in inviting them to see things from the viewpoint of the City of Ends so they may understand their age, let us not allow them to remain in ignorance of the aspects of this age which favour the realizing of their aim.

The theatre was formerly a theatre of 'characters'. More or less complex, but complete, figures appeared on the stage, and the situation had no other function than to put these characters into conflict and to show how each of them was modified by the action of the others. I have elsewhere shown how important changes have taken place in this domain; many authors are returning to the theatre of situation. No more characters; the heroes are freedoms caught in a trap like all of us. What are the issues? Each character will be nothing but the choice of an issue and will equal no more than the chosen issue. It is to be hoped that all literature will become moral and problematic like this new theatre. Moral —not moralizing; let it show simply that man is *also* a value and that the questions he raises are always moral. Above all, let it show the inventor in him. In a sense, each situation is a trap—there are walls everywhere. I've expressed myself poorly: there are no issues to *choose*. An issue is invented. And each one, by inventing his own issue, invents himself. Man must be invented each day.

The point is that all is lost if we want to *choose* between the powers which are preparing for war. To choose the U.S.S.R. is to give up civil liberties without even being able to hope to gain material freedom; the retardation of its industry prohibits it, in case of victory, from organizing Europe; hence, indefinite prolongation of dictatorship and misery.

But after the victory of the United States, when the C.P. would be annihilated and the working class discouraged, disoriented, and—if I may risk a neologism—atomized, when capitalism would be more pitiless since it would be master of the world, can anyone believe that a revolutionary movement which would start from zero would have much chance? But aren't there unknown factors to be reckoned with? That's just it! I reckon with what I know. But who is forcing us to choose? Does one really make history by choosing between given wholes simply because they are given, and by siding with the stronger? In that case in 1940 all Frenchmen should have sided with Germany as the collaborators proposed.

Now, it is obvious that, on the contrary, historical action can never be reduced to a choice between raw data, but that it has always been characterized by the invention of new solutions on the basis of a definite situation. Respect for 'wholes' is pure and simple empiricism. Man has long since gone beyond empiricism in science, ethics, and individual life; the fountain-makers of Florence 'chose between wholes'; Torricelli *invented* the weight of air—I say that he invented it rather than discovered it because when an object is concealed from all eyes, one must invent it out of whole cloth in order to be able to discover it. When it is a question of historical fact, why, out of what inferiority complex, do our realists deny this faculty of creation which they proclaim everywhere else? The historical agent is almost always the man who in the face of a dilemma suddenly causes a third term to appear, one which up to that time had been invisible. It is true that a *choice* must be made between the U.S.S.R. and the Anglo-Saxon bloc. As for socialist Europe, there's no 'choosing' it since it doesn't exist. It is *to be made.* Not by starting with the England of Mr. Churchill, nor even with that of Mr. Bevin, but by starting on the continent, by the union of all countries which have the same problems. It will be said that it is too late, but what does anyone know about it? Has anyone even tried? Our relations with our immediate neighbours always take place through Moscow, London, or

New York; doesn't anyone know that there are direct ways? Whatever the case may be and as long as circumstances do not change, the fortunes of literature are tied up with the coming of a socialist Europe, that is, of a group of states with a democratic and collectivist structure, each of which, while waiting for something better, would be deprived of part of its sovereignty for the sake of the whole. The hope of avoiding war dwells in this hypothesis only; in this hypothesis only will the circulation of ideas remain free and literature again find an object and a public.

Quite a number of jobs at the same time—and quite dissimilar. It's true. But Bergson has well shown that the eye—an extremely complicated organ if you regard it as a juxtaposition of functions—appears somewhat simple if it is replaced in the creative movement of evolution. The same with the writer; if you enumerate by analysis the themes which Kafka develops and the questions he raises in his books, and if you then go back to the beginning of his career and consider that for him these were themes *to be treated* and questions *to be raised*, you will be alarmed. But that's not the way he's to be taken. The work of Kafka is a free and unitary reaction to the Judaeo-Christian world of Central Europe. His novels are a synthetic act of going beyond his situation as a man, as a Jew, as a Czech, as a recalcitrant fiancé, as a tubercular, etc., as were also his handshake, his smile, and that gaze which Max Brod so admired. Under the analysis of the critic they break down into problems; but the critic is wrong; they must be read *in movement*.

I have not wanted to hand out extra impositions to the writers of my generation. What right would I have to do so, and has anybody asked me to? Nor do I have any taste for the manifestoes of a school. I have merely tried to describe a situation with its perspectives, its threats, and its demands. A literature of *praxis* is coming into being in the age of the unfindable public. That's the situation. Let each one handle it in his own way. His own way, that is, his own style, his own technique, his own subjects. If the writer is imbued, as I am, with the urgency of these problems, one can be sure that he will offer solutions to them in the *creative unity of his work*, that is, in the indistinctness of a movement of free creation.[45]

There is no guarantee that literature is immortal. Its chance today, its only chance, is the chance of Europe, of socialism, of democracy, and of peace. We must play it. If we writers lose it, too bad for us. But also, too bad for society. As I have shown, the collectivity passes to reflection and mediation by means of literature; it acquires an unhappy conscience, a lopsided image of itself which it constantly tries to modify and improve. But, after all, the art of writing is not protected by immutable decrees of Providence; it is what men make it; they choose it in choosing themselves. If it were to turn into pure propaganda or pure entertainment, society would wallow in the immediate, that is, in the life without memory of hymenoptera and gastropods. Of course, all of this is not very important. The world can very well do without literature. But it can do without man still better.

Writing for
One's Age

WE assert against certain critics and against certain authors that salvation is achieved on this earth, that it is of the whole man and by the whole man and that art is a meditation on life and not on death. It is true that for history talent alone counts. But I haven't entered into history and I don't know how I shall enter it; perhaps alone, perhaps in an anonymous crowd, perhaps as one of those names they put into footnotes in literary handbooks. At any rate, I do not have to bother myself with the judgements that the future will bring to bear upon my work since there's nothing I can do about them. Art cannot be reduced to a dialogue with the dead and with men not yet born; that would be both too difficult and too easy; and I see in this a last remnant of Christian belief in immortality: just as man's stay here below is presented as a moment of trial between limbo and hell or paradise, in like manner, for a book there is a transitory period coinciding approximately with that of its efficacy; after which, disembodied and gratuitous as a soul, it enters eternity. But at least, among Christians, it is this stay upon earth that decides everything and the final beatitude is only a sanction. Whereas it is commonly believed that the course run by our books, when we no longer exist, refers back to our life to justify it. This is true from the viewpoint of the objective mind. In the objective mind one classifies according to talent. But our descendants' view of us is not a privileged one, since others will come after them and will judge them in turn. It is obvious that we write out of a need for the absolute, and a work of the mind is indeed an absolute. But here one commits a double error. First of all, it is not true that a writer transmits his sufferings and his faults to the absolute when he writes about them; it is not true that he saves them. It is said that the unhappily married man who writes about marriage with talent has made a good book *with* his conjugal woes. That would be too easy: the bee makes honey *with* the

flower because it operates on the vegetal substance of *real* transformations; the sculptor makes a statue *with* marble. But it is
with words and not with his troubles that the writer makes his
books. If he wants to keep his wife from being disagreeable, it is
a mistake to write about her; he would do better to beat her. One
no more *puts* one's misfortunes into a book than one puts a model
on the canvas; one is inspired by them, and they remain what
they are. One gets perhaps a passing relief in placing oneself above
them in order to describe them, but once the book is finished,
there they are again. Insincerity begins when the artist wants to
ascribe a meaning to his misfortunes, a kind of immanent finality,
and when he persuades himself that they are there *in order* for him
to speak about them. When he justifies his own sufferings by this
ruse, he invites laughter; but he is contemptible if he seeks to
justify those of others. The most beautiful book in the world will
not save a child from pain; one does not redeem evil, one fights
it; the most beautiful book in the world redeems itself; it also
redeems the artist. But not the man. Any more than the man
redeems the artist. We want the man and the artist to work their
salvation together, we want the work to be at the same time an
act; we want it to be explicitly conceived as a weapon in the
struggle that men wage against evil.

The other error is just as grave. There is such a hunger for the
absolute in every heart that eternity, which is a non-temporal
absolute, is frequently confused with immortality, which is only
a perpetual reprieve and a long succession of vicissitudes. I understand this desire for the absolute; I desire it too. But what need is
there to go looking for it so far off: there it is, about us, under
our feet, in each of our gestures. We produce the absolute as
M. Jourdain produced prose. You light your pipe and that's an
absolute; you detest oysters and that's an absolute; you join the
Communist Party and that's an absolute. Whether the world is
mind or matter, whether God exists or whether He does not
exist, whether the judgement of the centuries to come is favourable to you or hostile, nothing will ever prevent your having
passionately loved that painting, that cause, that woman, nor that
love's having been lived from day to day; lived, willed, undertaken; nor your being completely committed to it. Our grand-
fathers were right in saying, as they drank their glass of wine,
'Another one that the Prussians won't get.' Neither the Prussians
nor anyone else. They can kill you, they can deprive you of wine

to the end of your days, but no God, no man, can take away that final trickling of the Bordeaux along your tongue. No relativism. Nor the 'eternal course of history' either. Nor the dialectic of the sensible. Nor the dissociations of psycho-analysis. It is a pure event, and we too, in the uttermost depths of historical relativity and our own insignificance, we too are absolutes, inimitable and incomparable, and our choice of ourselves is an absolute. All those living and passionate choices that we are and that we are constantly making with or against others, all those common enterprises into which we throw ourselves, from birth to death, all those bonds of love or hatred which unite us to one another and which exist only in so far as we feel them, those immense combinations of movements which are added to or cancel out one another and which are all lived, that whole discordant and harmonious life, concur in producing a new absolute which I shall call the *age*. The age is the intersubjectivity, the living absolute, the dialectical underside of history. . . . It gives birth in pain to events that historians will label later on. It lives blindly, distractedly, and fearfully the enthusiasm and the meanings that they will disengage rationally. Within the age, every utterance, before being a historical byword or the recognized origin of a social process, is first an insult or an appeal or a confession; economic phenomena themselves, before being the theoretical causes of social upheavals, are suffered in humiliation or despair, ideas are tools or evasions, facts are born of the intersubjectivity and overwhelm it, like the emotions of an individual soul. History is made with dead ages, for each age, when it dies, enters into relativity; it falls into line with other dead centuries; a new light is shed upon it; it is challenged by new knowledge; its problems are resolved for it; it is demonstrated that its most ardent pursuits were doomed to failure, that the results of the great undertakings of which it was so proud were the reverse of what it anticipated; its limits are suddenly apparent, and its ignorance too. But that is *because* it is dead; the limits and the ignorance did not exist 'at the time'; no deficiency was seen; or rather the age was a constant surpassing of its limits towards a future which was *its* future and which died with it; it was *this* boldness, *this* rashness, *this* ignorance of its ignorance; to live is to foresee at short range and to manage with the means at hand. Perhaps with a little more knowledge our fathers might have understood that a certain problem was insoluble, that a certain problem was badly stated.

But the human condition requires us to choose in ignorance; it is ignorance which makes morality possible. If we knew all the factors which condition phenomena, if we gambled on a sure thing, the risk would disappear; and with the risk, the courage and the fear, the waiting, the final joy and the effort; we would be listless gods, but certainly not men. The bitter Babylonian disputes about omens, the bloody and passionate heresies of the Albigenses, of the Anabaptists, now seem to us mistakes. At the time, man committed himself to them completely, and, in manifesting them at the peril of his life, he brought truth into being through them, for truth never yields itself directly, it merely appears through errors. In the dispute over Universals, over the Immaculate Conception or Transubstantiation, it was the fate of human Reason that was at stake. And the fate of Reason was again at stake when American teachers who taught the theory of evolution were brought to trial in certain states. It is at stake in every age, totally so, in regard to doctrines which the following age will reject as false. Evolution may some day appear to be the biggest folly of our century; in testifying for it against the clerics, the American teachers *lived* the truth, they lived it passionately and absolutely, at personal risk. Tomorrow they will be wrong, today they are absolutely right; the age is always wrong when it is dead, always right when it is alive. Condemn it later on, if you like; but first it had its passionate way of loving itself and lacerating itself, against which future judgements are of no avail. It had its taste which it tasted alone and which is as incomparable, as irremediable, as the taste of wine in our mouths.

A book has its absolute truth within the age. It is *lived* like an outbreak, like a famine. With much less intensity, to be sure, and by fewer people, but in the same way. It is an emanation of intersubjectivity, a living bond of rage, hatred or love among those who produce it and those who receive it. If it succeeds in commanding attention, thousands of people reject it and deny it: as everybody knows, to read a book is to re-write it. *At the time* it is at first a panic or an evasion or a courageous assertion; at the time it is a good or bad *action*. Later on, when the age is done with, it will enter into the relative, it will become a message. But the judgements of posterity will not invalidate those that were passed on it in its lifetime. I have often been told about dates and bananas: 'You don't know anything about them. In order to know what they are, you have to eat them on the spot, when they've just been picked.' And I have always considered bananas as dead fruit whose real, live taste escapes me. Books that are handed down from age to age are dead fruit. They had, in another time, another taste, tart and tangy. *Émile* or *The Persian Letters* should have been read when they were freshly picked.

Thus, one must write for one's age, as the great writers have done. But that does not mean that one has to lock oneself up in it. To write for one's age is not to reflect it passively; it is to want to maintain it or change it, thus to go beyond it towards the future, and it is this effort to change it that places us most deeply within it, for it is never reducible to the dead ensemble of tools and customs; it is in movement; it is constantly surpassing itself; the concrete present and the living future of all the men who compose it coincide rigorously within it. If, among other features, Newtonian physics and the theory of the noble savage concur in sketching the physiognomy of the first half of the eighteenth century, it should be borne in mind that one was a sustained effort to snatch some shreds of truth from the mists, to approach, beyond the state of contemporary knowledge, an ideal science in which phenomena might be mathematically deduced from the principle of gravitation, and that the other implied an attempt to restore, beyond the vices of civilization, the state of nature. They both drew up a rough sketch of a future; and if it is true that this future never became a present, that we have given up the golden age and the idea of making science a rigorous chain of reasons, still the fact remains that these live and deep hopes sketched out a future beyond everyday concerns and that, in order to interpret the meaning of the everyday, we must go back to it *on the basis* of that future. One cannot be a man or become a writer without tracing a horizon line beyond oneself, but the self-surpassing is in each case finite and particular. One does not surpass *in general* and for the proud and simple pleasure of surpassing; Baudelairean dissatisfaction represents only the abstract scheme of transcendence and, since it is dissatisfaction with everything, ends by being dissatisfaction with nothing. Real transcendence requires one to want to change certain specific aspects of the world, and the surpassing is coloured and particularized by the concrete situation it aims to modify. A man puts himself entirely into his project for emancipating the negroes or restoring the Hebrew language to the Jews of Palestine; he puts himself into it entirely and thereby realizes the human condition in its universality; but it is always on the occasion of a particular and dated enterprise. And if I am told, as by M. Schlumberger, that one also goes beyond the age when one aims at immortality, I shall reply that this is a false surpassing: instead of trying to change an intolerable situation, one attempts to evade it and seeks refuge in a future which is utterly foreign to us, since it is not the future that we are making, but the concrete present of our grandchildren. We have no means of action upon this present; they will live it on their own account and as they like; *situated* in their age, as we are in ours, if they make use of our writings, it will be for ends which are proper to them and which we had not foreseen, as one picks up stones along the way in order to throw them into the face of an aggressor. An attempt on our part to burden them with the responsibility of prolonging our existence would be vain; it is no duty or concern of theirs. And as we have no means of action over these strangers, it is as beggars that we shall present ourselves before them and that we shall beg them to lend us the appearance of life by using us however they like. If Christians, we shall accept humbly, provided they still speak of us, that they make use of us to testify that faith is inefficacious; if atheists, we shall be quite content if they are still concerned with our anguish and our faults, be it to prove that man without God is miserable. Would you be satisfied, M. Schlumberger, if our grandsons, after the Revolution, saw in your writings the most obvious example of the conditioning of art by economic structures? And if you do not have this literary destiny, you will have another which will hardly be worth more. If you escape dialectical materialism, it will be perhaps to become the subject of psycho-analysis. At all events, our grandchildren will be orphans who have their own concerns; why should they concern themselves with us? Perhaps Céline will be the only one of all of us to remain; it is highly improbable, but theoretically possible that the twenty-first century may retain the name of Drieu and drop that of Malraux; at any rate, it will not take up our quarrels, it will not mention what we call today the treason of certain writers; or, if it mentions it, it will do so without anger or contempt. But what does that matter to us? What Malraux, what Drieu are for us, that's the absolute. There is an absolute of contempt for Drieu in certain hearts, there was an absolute of friendship for Malraux that a hundred posthumous judgements will be unable to blemish. There was a living Malraux, a weight of hot blood in the age's heart; there will be a dead Malraux, a prey to history. Why does anyone expect the living man to be concerned with fixing the features of the dead man he will be? To be sure, he lives beyond himself; his gaze and his concerns exceed his death in the flesh. What measures the *presence* and weight of a man is not the fifty or sixty years of his organic life, nor the borrowed life he will lead throughout the centuries in minds foreign to his; it is the choice he himself will have made of the temporal cause which goes beyond him. It was said that the courier of Marathon had died an hour before reaching Athens. He had died and was still running; he was running dead, announced the Greek victory dead. This is a fine myth; it shows that the dead still act for a little while as if they were living. For a little while, a year, ten years, perhaps fifty years; at any rate, a *finite* period; and then they are buried a second time. This is the measure we propose to the writer: as long as his books arouse anger, discomfort, shame, hatred, love, even if he is no more than a shade, he will live. Afterwards, the deluge. We stand for an ethics and art of the finite.

Translated by Bernard Frechtman

Introducing
Les Temps
modernes

Introducing
Les Temps modernes

ALL WRITERS of middle-class origin have known the temptation of irresponsibility. For a century now, it has been a traditional part of the literary career. An author rarely establishes a link between his works and the income they bring. On the one hand, he writes, sings, or sighs; on the other, he is given money. The two facts have no apparent relation: the best he can do is tell himself that he's being paid in order to sigh. As a consequence, he is apt to regard himself more as a student enjoying a scholarship than as a worker receiving wages for his efforts. The theoreticians of Art for Art's Sake and of Realism have confirmed him in that opinion. Has it been noted that they share the same purpose and the same origin? According to the former, the author's principal concern is to produce works that serve no end; if they are quite gratuitous, thoroughly bereft of roots, they are not far from seeming beautiful to him. He thus situates himself at the margins of society; or rather, he consents to appear there only in his role as pure consumer: precisely as the scholarship holder. The Realist, for his part, is also a willing consumer. As for producing, that is a different matter: he has been told that science is not concerned with utility and he aspires to the sterile impartiality of the scholar. Have we not been told often enough that he "pores over" the social groups he is intent on describing? He pores *over*! Where was he, in that case? In the air? The truth is that unsure of his social position, too fearful to stand up to the bourgeoisie from whom he draws his pay, and too lucid to accept it without reservations, he has chosen to pass judgment on his century and has thereby convinced himself that he remains outside it, just as an experimenter remains outside the system of his experiment. Thus does the disinterestedness of pure science join with the gratuitousness of Art for Art's Sake. It is not by chance that Flaubert should be simultaneously a pure stylist, a purist in his love of forms, and the father of Naturalism; it is not by chance that the Goncourt brothers should flatter themselves for simultaneously knowing how to observe and having a highly aestheticized prose style.

That legacy of irresponsibility has troubled a number of minds. They suffer from a literary bad conscience and are no longer sure whether to write is admirable or grotesque. In former times, the poet took himself for a prophet, which was honorable. Subsequently, he became a pariah and an accused figure, which was still feasible. But today he has fallen to the rank of specialist, and it is not without a certain malaise that he lists his profession on hotel registers as "man of letters." Man of letters: that association of words is in itself sufficient to disgust one with writing. One thinks of an Ariel, a vestal virgin, an *enfant terrible*, and also of a fanatic similar in type to a numismatist or body builder. The whole business is rather ridiculous. The man of letters writes while others fight. One day he's quite proud of it, he feels himself to be a cleric and guardian of ideal values; the following day he's ashamed of it, and finds that literature appears quite markedly to be a special form of affectation. In relation to the middle-class people who read him, he is aware of his dignity; but confronted with workers, who don't, he suffers from an inferiority complex, as was seen in 1936 at the Maison de la Culture. It is certainly that complex which is the source of what Paulhan calls *terrorism*; it is what led the Surrealists to despise literature, on which they lived. After the other war, it was the occasion of a particular mode of lyricism: the best and purest writers confessed publicly to what might humiliate them the most and expressed their satisfaction whenever they succeeded in eliciting the disapproval of the bourgeoisie: they had produced a text which, through its consequences, bore a slight resemblance to an act. Those isolated attempts could not prevent words from undergoing a devaluation that increased by the day. There was a crisis of rhetoric, then one of language. On the eve of this war, most practitioners of literature were resigned to being no more than nightingales. Finally came a few authors who pressed their disgust with writing to an extreme. Outdoing their elders they declared that publishing a book that was merely useless was not enough: they maintained that the secret aim of all literature was the destruction of language, and that it was sufficient, in order to attain this end, to speak so as not to say anything. Such voluble silence was quite in fashion for a while, and Hachette used to distribute capsules of silence, in the form of voluminous novels, to many a railroad station bookstore. Today things have gone sufficiently far that we have seen writers who once were blamed or punished for renting their pens to the Germans express a pained astonishment. "What do you mean?" they ask. "Does the stuff someone writes actually commit him?"

We do not want to be ashamed of writing and we don't feel like writing so as not to say anything. Moreover, even if we wanted to we would not be able to: no one can. Every text possesses a meaning, even if that meaning is far removed from the one the author dreamed of inserting into it. For us, an author is indeed neither a vestal virgin nor Ariel: he is "implicated," whatever he does—tainted, compromised, even in his most distant retreat. If, at certain periods, he uses his art to forge what Mallarmé called "bibelots d'inanité sonore' (trinkets of sonorous inanity), this in itself is a sign—that there is a crisis of Letters and, no doubt, of Society, or even that the dominant classes have channeled him without his realizing it toward an activity that seems pure luxury, for fear that he might take off and swell the ranks of the revolutionaries. What is Flaubert— who so raged against the bourgeoisie and believed he had withdrawn outside the social machine—for us if not a talented man living off his investments? And does not his meticulous art presuppose the comfort of Croisset, the solicitude of a mother or a niece, an orderly regimen, a prosperous commercial endeavor, dividends received on schedule? Few years are needed for a book to become a social datum, to be questioned like an institution or recorded as a statistical reality; not much distance is needed for it to merge with the furnishings of an era, its habits, headgear, means of transport, and nourishment. A historian will say to us. "They ate this, read that, and dressed thus." The first railroads, cholera, the revolt of the Lyons silkworkers, Balzac's novels, and the rise of industry all contribute equally to characterizing the July Monarchy. All this has been said and repeated since Hegel; what we want to do is draw the practical consequences. Since the writer has no way of escaping, we want him to embrace his era—tightly. It is his only chance; it was made for him and he was made for it. We regret Balzac's indifference toward the revolutionary days of '48; we regret Flaubert's panicky incomprehension when confronted with the Commune. We regret them *for them*: those events are something that they missed out on forever. We don't want to miss out on anything of our time. There may be better ones, but this one is ours: we have only *this* life to live, amid *this* war, and perhaps *this* revolution. Let it not be concluded from this that we are preaching a variety of populism: quite the contrary. Populism is an offspring of the very old, the sad scion of the last Realists; it is yet another attempt to remove one's stakes from the board. We are convinced, on the contrary, that one *cannot* remove one's stakes from the board. Even if we were as deaf and dumb as pebbles, our very passivity would be an action. The abstention of whoever wanted to devote his life to writing novels about the Hittites would in itself constitute taking a position. The writer is *situated* in his time; every word he utters has reverberations. As does his silence. I hold Flaubert and the Goncourts responsible for the repression that followed the Commune because they didn't write a line to prevent it. Some will object that this wasn't their business. But was the Calas trial Voltaire's business? Was Dreyfus's sentence Zola's business? Was the administration of the Congo Gide's business? Each of those authors, at a particular time in his life, took stock of his responsibility as a writer. The Occupation taught us ours. Since we act upon our time by virtue of our very existence, we decide that our action will be voluntary. Even then, it must be specified: it is not uncommon for a writer to be concerned, in his modest way, with preparing the future. But there is a vague, conceptual future which concerns humanity in its entirety and on which we have no particular light to shed: Will history have an end? Will the sun be extinguished? What will be the condition of man in the socialist regime of the year 3,000? We leave such reveries to futurist novelists. It is the future of *our* time that must be the object of our concern: a limited future barely distinguishable from it— for an era, like a man, is first of all a future. It is composed of its ongoing efforts, its enterprises, its more or less long-term projects, its revolts, its struggles, its hopes: When will the war end? How will the country be rebuilt? How will international relations be organized? What social reforms will take place? Will the forces of reaction triumph? Will there be a revolution, and if so what will it be? That future we make our own; we don't want any other. No doubt some authors have concerns which are less contemporary, and visions which are less short-sighted. They move through our midst as though they were not there. Where indeed are they? With their grandnephews, they turn around to judge that bygone age which was ours and whose sole survivors they are. But they have miscalculated: posthumous glory is always based on a misunderstanding. What do they know of those nephews who will come fish them out of our midst! Immortality is a terrible alibi: it is not easy to live with one foot in the grave and another beyond it. How might one expedite current business if one saw it from such a distance? How might one grow excited over a battle, or enjoy a victory? Everything is equivalent. They look at us without seeing us: in their eyes we are already dead, and they return to the novel they are writing for men they will never see. They have allowed their lives to be stolen from them by immortality. We write for our contemporaries; we want to behold our world not with future eyes—which would be the surest means of killing it—but with our eyes of flesh, our real, perishable eyes. We don't want to win our case on appeal, and we will have nothing to do with any posthumous rehabilitation. Right here in our own lifetime is when and where our cases will be won or lost.

We are not, however, thinking of instituting a literary relativism. We have little taste for the purely historical. Besides, does the purely historical exist anywhere but in the manuals of Monsieur Seignobos? Each age discovers an aspect of the human condition; in every era man chooses himself in confrontation with other individuals, love, death, the world; and when adversaries clash on the subject of disarming the FFI or the help to be given the Spanish Republicans, it is that metaphysical choice, that singular and absolute project which is at stake.* Thus, by taking part in the singularity of our era, we ultimately make contact with the eternal, and it is our task as writers to allow the eternal values implicit in such social or political debates to be perceived. But we don't care to seek them out in some intelligible heaven: they are of interest only in their contemporary guise. Far from being relativists, we proclaim that man is an absolute. But he is such in his time, in his surroundings, on his parcel of earth. What is absolute, what a thousand years of history cannot destroy is *that* irreplaceable, incomparable decision which he makes at this moment concerning these circumstances. What is absolute is Descartes, the man who escapes us because he is dead, who lived in his time, who thought it through day by day with the means available to him, who formed his doctrine on the basis of a certain state of the sciences, who knew Gassendi, Caterus, and Mersenne, who in his childhood loved a girl who was cross-eyed, who waged war and impregnated a servant-girl, who attacked not the principle of authority in general but precisely the authority of Aristotle, and who emerges in his time, unarmed but unvanquished, like a milestone. What is relative is Cartesianism, that errant

* The Forces Françaises de l'Intérieur (FFI) were the combined underground paramilitary forces of the Resistance.—*Translator.*

philosophy, which is trotted out from century to century and in which everyone finds what he puts into it. It is not by running after immortality that we will make ourselves eternal; we will become absolutes not because we have allowed our writings to reflect a few emaciated principles (which are sufficiently empty and null to make the transition from one century to the next), but because we will have fought passionately within our own era, because we will have loved it passionately and accepted that we would perish entirely along with it.

In summary, our intention is to help effect certain changes in the Society that surrounds us. By which we do not mean changes within people's souls: we are happy to leave the direction of souls to those authors catering to a rather specialized clientele. As for us, who without being materialists have never distinguished soul from body and who know only one indivisible reality—human reality—we align ourselves on the side of those who want to change simultaneously the social condition of man and the concept he has of himself. Consequently, concerning the political and social events to come, our journal will take a position in each case. It will not do so *politically*—that is, in the service of a particular party—but it will attempt to sort out the conception of man that inspires each one of the conflicting theses, and will give its opinion in conformity with the conception it maintains. If we are able to live up to what we promise, if we succeed in persuading a few readers to share our views, we will not indulge in any exaggerated pride; we will simply congratulate ourselves for having rediscovered a good professional conscience, and for literature's having become again—at least for us—what it should never have stopped being: a social function.

Yet, some will ask, what is that conception of man that you pretend to reveal to us? We respond that it can be found on every street corner, and that we claim not to have discovered it but only to have brought it into better focus. I shall call this conception "totalitarian." But since the word may seem unfortunate, since it has been used to designate not the human individual but an oppressive and antidemocratic type of state, a few explanations are called for.

The bourgeoisie, it seems to me, may be defined intellectually by the use it makes of the analytic mode, whose initial postulate is that composite realities must necessarily be reducible to an arrangement of simple elements. In its hands, that postulate was once an offensive weapon allowing it to dismantle the bastions of the Old Regime. Everything was analyzed; in a single gesture, air and water were reduced to their elements, mind to the sum of impressions composing it, society to the sum total of individuals it comprised. Groups disappeared; they were no more than abstract agglomerations due to random combinations. Reality withdrew to the ultimate terms of the decomposition. The latter indeed—and such is the second postulate of analysis—retain unalterably their essential properties, whether they enter into a compound or exist in a free state. There was an immutable nature of oxygen, of hydrogen, or nitrogen, and of the elementary impressions composing our mind; there was an immutable human nature. Man was man the way a circle is a circle: once and for all. The individual, be he transported to the throne or plunged into misery, remained fundamentally identical to himself because he was conceived on the model of the oxygen atom, which can combine with hydrogen to produce water, or with nitrogen to produce air, without its internal structure being changed. Those principles presided over the Declaration of the Rights of Man. In society as conceived by the analytic cast of mind, the individual, a solid and indivisible participle, the vehicle of human nature, resides like a pea in a can of peas: he is round, closed in on himself, uncommunicative. All men are *equal*, by which it should be understood that they all participate equally in the essence of man. All men are *brothers*: fraternity is a passive bond among distinct molecules, which takes the place of an active or class-bound solidarity that the analytic cast of mind cannot even imagine. It is an entirely extrinsic and purely sentimental relation which masks the simple juxtaposition of individuals in analytic society. All men are *free*—free *to be men*, it goes without saying. Which means that political action ought to be strictly negative. A politically active individual has no need to forge human nature; it is enough for him to eliminate the obstacles that might prevent him from blossoming. Thus it was that, intent on destroying divine right, the rights of birth and blood, the right of primogeniture, all those rights based on the notion that there are differences in men's natures, the bourgeoisie confused its own cause with that of analysis and constructed for its use the myth of the universal. Unlike today's revolutionaries, they were able to achieve their goals only by abdicating their class consciousness: the members of the Third Estate at the Constituent Assembly were bourgeois precisely to the extent that they considered themselves to be simply men.

A hundred and fifty years later, the analytic cast of mind remains the official doctrine of bourgeois democracies, with the difference that is has now become a defensive weapon. It is entirely in the interest of the bourgeoisie to blind itself to the existence of classes even as it formerly failed to perceive the synthetic reality of the institutions of the Old Regime. It persists in seeing no more than men, in proclaiming the identity of human nature in every diverse situation; but it is against the proletariat that it makes that proclamation. A worker, for the bourgeoisie, is first of all a man—a man like any other. If the Constitution grants that man the right to vote and freedom of expression, he displays his human nature as fully as does a bourgeois. A certain polemical tradition has too often presented the bourgeois as a calculating drone whose sole concern is to defend his privileges. In fact, though, one *constitutes* oneself as a bourgeois by choosing, once and for all, a certain analytic perspective on the world which one attempts to foist on all men and which excludes the perception of collective realities. To that extent, the bourgeois defense is in a sense permanent, and is indistinguishable from the bourgeoisie itself. But it is not revealed in sordid calculations; within the world that the bourgeoisie has constructed, there is room for carefreeness, altruism, and even generosity—except that the good deeds of the bourgeois are individual acts addressed to universal human nature insofar as it is incarnated in an individual. In this sense, they are about as effective as a skillful piece of propaganda, since the beneficiary of the good deeds is obliged to receive them on the terms on which they are offered—that is, by thinking of himself as an isolated human being confronting another human being. Bourgeois charity sustains the myth of fraternity.

But there is another form of propaganda which is of more specific interest to us, since we are writers, and writers have turned themselves into its unwitting agents. The legend of the irresponsibility of the poet, which we were criticizing a while ago, derives its origin from the analytic cast of mind. Since bourgeois authors themselves think of themselves as peas in a can, the solidarity binding them to other men seems strictly *mechanical* to them—a matter, that is, of mere juxtaposition. Even if they have an exalted sense of their literary mission, they think they have done enough once they have described their own nature or that of their friends: since all men are made the same, they will have rendered a service to all by teaching each man about himself. And since the initial postulate from which they speak is the primacy of analysis, it seems quite simple to make use of the analytic method in order to attain self-knowledge. Such is the origin of intellectualist psychology, whose most polished exemplar we find in the works of Proust. As a pederast, Proust thought he could make use of his homosexual experience in depicting Swann's love for Odette; as a bourgeois, he presents the sentiments of a rich and idle bourgeois for a kept woman as the prototype of love, the reason being that he believes in the existence of universal passions whose mechanism does not vary substantially when there is a change in the sexual characteristics, social condition, nation, or era of the individuals experiencing them. Having thus "isolated" those immutable emotions, he can attempt to reduce them, in turn, to elementary particles. Faithful to the postulates of the analytic cast of mind, he does not even imagine that there might be a dialectic of feelings—he imagines only a mechanics. Thus does social atomism, the entrenched outpost of the contemporary bourgeoisie, entail psychological atomism. Proust *chose himself* to be a bourgeois. He made himself into an accomplice of bourgeois propaganda, since his work contributes to the dissemination of the myth of human nature.

We are convinced that the analytic spirit has had its day and that its sole function at present is to confuse revolutionary consciousness and to isolate men for the benefit of the privileged classes. We no longer believe in Proust's intellectualist psychology, and we regard it as nefarious. Since we have chosen as an example his analysis of the passion of love, we shall no doubt contribute to the reader's enlightenment by mentioning the essential points on which we are totally at odds with him.

First of all, we do not accept *a priori* the idea that romantic love is a constitutive affect of the human mind. It may well be the case, as Denis de Rougemont has suggested, that it originated historically as a correlate of Christian ideology. More generally, we are of the opinion that a feeling always expresses a specific way of life and a specific conception of the world that are shared by an entire class or an entire era, and that its evolution is not the effect of some unspecified internal mechanism but of those historical and social factors.

Second, we cannot accept the idea that a human emotion is composed of molecular elements that may be juxtaposed without modifying each other. We regard it not as a well-constructed machine but as an organized form. The possibility of undertaking an *analysis* of love seems inconceivable to us, because the development of that feeling, like that of all others, is *dialectical*.

Third, we refuse to believe that the love felt by a homosexual offers the same characteristics as that felt by a heterosexual. The secretive and forbidden character of the former, its Black Mass side, the existence of a homosexual freemasonry, and that damnation toward which the homo-sexual is aware of dragging his partner are all elements that seem to us to exercise an influence on the feeling in its entirety and even in the very details of its evolution. We maintain that the various sentiments of an individual are not juxtaposed, but that there is a synthetic unity of one's affectivity and that every individual moves within an affective world specifically his own.

Fourth, we deny that the origin, class, environment, and nation of an individual are simple accessories of his emotional life. It seems to us, on the contrary, that every affect—like, for that matter, every other form of psychical life—*manifests* his social situation. A worker who receives a salary, who does not own the instruments of his craft, whose work isolates him from material reality, and who defends himself from oppression by becoming aware of his class can in no way *feel* the same way as does a bourgeois of analytic propensities, whose profession puts him into relations of *politesse* with other members of his class.

Thus do we have recourse, against the spirit of analysis, to a synthetic conception of reality whose principle is that a whole, whatever it may be, is different in nature from the sum of its parts. For us, what men have in common is not a nature but a metaphysical condition—by which we mean the totality of constraints that limit them *a priori*, the necessity of being born and dying, that of being *finite* and of existing in the world among other men. In addition, they constitute indivisible totalities whose ideas, moods, and acts are secondary, dependent structures and whose essential characteristic lies in being *situated*, and they differ from each other even as their situations differ in relation to each other. The unity of those signifying wholes is the meaning which they manifest. Whether writing or working on an assembly line, whether choosing a wife or a tie, a man constantly manifests . . . He manifests his professional surroundings, his family, his class, and ultimately (since he is situated in relation to the world in its entirety) the world itself. A man is the whole earth. He is everywhere present, everywhere active. He is responsible for all, and his destiny is played out everywhere—Paris, Potsdam, Vladivostok. We adhere to these views because to us they seem true, because to us they seem socially useful at the present time, and because to us a majority of people seem to intuit them in their thinking and indeed to call them forth. We would like our journal to contribute in a modest way to the elaboration of a synthetic anthropology. But it is not, we repeat, simply a question of effecting an advance in the domain of pure knowledge: the more distant goal we are aiming at is a *liberation*. Since man is a totality, it is indeed not enough to grant him the right to vote without dealing with the other factors that constitute him. He must free himself totally—that is, make himself *other*, by acting on his biological constitution as well as on his economic condition, on his sexual complexes as well as on the political terms of his situation.

This synthetic perspective, however, presents some grave dangers. If the individual is the result of an arbitrary selection effected by the analytic cast of mind, doesn't one run the risk, in breaking with analytic conceptions, of substituting the domination of collective consciousness for the domination of the person? The spirit of synthesis cannot be apportioned its mere share: no sooner is he glimpsed than man as a totality would be submerged by his class. Only the class exists, and it alone must be delivered. But, it will be objected, in liberating a class is one necessarily freeing the men it comprises? Not necessarily. Would the triumph of Hitler's Germany have been the triumph of every German? Where, moreover, would the synthesis stop? Tomorrow we may be told that the class is a secondary structure dependent on a larger totality which will be, say, the nation. The great attraction which Nazism exercised on certain minds of the left undoubtedly came from the fact that it pressed the totalitarian conception to the absolute. Its theoreticians also denounced the ill effects of analysis, the abstract character of democratic freedoms; its propaganda also promised to forge a new man and retained the words "revolution" and "liberation." Except that for a class-proletariat a proletariat of nations was substituted. Individuals were reduced to mere dependent functions of their class, classes to mere functions of their nation, nations to mere functions of the European continent. If, in occupied countries, the entire working class rose up against the invader, it was undoubtedly because it felt wounded in its revolutionary aspirations, but also because it felt an invincible repugnance to allowing the individual to be dissolved in the collectivity.

Thus does the contemporary mind appear divided by an antinomy. Those who value above all the dignity of the human being, his freedom, his inalienable rights, are as a result inclined to think in accordance with the analytic cast of mind, which conceives of individuals outside their actual conditions of existence, which endows them with an unchanging, abstract nature, and which isolates them and blinds itself to their solidarity. Those who have profoundly understood that man is rooted in the collectivity and who want to affirm the importance of historical, technical, and economic factors are inclined toward the synthetic mode, which, blind to individuals, has eyes only for groups. This antinomy may be perceived, for example, in the widely held belief that socialism is diametrically opposed to individual freedom. Thus, those holding fast to the autonomy of the individual would be trapped in a capitalist liberalism whose nefarious consequences are clear; those calling for a socialist organization of the economy would be requesting it of an unspecified totalitarian authoritarianism. The current malaise springs from the fact that no one can accept the extreme consequences of these principles: there is a "synthetic" component to be found in democrats of good will, and there is an "analytic" component in socialists. Recall, for instance, what the Radical Party was in France. One of its theoreticians wrote a book entitled *The Citizen* versus *the Powers That Be*.* The title sufficiently indicates how he envisaged politics: everything would be better if the isolated citizen,

* Alain published *Le Citoyen contre les pouvoirs* in 1926. *Translator.*

the molecular representative of human nature, controlled those he elected and, if need be, exercised his own judgment against them. But the Radicals, precisely, could not avoid acknowledging their own failure. In 1939 the great party had no will, no program, no ideology; it was sinking into the depths of opportunism, because it was intent on solving politically problems that were not amenable to a political solution. The best minds were astonished. If man was a political animal, how could it be that in granting him political freedom his fate had not been settled once and for all? How could it be that the unhampered interaction of parliamentary institutions had not succeeded in eliminating poverty, unemployment, and oppression by monopolies? How could it be that a class struggle had emerged on the far side of the fraternal competition between parties? One would not have to push things much further to perceive the limits of the analytic cast of mind. The fact that the Radicals consistently sought an alliance of leftist parties clearly indicates the direction in which their sympathies and confused aspirations were taking them, but they lacked the intellectual technique that would have allowed them not only to solve but even to formulate the problems they intuited obscurely.

In the other camp, there is no less perplexity. The working class has made itself heir to the traditions of democracy. It is in the name of democracy that it demands its liberation. Now the democratic ideal, as we have seen, has manifested itself historically in the form of a social contract among free individuals. Thus do the analytic demands of Rousseau frequently interfere in many minds with the synthetic demands of Marxism. Moreover, the worker's technical training develops his analytic propensities. Similar in that regard to the scientist, he would resolve the problems of matter by way of analysis. Should he turn toward human realities, he will tend, in order to understand them, to appeal to the same reasoning that has served him in his work. He thus applies to human behavior an analytic psychology related to that of the French seventeenth century.

The simultaneous existence of those two modes of explanation reveals a certain uncertainty. The perpetual recourse to the phrase "as though . . ." indicates sufficiently that Marxism does not yet have at its disposal a synthetic psychology adequate to its totalitarian conception of classes.

Insofar as we are concerned, we refuse to let ourselves be torn between thesis and antithesis. We can easily conceive that a man, although totally conditioned by his situation, can be a center of irreducible indeterminacy. The window of unpredictability that stands out within the social domain is what we call freedom, and a person is nothing other than his freedom. This freedom ought not to be envisaged as a metaphysical endowment of human "nature." Neither is it a license to do whatever one wants, or some unspecified internal refuge that would remain to us even in our chains. One does not do whatever one wants, and yet one is responsible for what one is: such are the facts. Man, who may be explained simultaneously by so many causes, is nevertheless alone in bearing the burden of himself. In this sense, freedom might appear to be a curse; it *is* a curse. But it is also the sole source of human greatness. On this score, the Marxists will agree with us in spirit, if not in letter, since as far as I know they are not reluctant to issue moral condemnations. What remains is to explain it—but this is the philosophers' business, not ours. We would merely observe that if society constitutes the individual, the individual, through a reversal analogous to the one Auguste Comte termed "the transition of subjectivity," constitutes society. Without its future, society is no more than an accumulation of raw data, but its future is nothing other than the self-projection beyond the status quo of the millions of men composing it. Man is no more than a situation; a worker is not *free* to think and feel like a bourgeois. But for that situation *to be a man*, an integral man, it must be lived and transcended toward a specific aim. In itself, it remains a matter of indifference to the extent that a human freedom does not charge it with a specific sense. It is neither tolerable nor unbearable, insofar as a human freedom neither resigns itself to it nor rebels against it—that is, insofar as a man does not choose himself within it, by choosing its meaning. And it is only then, within this free choice, that the freedom becomes a determinant, because it is overdetermined. No, a worker cannot live like a bourgeois. In today's social organization, he is forced to undergo to the limit his condition as an employee. No escape is possible; there is no recourse against it. But a man does not exist in the same way that a tree or a pebble does: he must *make himself* a worker. Though he is completely conditioned by his class, his salary, the nature of his work, conditioned even in his feelings and his thoughts, it is nevertheless up to him to decide on the meaning of his condition and that of his comrades. It is up to him, freely, to give the proletariat a future of constant humiliation or one of conquest and triumph, depending on whether he chooses to be resigned or a revolutionary. And this is the choice for which he is responsible. He is not at all free to choose: he is implicated, forced to wager; abstention is also a choice. But he is free to choose at the same time his destiny, the destiny of all men, and the value to be attributed to humanity. Thus does he choose himself simultaneously as a worker and as a man, while at the same time conferring a meaning upon the proletariat. Such is man as we conceive him: integral man. Totally committed and totally free. And yet it is the free man who must be *delivered*, by enlarging his possibilities of choice. In certain situations there is room for only two alternatives, one of which is death. It is necessary to proceed in such a way that man, in every circumstance, can choose life.

Our journal will be devoted to defending that autonomy and the rights of the individual. We consider it to be above all an instrument of inquiry. The ideas I have just presented will serve as our guiding theme in the study of concrete contemporary problems. All of us approach the study of those problems in a common spirit, but we have no political or social program; each article will commit its author alone. We hope only to set forth, in the long run, a general line.

At the same time, we will draw from every literary genre in order to familiarize the reader with our conceptions; a poem or a novel, if inspired by them, may well create a more favorable climate for their development than a theoretical text. But that ideological content and those new intentions may also influence the very form and techniques of novelistic production; our critical essays will attempt to define in their broad lines the—new or ancient—literary techniques best suited to our designs. We will attempt to support our examination of contemporary issues by publishing as often as we can historical studies, when (as in the efforts of Marc Bloch or Pirenne on the Middle Ages) they spontaneously apply those principles and the method they entail to past centuries; that is, when they forsake an arbitrary division of history into histories—whether political, economic, ideological, the history of institutions, the history of individuals—in order to attempt to restore a vanished age as a totality, one that they will consider as the age expresses itself in and through individuals and as individuals choose themselves in and through their age. Our chronicles will strive to consider our own era as a meaningful synthesis and will consequently envisage in a synthetic spirit the diverse manifestations of our contemporaneity—styles and criminal trials as well as political events and works of the mind—always seeking to discover in them a common meaning far more than to appreciate them individually. Which is why, contrary to custom, we will no more hesitate to pass over in silence an excellent book which, from our point of view, teaches us nothing new about our era, than to linger, on the contrary, over a mediocre book which, in its very mediocrity, may strike us as revealing. Each month we will assemble, in addition to such studies, raw documents which will be selected in as various a manner as possible, simply requiring of them that they clearly demonstrate the interrelation of the collective and the individual. We will supplement those documents with polls and news reports. It strikes us, in fact, that journalism is one of the literary genres and that it can become one of the most important of

them. The ability to grasp meanings instantly and intuitively, and a talent for regrouping them in order to offer the reader immediately comprehensible synthetic wholes, are the qualities most crucial to a reporter; they are the ones we ask of all our collaborators. We are aware, moreover, that among the rare works of our age destined to endure are several works of journalism, such as *Ten Days That Shook the World* and, above all, the admirable *Spanish Testament* . . .*
Finally, in our chronicles we will devote a good deal of space to psychiatric studies, when they are written in the perspective that interests us. Our project is obviously ambitious: we cannot implement it by ourselves. At the start, we are a small crew, who will have failed if, in a year, we have not increased our numbers considerably. We appeal to all men of good will; all manuscripts will be accepted, whatever their source, provided they be inspired by preoccupations related to our own and provided they possess, in addition, literary merit. I recall, in fact, that in "committed literature," *commitment* must in no way lead to a forgetting of *literature*, and that our concern must be to serve literature by infusing it with new blood, even as we serve the collectivity by attempting to give it the literature it deserves.

Translated by Jeffrey Mehlman

---

* Written respectively by John Reed and Arthur Koestler.—*Translator.*

The
Nationalization
of Literature

The Nationalization
of Literature

IN THOSE SPLENDID YEARS of anarchy following the
Versailles Treaty, authors were ashamed of writing and
critics disliked reading. In literary salons, one met few
writers any more—only professionals at eroticism, crime,
despair, revolt, or mystical intuition who consented, once or
twice a year at the behest of their publishers, to deliver
themselves of a message. Since they were not at all worried
about their readers and it was agreed, in addition, that
words could not express thought, many books were bought
but rather little reading was done. When a chronicler, out
of professional scruple, devoted a few hours to his craft, his
gaze passed through the text like sunlight through a
windowpane and tackled the man directly. For terrorism
was the rage in those days. One pretended that authors had
never written, if their works were considered, it was solely
as an assemblage of diverse bits of information about their
mores. Their techniques and rhetoric were discussed as
though it were a matter not of artifice and frills but of
piquant and licentious details about their intimate lives. Of
Giraudoux it was said not that he published *Bella* or
Eglantine but: "He takes us with him by the hand and bids
us accompany him in his pirouette; we think we're following
him to Bellac, and there we are in China; he shoots at a
target in Berlin, and a bird of paradise comes tumbling from
the sky in Milwaukee," so great was the contempt in which
the literary thing was then held.

Today, the wind has shifted: literature and rhetoric have
been restored in their dignity and their powers. It is no
longer a matter of lighting a fire in the brush of language,
or marrying off "words on fire" and achieving the absolute
through the combustion of the dictionary; it has become a
matter of communicating with other men by modestly

making use of the means available. Since pride is no longer taken in separating thought from words, one cannot even conceive how words might betray thought. Sufficient probity has returned for there to be no desire to be judged on some unspecified ineffability that neither words nor actions might exhaust; intentions are said to be known only through the acts that realize them and thoughts only by the words that express them. Whereupon critics have begun to read again. All would be well did one not discern in the tone they adopt in speaking of works of the mind the omen of a new fashion that is still more disquieting than the previous one. To be sure, the author is no longer looked on as a madman, a murderer, or a miracle worker—that is, as a buffoon; no occasion is missed to remind him of his greatness and his obligations. But ultimately I am unsure whether it is not better to pass for a buffoon than for a subprefect; for the respect accorded the writer is strangely reminiscent of that displayed toward charitable benefactresses and government agents. An official once said to me, concerning Dullin, "He is a national treasure." It didn't at all make me laugh: I fear that at present some subtle maneuver will be sought to transform writers and artists into national treasures. No doubt we should be happy that there is less talk of their loves and more of their works. But the talk is too deferential. Not that criticism has become more indulgent or more generous in distributing bouquets, but it situates differently the works it discusses. There was a time when simply daring to publish a book—after Racine, Fénelon, or Pascal—was regarded as a rare impertinence, and an author needed, at the least, all his talent in order to be pardoned for writing. Today it's quite the opposite, and new works, even before appearing, benefit from favorable prejudice. But that benevolence is not directed at the author's invariably solitary and uncertain effort to express his feelings. It stems from the fact that every new text is considered an official ceremony and, in the last analysis, a beneficial contribution to the festivities of the Fourth Republic.

It is received not as one would receive an unripe fruit that needs time to mature and to evolve its full meaning, but simultaneously as a veterans' banquet and a gala car show. The literate public has followed suit. In certain circles, one no longer says of a novel or a poem that it is beautiful or amusing or moving. One adopts a rich, concerned tone and advises, "Read it; it's very *important.*" Important, like an interview with a labor leader, or like a speech by Poincaré defining his monetary policy on the occasion of inaugurating a monument to the war dead. Imagine Madame de Sévigné writing to her daughter, "I have seen *Esther*; it's very important." Are *littérateurs* about to become important?

How can one determine the importance of works that have just begun their careers? Is it not a hundred years later, through their effects and their offspring, that such importance can be recognized? We can grasp here, in the act, the tactic of the critic and the refined public: they are less concerned with appreciating the value of a text than with calculating from the start its effects and its posterity. They define point-blank the literary trends it will determine, and analyze the role it will play in such and such a social movement that has not yet seen the light of day. Has Monsieur Julien Gracq published *Un Beau Ténébreux?* There go our critics talking about a "return to Surrealism." A return by whom? For, after all, Monsieur Gracq had never left it. Indeed, if we refer to *Au Château d'Argol*, he seems, on the contrary, to have moved quite far from his early style. But our clever readers are not at all concerned with throwing into relief the continuity of views or the slow evolution of an individual transforming himself while remaining faithful to a general line. They consider the work in itself, as though cut off from its author. In 1945, six months after the Liberation, a "surrealist demonstration" took place: this is what interests them. They proceed similarly even before the war, when upon the appearance of *Saint-Saturnin* they said, "An important landmark. This novel marks the return of order within literature." What a strange sentence! For Monsieur Schlumberger, there was no separation between being born and enrolling in the party of order. And as for the fomentors of disorder—the Bretons and the Cocteaus— I am not at all aware that *Saint-Saturnin* had much influence on them. They may even have neglected to read it. But the critic cannot be bothered by such trifles; each year, each new publication signifies to him a departure, a return—a coming or going. Here is one of our chroniclers predicting that we will have twenty years of famine—no great works for twenty years. At the same time, another bets on prosperity: he explains quite well how tomorrow's literature has been fertilized by the sufferings of the Occupation. A third denounces the danger to French letters posed by American influence. Twenty years of American novels. But a fourth one reassures us: the publication of I forget which novel has sounded the death knell of that nefarious influence. A fifth, sixth, and seventh detect literary schools in the current confusion: there is Existentialism, which extends, we are told, as far as the graphic arts, since there are known Existentialist painters and artists. And even musicians. It appears—my apologies for speaking of myself— that I have something to do with all this. No, not quite, since (if we believe another critic) I am the leader of Neo-Surrealism, counting in my ranks Eluard and Picasso (of whom I ask forgiveness, having not forgotten, thank God, that I was still in short pants when they had already acquired self-mastery). And here is the last to surface, the Miserabilist school, which is so new that it has not yet, to my knowledge, acquired any representatives. There are other games. Some critics, for example, delight in depicting the book we are waiting for. They see it as Geoffroy Rudel saw his distant princess and find such persuasive accents to speak to us of it that we see it along with them. Here then is the world in wait: already the future and oh-so-hoped-for novel takes on the dignity of a sacred ceremony. We rediscover it in our features, our hopes, and our furies. After which, all that remains is to find a volunteer to write it. We are in revolution, claims another. Consequently, our literature has all the traits of a revolutionary literature. And he

enumerates them. Who could fail to understand his scorn
when he subsequently observes that young writers are so
frivolous that they do not bear out his prophecies? That's
because they are false writers, saboteurs, maybe even
Trotskyists. Another, referring last month to a very good
French novel about the Polish partisan forces, wrote se-
renely, "This is *the* novel of the Resistance." Formerly, one
would have held the future in reserve; one would have given
an opportunity to the Russians, the Belgians, the Dutch,
the Czechs, the Italians, and even the Poles, as well as to
some two thousand Frenchmen who have a work in store on
the subject. The contemporary critic cannot be bothered by
such inane prudence: his pleasure lies in extrapolating. After
each new work he takes stock, as though that work marked
the end of history and of literature. *Balance-Sheet of the
Occupation, Balance-Sheet of the Year 1945, Balance-Sheet of
Contemporary Theater*: he adores balance sheets. In order to
produce them more conveniently, he halts careers with a
stroke of his pen. Several journalists, after *L'Invitée*, after
Enrico, decreed that Simone de Beauvoir and Mouloudji
would write nothing more. I am reminded that Monsieur
Lalou was concerned to know whether *La Nausée*, which was
my first work, was not also my "literary testament." It was
a discreet invitation: an author who knows how to live draws
up his literary testament at age thirty and sticks to it. The
scandal with those compulsive workers who produce a book
every two years is that the critics each time are obliged to
call their previous judgment into question. Failing to guess
with any certainty the careers of new writers, they find
themselves before every beginner in the situation of that
"reader" for a large publishing house who wrote, after
reading a manuscript recommended to him by Pierre Bost,
"Ask Pierre Bost if the author has any talent." Talent,
which means in the language of publishers: How many
books does he have in him? In Mouloudji, the critics
decided that there was only one. That is, they overtook the
young man with blinding speed and were there waiting for
him in the future, at the end of his long life. From there,

solidly entrenched in that privileged instant in which Mouloudji would breathe his last, and in which, according to ancient wisdom, it would be possible to decide whether he was happy or unhappy, foolish or wise, they looked on *Enrico*, the dead man's sole literary production, which no subsequent work had called into question, and rendered a definitive judgment. After that, you will say, Mouloudji wrote a second book. Agreed, but he was wrong to do so, and the critics have certainly let him know as much.

What does this mean? And what is there in common among the various comments we have just made? When a newspaper article infuriates you, it is rare for you to think of its author. Were you to think of him, your indignation would be disarmed unless he was a famous individual. But if the article seems like a task imposed on some poor bugger who wrote it at night amid the confusion of the newsroom, your anger will turn to pity. And that is because you will not consider the words that irritate you as signs traced on the sheet you have in your hands; you seem to hear them repeated by a thousand mouths, like the murmur of the wind in the reeds. Each of them is a social event, since it has passed from one person's lips to another's ears, since it has been the occasion of repeated contacts among different members of the community. And finally, the article no longer has anything in common with the nocturnal lucubrations of an irresponsible journalist; it's an immense collective representation spreading through a hundred thousand heads. It's as a collective representation that it strikes you as nefarious and sacred. Today, critics and men of letters agree in considering a book as though it were the editorial of a daily newspaper. They are not concerned with what the author *meant*, and in truth they envisage it as though it didn't have an author. It interests them only as a slogan with which to rally an army of readers for a few days or a few months. They see in it a spontaneous production of the collective consciousness, something like an institution. In order to better account for that institution, to plot its fate and enumerate its repercussions, the critic chooses to observe it with the eyes of his grandchildren and to expatiate on it as a literature manual might on a text a hundred and fifty years old. Only a manual, in fact, can appreciate the influence *exercised* by a production of the mind; it alone can explain its fortune and judge its posterity because it alone is qualified to write its history at a hundred years' distance. In a hundred years, we will be able to decide for good if Surrealism made an offensive comeback around 1945, if *L'Education européenne* was or wasn't *the* book of the Resistance. In a hundred years we will nail down the literary trends of this postwar period; in a hundred years, we'll be able to give an appropriate description of the novelistic form we have been waiting for—if, indeed, we are waiting for it—by comparing the diverse degrees of success that the novels about to appear in this decade will have had. But we are in a hurry. We are in a rush to know and to pass judgment on ourselves. And that is because during the last twenty years Western consciousness has made significant progress. Under the pressure of history we have learned that we were historical. Cartesian mathematics conditioned the various branches of knowledge and letters in the seventeenth century; in the same way, Newtonian physics conditioned them in the eighteenth century, Claude Bernard's and Lamarck's biology in the nineteenth, and history in our own. We know that the most intimate of our gestures helps constitute history, that the most subjective of our opinions helps form what the historian will call the public opinion of 1945; we know that we belong to an era that will later have a name and a physiognomy and whose broad features, principal dates, and deep meaning will be easily deciphered. We live in history like fish in water; we have an acute awareness of our historical responsibility. Were we not told in San Francisco that the fate of civilization would be determined in the coming years? Didn't Hitler repeat that the war he had just lost would fix human destiny for a thousand years? But the more exquisite our historical awareness, the more we are irritated at floundering in the dark, at being subject to a jurisdiction that we will never know, at sensing that we are caught in a Kafkaesque trial whose outcome will elude us and which will perhaps never end. Is it not offensive that the secret of our era and the exact appreciation of our errors belong to individuals who have not yet been born and to whom our children and grandchildren will still be giving spankings long after we have died? We would like to snatch the rug from under the feet of those snot-noses and establish immediately and forever what they should think of us. If we could turn back toward ourselves and sift out the historical import of our deeds at the same time we accomplish them, it seems to us that we would close the circle and offer our nephews so complete and so pertinent an appreciation of our era that they could do nothing but concur. Thus it is that we spend our time circumscribing, classifying, and labeling the events we are living, writing for posterity a history manual of the twentieth century. There was much laughter at the moment in that melodrama when the author has his soldiers from Bouvines say, "We knights of the Hundreds Years' War." Which is fine, but in that case we should be laughing at ourselves: our youth were calling themselves the "interwar generation" four years before the Munich Pact. They should be laughed at even though events proved them right, for they had chosen to speak to themselves as if they were their own grandchildren. Which is yet another way of conferring importance on that odious ego we were taught to conceal: one always respects one's grandfather. We should imbue ourselves, on the contrary, with this austere truth: from whatever heights we pretend to judge ourselves, a future historian will judge us from an even greater height; the mountain on which we believe we have built our eagle's nest will be but a molehill for him. The verdict we have delivered concerning our era will figure as only part of the evidence of our case. In vain would we attempt to be our own historians: the historian himself is a historical creature. We are obliged to be satisfied with *forging* our history blindly, one day at a time, choosing from all the options the one which seems best to us at present. But we can never hold, concerning history, those cavalier views that helped make the fortunes of Taine and Michelet. We are *inside.* The same can be said of the critic. In vain does he envy the historian of ideas. Hazard can speak of the intellectual crisis of 1715, but we cannot at all pretend to treat the "crisis of the novel in 1945." Do we even know whether or not the novel is in crisis? We can clearly discern what each author or school intends to do, and we can also judge whether in their works they remain faithful to their purpose. We can sift out certain secret aims, certain hidden intentions. But we cannot discover the figure the work will cut for the readers of tomorrow; we cannot consider it already as an acquisition of the objective spirit of the era. Its objective physiognomy is still veiled for us, for it is nothing other than the aspect it will take on in the eyes of others. We cannot be simultaneously inside and outside. In treating the productions of the mind with the kind of respect formerly reserved only for the distinguished dead, one runs the risk of killing them. There is not a single petty novelist who is not discussed in tones Lanson used for Racine and Bédier for *La Chanson de Roland.* Some may feel flattered by this, but not without a measure of resentment, for it is ultimately not very agreeable to be treated during one's lifetime as a public monument. We should be cautious. This literary year, which is not particularly distinguished for the quality of its works, is already studded with monuments; it's like the Appian Way. We have to relearn modesty and reacquire a taste for taking risks. Since we cannot step out of subjectivity—not individual subjectivity, but that of the era—the critic ought to renounce passing judgment with complete assurance and share the uncertainty of authors. After all, a novel is not first and foremost an application of the American technique, or an illustration of Heidegger's theories, or a Surrealist manifesto. Neither is it an evil action, or an event heavy with international consequences. It is the precarious undertaking of a single man. To read as would a contemporary of the author's, caught up in the same historical subjectivity, is to share the risks of the undertaking. The book is new, unknown, without importance; it must be entered without a guide. Perhaps we will let the rarest qualities pass without noticing them. Perhaps, on the contrary, a superficial brilliance will lead us astray. Perhaps we will find, negligently cast at the bottom of a page, one of those ideas that suddenly cause the heart to beat faster, as happened to Daniel de Fontanin when he encountered *Les Nourritures terrestres.* And then, after all, one has to wager. Is the book good? Is it bad? Let us bet; it's all we can do. Out of fear, out of a taste for social consecration, today's critic reads the way one rereads. If I were in his place I would fear that the petrification caused by his Medusa's eye might be an omen of the death of Art foreseen by Hegel.

But why, it may be asked, does he proceed in this manner? Why is the critic, who affected twenty years ago to grasp the most idiosyncratic virtues of an author through a quasi-Bergsonian act of intuition, solely preoccupied at present with collecting the social resonances of a work? It's because the author himself has been socialized. He no longer appears to the world's gaze like the white blackbird he used to be; he now serves as an ambassador. Formerly, a new writer felt superfluous on earth: he was not awaited. The public never awaits anything. Or rather, yes, it awaits the next book by the novelist it already knows, whose style and way of viewing things it has assimilated. But between the problems of any particular era and the random or traditional solutions they are given, for better or worse, a certain balance is invariably reached, and any newcomer arrives on the scene as an intruder. No one was waiting for Freud; the psychology of Ribot and Wundt sufficed as best it could to explain everything except one or two little rebellious points, which people hoped would soon be absorbed into the reigning order. No one was waiting for Einstein; it was thought that the Michelson-Morley experiment could be interpreted without abandoning Newton's physics. No one was waiting for Proust or Claudel; Maupassant, Bourget, and Leconte de Lisle sufficed to ravish sensitive souls. Today ideas or styles are not awaited any more than previously, but one waits for men. One goes to search out the author at home; he is solicited. With his first book, people say to themselves, "Well, now! This could be our man." With his second, they're sure of it. With his third, he is already reigning: he presides over committees, writes for political newspapers, is already thought of as a candidate for the Chamber or the Academy. What is essential is that he be consecrated as quickly as possible. We already have a habit of publishing a writer's posthumous works during his lifetime; before long we may be casting his statue before he is dead. This is, in the strict sense of the term, literary inflation. In periods of calm, there is a normal and constant gap between fiduciary circulation and the gold which covers it, between an author's reputation and the works he has produced. When the gap grows, there is inflation. At present it has grown to an extreme. It is as though France had a desperate need for great men.

Such a need is first of all a function of the difficulties of maintaining our cultural continuity. Normally, this is ensured by the continual infiltration into the oldest strata of elements from the younger generations. As a result, changes are not particularly perceptible, and the old, who tend to hold on to their privileges, put a more than sufficient damper on the ardor of the newcomers. After 1918 the balance was broken to the benefit of the elders: the young stayed on at Verdun, and the Marne and the Yser. Nowadays, the inverse tends to occur. To be sure, France has lost many young men. But the defeat and the Occupation hastened the liquidation of the earlier generations. Many an old star strayed off course; others sought refuge abroad and were quite willingly forgotten; still others elected to die. A poet, who was nevertheless quite famous, observed sadly one day after seeing the— incomplete—list of collaborationist writers, "Our glory does not weigh much when compared with theirs." Traitors or suspects: Montherlant, Céline, Chardonne, Drieu, Fernandez, Abel Hermant, André Thérive, Henri Bordeaux. Forgotten: Maurois, Romains, Bernanos (who are presently doing whatever they can to recommend themselves to our memories). Dead: Romain Rolland and Giraudoux. When Maritain returned to New York after a brief trip to France, he was asked of his impression of the Fourth Republic. He replied, "France lacks men." By which he meant, it goes without saying, "She lacks men of my age." But it is no less true that this sudden slaughter of the deans has left enormous voids. We are at present making hasty efforts to fill them up, just as in certain countries, when a new party seizes power, it usually outlaws half the senate and creates as an emergency measure a new crop of senators to fill the gaps. Peerdom or the field marshal's baton has thus been conferred on writers who, in normal times, would still have a long time to wait for such honors. There is nothing in this that deserves blame. Quite the contrary: when, during the Occupation, the public, disconcerted by the disloyalty of several great writers, turned toward men who were younger and more sure, gave them its trust, and in the process, in order to counterbalance the weight of the traitors, conferred on the newcomers a glory they did not yet deserve on the basis of their works, there were, in that surge of feeling, a moving greatness and energy. I know some who have been elevated—not morally, as might be expected, but literarily—by their silence. That is proper; the duty of the man of letters is not only to write but also to know how to keep silent when he should. But now that the war is over, it's dangerous to fish for great men on the basis of the same principles. With collaborationist authors temporarily forced into retirement, there is not a single writer practicing today who did not cooperate directly or indirectly with one resistance movement or another; at the very least he had a cousin in the underground. As a result, in literary circles, writing and having resisted are now synonymous. No author offers up his new book bare as a newborn babe: new works come with a halo of courage. A rather singular form of fraternity has resulted. "How could I," the critic wonders, "a member of the Resistance, tell this former Resister that I don't find his last book on the Resistance any good?" He tells him so nevertheless, because he's honest; but he implies that the book, although unsuccessful, contains a rarer and more exquisite quality than it would have had it succeeded—something like the fragrance of virtue. The slightest bit more pressure and that inevitable confusion between a soul's value and talent accrues to the benefit of politics. And why stop midway? Why should he who in all purity has chosen to love such and such a novelist because he resisted the enemy not choose to love some other one who is his comrade in the same party? Occasionally, judgments will interfere with each other: this bourgeois, Catholic writer should have no talent in the eyes of the leftist critic; and yet, yes, indeed he has, since he was in the Resistance. The critic will extricate himself by assigning proportions. A quivering cordiality reigns in the world of letters. Which is why I won't accuse those who compensate works on account of their political meaning—rather than the real value of their content—of cowardice. We are all more or less at this juncture now and I am not sure that those who protest the most against this state of affairs are not themselves also inspired by political motives. An author thus selected, and promoted (occasionally in spite of himself) to the first rank, represents the underground or the prisoners of war, the Communist Party or the Christian-Democrats, everyone except himself. And how is one to know whether his prestige accrues to him from his years of exile, prison, deportation, clandestine activity, or, quite bluntly, from his talent? On that basis, to be sure, the parties consume great men at a frightening rate. In 1939 the Communist Party won Paul Nizan the Prix Interallié; he was the great favorite, the challenger to Aragon. He left the Party at the time of the German-Soviet Pact. He was wrong, I'm willing to admit; moreover, that doesn't concern me here. But consider: first of all he died in combat, and then he was a writer of the first rank. Today there is silence around his name; those who speak of our losses mention Prévost

and Decour, never Nizan. Need we conclude that if
Aragon left the Party (an absurd hypothesis, I realize), after
having been Béranger, he would abruptly fall to the level
of Déroulède?

The entire public is an accomplice. We have just
discovered to our humiliation that France will no longer
play in tomorrow's world the role it played in yesterday's.
In point of fact, no one is guilty: our country didn't have
enough men; our subsoil was not sufficiently rich. The
slippage of France, accompanied moreover by that of
Western Europe, is the result of a long evolution. Had we
perceived it gradually, there is no doubt that we would
have adapted to it with courage; the role we are given to
play remains quite fine. But the truth was revealed to us in
a moment of disaster. Until 1939 our previous victory—
which had only precipitated things by decimating our
population—and the brilliance of our intellectual and
artistic life had papered over our actual importance. We
have trouble tolerating so brutal a revelation; the shame of
losing the battle of 1940 and the pain of giving up our
hegemony over Europe fuse in our hearts. At times we are
tempted to believe that we buried our country with our
own hands; at others, we raise our heads and affirm that
eternal France will never perish. In other words, in five
years we have acquired a formidable inferiority complex.
The attitude of the world's masters is in no way disposed to
cure us of it. We recall our past greatness, and we are told
that it is, precisely, past. On only one score have we
surprised foreigners: they have never stopped admiring the
vitality of our literature. "How can it be?" they ask. "You
were beaten, occupied, ruined, yet you've written so
much!" That admiration is easy enough to explain: if the
English and the Americans have produced few new works,
it's because they were mobilized, and their writers
dispersed to the four corners of the globe. We, on the
contrary, though persecuted, hunted, and in many cases
threatened with death, at least were in France, in our
homes; our writers could write, if not in broad daylight, at

least in hiding. And then Anglo-Saxon intellectuals, who form a caste apart, cut off from the rest of the nation, are always dazzled upon rediscovering in France men of letters and artists who are intimately involved in the life and affairs of the country. Finally, many of them share the opinion recently expressed to me by an English lady. "The French," she said, "are suffering in their pride. They have to be persuaded that they have friends in the world, and thus for the time being one should speak to them only about what one admires in them—for example, their literature." As a result of that admiration, which is both spontaneous and accommodatingly displayed, the United States, England, and twenty other countries are showing a profound interest in our writers. Our novelists and poets have never received so many invitations—to be seen, to be heard, and also to be fed. Switzerland has fattened up a few, as has America. Great Britain will do its best. At which point we too are beginning to take our literature seriously. Those who previously saw in it no more than a pastime for the idle or a guilty activity have now come to realize that it is an instrument of propaganda. People cling to its prestige, since it is recognized abroad. Many would prefer that we be admired for our industrial might or the number of our guns. But we are so in need of esteem that they make do in the end with an admiration of our literature. They have not stopped wishing in their hearts that France might again become the country of Turenne and Bonaparte, but in the meantime they fall back on Rimbaud or Valéry. In their eyes, literature becomes a surrogate activity. It was permissible to treat the writer as accursed so long as the factories were working and the generals had soldiers obeying them. Today they hastily gather up young authors and shove them into an incubator in order to transform them rapidly into great men to be sent on missions to London, Stockholm, or Washington.

Never has literature been threatened by a graver danger: formal and informal powers that be, the government, newspapers, perhaps even the central banks and heavy industry have just discovered its might and are about to turn it to their profit. If they succeed, the writer will be able to choose—to devote himself to electoral propaganda or to enter into a special section of the Ministry of Information. Critics are concerned no longer with appreciating his works but with calculating their national importance and effectiveness; as soon as they learn how to manipulate statistics, their discipline will progress rapidly. The author, henceforth a functionary and overcome with honors, will be discreetly eclipsed by his work. At the very most, mention will be made of "Malraux's" or "Chamson's" novel the way one speaks of Fowler's liquor or Ohm's law: as a mnemic device. On the outskirts of large cities are factories whose job is to retrieve trash; old rags burn well, provided the temperature is sufficiently high. Expanding that effort, society wants to retrieve materials for which until now it has scarcely had any use: its writers. We should be careful: among them are some rather superb specimens of trash. What would we gain by allowing them to go up in smoke? That is not our understanding of literary commitment. There is no doubt that the written work is a social fact, and the writer before ever taking up his pen should be deeply convinced of it. He should, in fact, imbue himself with his responsibility. He is responsible for everything: lost or victorious wars, rebellions and repressions. He is the accomplice of the oppressors if he is not the natural ally of the oppressed. But not simply because he is a writer: because he is a man. He should live and desire that responsibility (and, for him, living and writing ought to be the same thing—not because art redeems life, but because life expresses itself in one's undertakings and his is to write). But he should not look back and consider his activity in order to discern what it will mean to his nephews. For him it is a matter not of knowing whether he will orient a literary movement, an "ism," but of committing himself *in the present*; not of foreseeing a distant future from which he would be able to pass judgment on himself after the fact, but of desiring, one day at a time, the immediate future. The historian may determine that the armistice of 1940 allowed the war to be won. He may say that Germany never would have attacked the Soviet Union—which was the beginning of its defeat—if the English had already entrenched themselves by 1940 in Algiers and Bizerte. Perhaps. But these considerations could not intervene in 1940: no one could predict the German-Russian conflict in the short term, and consequently, given the *actual* information at our disposition, *it was imperative to continue the war.* In this the writer is no different from the statesman: he knows little, and he is obliged to decide on the basis of what he knows. The rest—that is, the fate of his work throughout the centuries—is the devil's part. And one ought not to play with the devil. Let us acknowledge that there is an aspect of our books that will escape us forever. Love, a career, a revolution—we begin so many undertakings in ignorance of their outcome. Why should the writer elude the common fate? Thus it is that he ought to accept running the risk, losing himself. He is told on all sides that he was awaited. Let him know unequivocally that it's not ture. People were awating an ambassador of French thought, not a man struggling to express in words a new thought. His current notoriety is based on a misunderstanding. A great man is always awaited, because it is flattering for a nation to have produced him. But a great thought is never awaited, because it offends. Let him then accept industry's motto: create needs in order to satisfy them. Let him create the need for justice, freedom, and solidarity, and strain to satisfy these needs with his susbsequent works. Let us hope that he will be able to shake off the numerous tributes raining down on him and rediscover within himself the strength to scandalize; let him blaze paths rather than embark on national highways, even if he is furnished with a racing car. I have never believed that good literature can be made with bad sentiments. But I think that the right sentiments are never given in advance; every man has to invent them in turn. Perhaps criticism might help save literature if it concerned itself with understanding works rather than consecrating them. In any event, we in this forum are firmly committed to literary deflation. We probably won't make many friends. But literature is falling asleep. The right passion—even anger—will have the good fortune perhaps to awaken it.

Translated by Jeffrey Mehlman

Black
Orpheus

Black Orpheus

WHEN YOU REMOVED the gag that was keeping these black mouths shut, what were you hoping for? That they would sing your praises? Did you think that when they raised themselves up again, you would read adoration in the eyes of these heads that our fathers had forced to bend down to the very ground? Here are black men standing, looking at us, and I hope that you—like me—will feel the shock of being seen. For three thousand years, the white man has enjoyed the privilege of seeing without being seen; he was only a look—the light from his eyes drew each thing out of the shadow of its birth; the whiteness of his skin was another look, condensed light. The white man—white because he was man, white like daylight, white like truth, white like virtue—lighted up the creation like a torch and unveiled the secret white essence of beings. Today, these black men are looking at us, and our gaze comes back to our own eyes; in their turn, black torches light up the world and our white heads are no more than Chinese lanterns swinging in the wind. A black poet—unconcerned with us—whispers to the woman he loves:

> Naked woman, black woman
> Dressed in your color which is life . . .
> Naked woman, dark woman,
> Firm fleshed ripe fruit, somber ecstasies of black wine

and our whiteness seems to us to be a strange livid varnish that keeps our skin from breathing—white tights, worn out at the elbows and knees, under which we would find real human flesh the color of black wine if we could remove them. We think we are essential to the world—suns of its harvests, moons of its tides; we are no more than its fauna, beasts. Not even beasts:

These gentlemen from the city
These proper gentlemen
Who no longer know how to dance in the evening by moonlight
Who no longer know how to walk on the flesh of their feet
Who no longer know how to tell tales by the fireside . . .

Formerly Europeans with divine right, we were already feeling our dignity beginning to crumble under American or Soviet looks; Europe was already no more than a geographic accident, the peninsula that Asia shoves into the Atlantic. We were hoping at least to find a bit of our greatness reflected in the domesticated eyes of the Africans. But there are no more domesticated eyes: there are wild and free looks that judge our world.

Here is a black man wandering:
  to the end of
  the eternity of their endless boulevards
  with cops . . .
Here is another one shouting to his brothers:
  Alas! Alas! Spidery Europe is moving its fingers and its
  phalanxes of ships . . .
Here is:
  the cunning silence of Europe's night . . .

in which

  . . . there is nothing that time does not dishonor.

A Negro writes:

  At times, we will haunt Montparnasse and Paris,
  Europe and its endless torments, like memories
  or like malaises . . .

and suddenly France seems exotic in our own eyes. She is no more than a memory, a malaise, a white mist at the bottom of sunlit souls, a back-country unfit to live in; she has drifted toward the North, she is anchored near Kamchatka: the essential thing is the sun, the sun of the tropics and the sea "lousy with islands" and the roses of Imangue and the lilies of Iarive and the volcanos of Martinique. Being [l'Etre] is black, Being is made of fire, we are accidental and far away, we have to justify our mores, our technics, our undercooked paleness of our verdigris vegetation. We are eaten away to the bones by these quiet and corrosive looks:

> Listen to the white world
> horribly weary of its immense effort
> its rebel articulations crackling under hard stars,
> its steel-blue stiffnesses piercing mystical flesh
> listen to its exhibitionist victories trumpeting its defeats
> listen to its wretched staggering with grandiose alibis
> Have pity on our naïve omniscient conquerors.

There we are, *finished*; our victories—their bellies sticking up in the air—show their guts, our secret defeat. If we want to crack open this finitude which imprisons us, we can no longer rely on the privileges of our race, of our color, of our technics: we will not be able to become a part of the totality from which those black eyes exile us, unless we tear off our white tights in order to try simply to be men.

If these poems shame us, however, they were not intended to: they were not written for us; and they will not shame any colonists or their accomplices who open this book, for these latter will think they are reading letters over someone's shoulder, letters not meant for them. These black men are addressing themselves to black men about black men; their poetry is neither satiric nor imprecatory: it is an awakening to consciousness. "So," you will say, "in what way does it interest us, if it is only a document? We cannot enter into it." I should like to show in what way we *can* gain access to this world of jet; I should like to show that this poetry—which seems racial at first—is actually a hymn by everyone for everyone. In a word, I am talking now to white men, and I should like to explain to them what black men already know: why it is necessarily through a poetic experience that the black man, in his present condition, must first become conscious of himself; and, inversely, why black poetry in the

French langauge is, in our time, the only great revolutionary poetry.

It is not just by accident that the white proletariat rarely uses poetic language to speak about its sufferings, its anger, or its pride in itself; neither do I think that workers are less gifted than our bourgeois sons: "talent"—the efficacious grace—loses all meaning when one claims that it is more widespread in one class than in another. Nor is it hard work that takes away their capacity for song: slaves used to drudge even harder and yet we know of slave hymns. It must therefore be recognized that it is the present circumstances of the class struggle that keep the worker from expressing himself poetically. Oppressed by technics, he wants to be a technician because he knows that technics will be the instrument of his liberation; he knows that it is only by gaining professional, economic, and scientific know-how that he will be able someday to control business management. He now has a profound practical knowledge of what poets have called *Nature*, but it is a knowledge he has gained more through his hands than through his eyes: Nature is Matter for him—that crafty, inert adversity that he works on with his tools; Matter has no song. At the same time, the present phase of his struggle requires of him continual, positive action: political calculation, precise forecasting, discipline, organization of the masses; to dream, at this point, would be to betray. Rationalism, materialism, positivism—the great themes of his daily battle—are least propitious for the spontaneous creation of poetic myths. The last of these myths—the famous "Upheaval"—has withdrawn under the circumstances of the struggle: one must take up the matter that is most urgent, gain this and that position, raise this salary, decide on that sympathy strike or on some protest against the war in Indochina: efficiency alone matters. And, without a doubt, the oppressed class must first find itself. This self-discovery, however, is the exact opposite of a subjective examination of oneself: rather, it is a question of recognizing—in and by action—the objective situation of the proletariat, which can be determined by the circumstances of production or of redistribution of property. Unified by an oppression which is exerted on each and every one, and reduced to a common struggle, workers are hardly acquainted with the inner contradictions that fecundate the work of art and that are harmful to the praxis. As far as they are concerned, to know themselves is to situate themselves within the context of the great forces that surround them; it requires them to determine both their exact position in their class and their function in the Party. The very language they use is free from the slight loosening of the screws, the constant frivolous impropriety, the game of transmissions which create the poetic Word. In their business, they use well-defined technical terms; and as for the langauge of revolutionary parties, Parain has shown that it is *pragmatic*: it is used to transmit orders, watchwords, information; if it loses its exactness, the Party falls apart. All of this tends more and more rigorously to eliminate the subject; poetry, however, must in some way remain subjective. The proletariat has not found a poetry that is sociological and yet finds its source in subjectivity, that is just as subjective as it is sociological, that is based on ambiguous or uncertain language, and that is nevertheless as exalting and as generally understood as the most precise watchwords or as the phrase "Workers of all countries, unite" which one reads on doors in Soviet Russia. Lacking this, the poetry of the future revolution has remained in the hands of well-intentioned young bourgeois who found their inspiration in their personal psychological contradictions, in the dichotomy between their ideal and their class, in the uncertainty of the old bourgeois language.

Like the white worker, the Negro is a victim of the capitalist structure of our society. This situation reveals to him his close ties—quite apart from the color of his skin—with certain classes of Europeans who, like him, are opposed; it incites him to imagine a privilege-less society in which skin pigmentation will be considered a mere fluke. But even though oppression itself may be a mere fluke, the circumstances under which it exists vary according to history and geographic conditions: the black man is a victim of it *because he is a black man* and insofar as he is a colonized native or a deported African. And since he is oppressed within the confines of his race and because of it, he must first of all become conscious of his race. He must oblige those who have vainly tried throughout the centuries to reduce him to the status of a beast, to recognize that he is a man. On this point, there is no means of evasion, or of trickery, no "crossing line" that he can consider: a Jew—a white man among white men—can deny that he is a Jew, can declare himself a man among men. The Negro cannot deny that he is Negro, nor can he claim that he is part of some abstract colorless humanity: he is black. Thus he has his back up against the wall of authenticity: having been insulted and formerly enslaved, he picks up the word "nigger" which was thrown at him like a stone, he draws himself erect and proudly proclaims himself a black man, face to face with white men. The unity which will come eventually, bringing all oppressed peoples together in the same struggle, must be preceded in the colonies by what I shall call the moment of separation or negativity: this antiracist racism is the only road that will lead to the abolition of racial differences. How could it be otherwise? Can black men count on a distant white proletariat—involved in its own struggles—before they are united and organized on their own soil? And furthermore, isn't there some need for a thorough work of analysis in order to realize the identity of the interests that underlie the obvious difference of condition? The white worker benefits somewhat from colonization, in spite of himself: low as his standard of living may be, it would be even lower if there were no colonization. In any case, he is less cynically exploited than the day laborer in Dakar or Saint-Louis. The technical equipment and industrialization of the European countries make it possible for measures of socialization to be immediately applicable there; but as seen from Senegal or the Congo, socialism seems more than anything else like a beautiful dream: before black peasants can discover that socialism is the necessary answer to their present local claims, they must learn to formulate these claims jointly; therefore, they must think of themselves as black men.

But this new self-discovery is different from that which Marxism tries to awaken in the white worker. In the European worker, class consciousness is based on the nature of profit and unearned increment, on the present conditions of the ownership of the instruments for work; in brief, it is based on the objective characteristics of the *position* of the proletariat. But since the selfish scorn that white men display for black men—and that has no equivalent in the attitude of the bourgeois toward the working class—is aimed at the deepest recesses of the heart, black men must oppose it with a more exact view of black *subjectivity*; consequently race consciousness is based first of all on the black soul, or, rather—since the term is often used in this anthology—on a certain quality common to the thoughts and conduct of Negroes which is called *negritude*. There are only two ways to go about forming racial concepts: either one causes certain subjective characteristics to become objective, or else one tries to interiorize objectively revealed manners of conduct; thus the black man who asserts his negritude by means of a revolutionary movement immediately places himself in the position of having to meditate, either because he wishes to recognize in himself certain objectively established traits of the African civilizations, or because he hopes to discover the Essence of blackness in the well of his heart. Thus subjectivity reappears: the relation of the self with self; the source of all poetry, the very poetry from which the worker had to disengage himself. The black man who asks his colored brothers to "find themselves" is going to try to present to them an exemplary image of their negritude and will look into his own soul to grasp it. He wants to be both a beacon and a mirror; the first revolutionary will be the harbinger of the black soul, the herald—half prophet and half follower—who will tear Blackness out of himself in order to offer it to the world; in brief, he will be a poet in the literal sense of *vates*. Furthermore, black poetry has nothing in common with heartfelt effusions: it is functional, it answers a need which is defined in precise terms. Leaf through an anthology of contemporary white poetry: you will find a hundred different subjects, depending upon the mood and interests of the poet, depending upon his position and his country. In the anthology which I am introducing to you here, there is only one subject that all the poets attempt to treat, more or less successfully. From Haiti to Cayenne, there is a single idea: *reveal* the black soul. Black poetry is evangelic, it announces good news: Blackness has been rediscovered.

However, this negritude, which they wish to fish for in their abyssal depths, does not fall under the soul's gaze all by itself: in the soul, nothing is gratuitous. The herald of the black soul has gone through white schools, in accordance with a brazen law which forbids the oppressed man to possess any arms except those he himself has stolen from the oppressor; it is through having had some contact with white culture that his blackness has passed from the immediacy of existence to the meditative state. But at the same time, he has more or less ceased to live his negritude. In choosing to see what he is, he has become split, he no longer coincides with himself. And on the other hand, it is because he was already exiled from himself that he discovered this need to reveal himself. He therefore begins by exile. It is a double exile: the exile of his body offers a magnificent image of the exile of his heart; he is in Europe most of the time, in the cold, in the middle of gray crowds; he dreams of Port-au-Prince, of Haiti. But in Port-au-Prince he was *already* in exile; the slavers had torn his fathers out of Africa and dispersed them. And all of the poems in this book—except those which were written in Africa—show us the same mystical geography. A hemisphere: in the foreground—forming the first of three concentric circles—extends the land of exile, colorless Europe; then comes the dazzling circle of the Islands and of childhood, which dance the roundelay around Africa; the last circle is Africa, the world's navel, pole of all black poetry—dazzling Africa, burnt, oily like a snake's skin, Africa of fire and rain, torrid and tufted; Africa—phantom flickering like a flame, between being and nothingness, more *real* than the "eternal boulevards with cops" but absent, beyond attainment, disintegrating Europe with its black but invisible rays; Africa, an *imaginary* continent. The extraordinary good luck of black poetry lies in the fact that the anxieties of the colonized native have their own grandiose and obvious symbols which need only to be gone into deeply and to be meditated upon: exile, slavery, the Africa-Europe couple and the great Manichaean division of the world into black and white. This ancestral bodily exile represents the other exile: the black soul is an Africa from which the Negro, in the midst of the cold buildings of white culture and technics, is exiled. And ever-present but concealed negritude haunts him, rubs against him; he himself rubs up against its silky wing; it palpitates and is spread throughout him like his searching memory and his loftiest demands, like his shrouded, betrayed childhood, and like the childhood of his race and the call of the earth, like the swarming of insects and the indivisible simplicity of Nature, like the pure legacy of his ancestors, and like the Ethics that ought to unify his truncated life. But if he turns around to look squarely at his negritude, it vanishes in smoke; the walls of white culture—its silence, its words, its mores—rise up between it and him:

> Give me back my black dolls, so that I may play with them
> My instinct's simple games
> that I may remain in the shadow of its laws
> cover up my courage
> my audacity
> feel me as me
> me renewed through what I was yesterday
>   yesterday
>   without complexity

> yesterday
> when the uprooting hour came . . .
> they have ransacked the space that was mine

However, the walls of this culture prison must be broken down; it will be necessary to return to Africa some day: thus the themes of return to the native country and of re-descent into the glaring hell of the black soul are indissolubly mixed up in the *vates* of negritude. A quest is involved here, a systematic stripping and an *ascèse** accompanied by a continual effort of investigation. And I shall call this poetry "Orphic" because the Negro's tireless descent into himself makes me think of Orpheus going to claim Eurydice from Pluto. Thus, through an exceptional stroke of poetic good luck, it is by letting himself fall into trances, by rolling on the ground like a possessed man tormented by himself, by singing of his angers, his regrets, or his hates, by exhibiting his wounds, his life torn between "civilization" and his old black substratum; in short, by becoming most lyrical, that the black poet is most certain of creating a great collective poetry. By speaking only of himself, he speaks for all Negroes; it is when he seems smothered by the serpents of our culture that he is the most revolutionary, for he then undertakes to ruin systematically the European knowledge he has acquired, and this spiritual destruction symbolizes the great future taking-up of arms by which black men will destroy their chains. A single example will suffice to clarify this last remark.

In the twentieth century, most ethnic minorities have passionately endeavored to resuscitate their national languages while struggling for their independence. To be able to say that one is Irish or Hungarian, one must belong to a collectivity which has the benefit of a broad economic and political autonomy; but to *be* Irish, one must also *think Irish*, which means above all: think *in* Irish. The specific traits of a Society correspond exactly to the untranslatable

---

* The ascetic's movement of interiorization.—*Translator.*

locutions of its language. The fact that the prophets of negritude are forced to write their gospel *in French* means that there is a certain risk of dangerously slowing down the efforts of black men to reject our tutelage. Having been dispersed to the four corners of the earth by the slave trade, black men have no common language; in order to incite the oppressed to unite, they must necessarily rely on the words of the oppressor's language. And French is the language that will furnish the black poet with the largest audience, at least within the limits of French colonization. It is in this goose-pimply language—pale and cold like our skies, and which Mallarmé said was "the neutral language *par excellence*, since our spirit demands an attenuation of variegation and of all excessively brilliant color"—in this language which is half dead for them, that Damas, Diop, Laleau, Rabéarivelo are going to pour the fire of their skies and of their hearts; it is through this language alone that they can communicate; like the sixteenth-century scholars who understood each other only in Latin, black men can meet only on that trap-covered ground that the white man has prepared for them. The colonist has arranged to be the eternal mediator between the colonized; he is there—always there—even when he is absent, even in the most secret meetings. And since words are ideas, when the Negro declares in French that he rejects French culture, he accepts with one hand what he rejects with the other; he sets up the enemy's thinking-apparatus in himself, like a crusher. This would not matter: except that this syntax and vocabulary—forged thousands of miles away in another epoch to answer other needs and to designate other objects—are unsuitable to furnish him with the means of speaking about himself, his own anxieties, his own hopes. The French language and French thought are analytic. What would happen if the black spirit were above all synthetic? The rather ugly term "negritude" is one of the few black contributions to our dictionary. But after all, if this "negritude" is a definable or at least a describable concept, it must subsume other more elementary concepts which correspond to the immediate fundamental ideas directly involved with Negro consciousness. But where are the words to describe them? How well one understands the Haitian poet's complaint:

> This obsessing heart which does not correspond
> To my language, or to my customs,
> And on which encroach, like a clinging-root,
> Borrowed feelings and the customs
> Of Europe, feel this suffering
> And this despair—equal to no other—
> Of ever taming with words from France
> This heart which came to me from Senegal.

It is not true, however, that the black man expresses himself in a "foreign" language, since he is taught French from childhood and since he is perfectly at ease when he thinks in the terms of a technician, of a scholar, or of a politician. Rather, one must speak about the slight but patent difference that separates what he says from what he would like to say, whenever he speaks about himself. It seems to him that a Northern Spirit steals his ideas from him, bends them slightly to mean more or less what he wanted; that white words drink his thoughts as sand drinks blood. If he suddenly gorges himself, if he pulls himself together and takes a step backward, there are the sounds lying prostrate *in front of him*—strange: half signs and half things. He will not speak his negritude with precise, efficacious words which hit the target every time. He will not speak his negritude *in prose.* As everyone knows, every poetic experience has its origin in this feeling of frustration that one has when confronted with a language that is supposed to be a means of direct communication.

The reaction of the *speaker* frustrated by prose is in effect what Bataille calls the holocaust of words. As long as we can believe that a preestablished harmony governs the relationship between a word and Being, we use words without seeing them, with blind trust; they are sensory organs, mouths, hands, windows open on the world. As soon as we experience a first frustration, this chattering falls beyond us;

we see the whole system, it is no more than an upset, out-of-order mechanism whose arms are still flailing to INDICATE EXISTENCE in emptiness; in one fell swoop we pass judgment on the foolish business of naming things; we understand that language is in essence prose, and that prose is in essence failure; Being stands erect in front of us like a tower of silence, and if we still want to catch it, we can do so only through silence: "evoke, in an intentional shadow, the object *tu* by allusive words, never direct, reducing themselves to the same silence."[1] No one has better stated that poetry is an incantatory attempt to suggest Being in and by the vibratory disappearance of the word: by insisting on his verbal impotence, by making words mad, the poet makes us suspect that beyond this chaos which cancels itself out, there are silent densities; since we cannot keep quiet, we must *make silence with language.* From Mallarmé to the Surrealists, the final goal of French poetry seems to me to have been this autodestruction of language. A poem is a dark room where words are knocking themselves about, quite mad. Collisions in the air: they ignite each other with their fire and fall down in flames.

It is in this perspective that we must situate the efforts of the "black evangelists." They answer the colonist's ruse with a similar but inverse ruse: since the oppressor is present in the very language that they speak, they will speak this language in order to destroy it. The contemporary European poet tries to dehumanize words in order to give them back to nature; the black herald is going to *de-Frenchify* them; he will crush them, break their usual associations, he will violently couple them

> with little steps of caterpillar rain
> with little steps like mouthfuls of milk
> with little steps like ball-bearings
> with little steps like seismic shocks
> Yams in the soil stride like gaps of stars[2] . . .

Only when they have regurgitated their whiteness does he adopt them, making of this ruined language a solemn, sacred super-langauge, Poetry. Only through Poetry can the black men of Tenanarive and of Cayenne, the black men of Port-au-Prince and of Saint-Louis, communicate with each other in private. And since French lacks terms and concepts to define negritude, since negritude is silence, these poets will use "allusive words, never direct, reducing themselves to the same silence" in order to evoke it. Short-circuits of language: behind the flaming fall of words, we glimpse a great black mute idol. It is not only the black man's self-portrayal that seems poetic to me; it is also his personal way of utilizing the means of expression at his disposal. His position incites him to do it: even before he thinks of writing poetry, in him the light of white words is refracted, polarized, and altered. This is nowhere more manifest than in his use of two connected terms, "white" and "black," that cover both the great cosmic division of day and night and the human conflict between the native and the colonist. But it is a connection based on a hierarchical system: by giving the Negro this term, the teacher also gives him a hundred language habits which consecrate the white man's rights over the black man. The Negro will learn to say "white like snow" to indicate innocence, to speak of the blackness of a look, of a soul, of a deed. As soon as he opens his mouth, he accuses himself, unless he persists in upsetting the hierarchy. And if he upsets it in *French*, he is already poetizing: can you imagine the strange savor that an expression like "the blackness of innocence" or "the darkness of virtue" would have for us? That is the savor which we taste on every page of this book, when, for example, we read:

Your round, shining, black satin breasts . . .
this white smile
of eyes
in the face's shadow
awaken in me this evening
deaf rhythms . . .
which intoxicate, there in Guinée,
our sisters

black and naked
and inspire in me
this evening
black twilights heavy with sensual anxiety
for
the soul of the black country where the ancients
are sleeping
lives and speaks
this evening
in uneasy strength, along the small of
your back . . .

Throughout this poem, black is color; better still, light. Its soft diffuse radiance dissolves our habits; the *black* country where the ancients are sleeping is not a dark hell: it is a land of sun and fire. Then again, in another connection, the superiority of white over black does not express only the superiority that the colonist claims to have over the native: more profoundly, it expresses a universal adoration of *day* as well as our night terrors, which also are universal. In this sense, these black men are reestablishing the hiararchy they have just upset. They don't want to be poets of *night*, poets of vain revolt and despair: they give the promise of dawn; they greet

the transparent dawn of a new day.

At last, the black man discovers, through the pen, his baleful sense of foreboding:

Nigger black like misery

one of them, and then another, cries out:

Deliver me from my blood's night . . .

Thus the word *black* is found to contain *all Evil* and *all Good*; it covers up almost unbearable tension between two contradictory classifications: solar hierarchy and racial hierarchy. It gains thereby an extraordinary poetry, like self-destructive objects from the hands of Duchamp and the Surrealists; there is a secret blackness in white, a secret whiteness in black, a vivid flickering of Being and of Nonbeing which is perhaps nowhere expressed as well as in this poem of Césaire's:

> My tall wounded statue, a stone in its fore-
> head; my great inattentive day flesh with
> pitiless spots, my great night flesh with
> day spots.

The poet will go even further. He writes:

> Our beautiful faces like the true operative
> power of negation.

Behind this abstract eloquence evoking Lautréamont is seen an extremely bold and subtle attempt to give some sense to black skin and to realize the poetic synthesis of the two faces of night. When David Diop says that the Negro is "black like misery," he makes black represent deprivation of light. But Césaire develops and goes into this image more deeply: night is no longer absence, it is refusal. Black is not color, it is the destruction of this borrowed clarity which falls from the white sun. The revolutionary Negro is negation because he wishes to be complete nudity: in order to build his Truth, he must first destroy others' Truth. Black faces—these night memories which haunt our days— embody the dark work of Negativity which patiently gnaws at concepts. Thus, by a reversal which curiously recalls that of the humiliated Negro—insulted and called "dirty nigger" when he asserts his rights—it is the privative aspect of darkness that establishes its value. Liberty is the color of night.

Destructions, *autos-da-fé* of language, magic symbolism, ambivalence of concepts: all the negative aspects of modern poetry are here. But it is not a matter of some gratuitous game. The black man's position, his original "rending," the alienation that a foreign way of thinking imposes on him, all oblige him to reconquer his existential unity as a Negro—or, if you prefer, the original purity of his plan—through a gradual *ascèse*, beyond the language stage. Negritude—like liberty—is a point of departure and an ultimate goal: it is a matter of making negritude pass from the immediate to the mediate, a matter of *thematicizing* it. The black man must therefore find death in white culture in order to be reborn with a black soul, like the Platonic philosopher whose body embraces death in order to be reborn in truth. This dialectical and mystical return to origins necessarily implies a method. But this method is not presented as a set of rules to be used in directing the spirit. Rather, it becomes *one* with whoever applies it; it is the dialectical law of successive transformations which lead the Negro to coincidence with himself in negritude. It is not a matter of his *knowing*, or of his ecstatically tearing himself away from himself, but rather of both discovering and becoming what he is.

There are two convergent means of arriving at this primordial simplicity of existence: one is objective, the other subjective. The poets in our anthology sometimes use one, sometimes the other, and sometimes both of them together. In effect, there exists an objective negritude that is expressed by the mores, arts, chants, and dances of the African populaces. As a *spiritual exercise*, the poet will prescribe allowing himself to be fascinated by primitive rhythms, letting his thoughts run in traditional forms of black poetry. Many of the poems included here are called *tam-tams*, because they borrow from the nighttime tambourine players a percussive rhythm which is sometimes sharp and regular, sometimes torrential and bounding. The poetic act, then, is a dance of the soul; the poet turns round and round like a dervish until he faints; he has established his ancestors' time in himself, he feels it flowing with its peculiar violent pulls; he hopes to "find" himself in this rhythmic pulsation; I shall say that he tries to make himself "possessed" by his people's negritude; he hopes that the echoes of his tam-tam will come to awaken timeless instincts sleeping within him. Upon leafing through this collection, one will get the impression that the *tam-tam* tends to become a *genre* of black poetry, just as the sonnet or the ode was a *genre* of our poetry. Others, like Rabemananjara, will be inspired by royal proclamations. Still others will draw from the popular well of the Haintenys. The calm center of this maelstrom of rhythms, chants, shouts, is the poetry of Birago Diop, in all its majestic simplicity: it alone is at *rest* because it comes directly from Griot narratives and oral tradition. Almost all the other attempts have something contorted, taut, and desperate about them because they aim at *becoming a part* of folkloric poetry rather than emanating from it. But however far he may be from "the black country where ancestors sleep," the black man is closer than we are to the great period when, as Mallarmé says, "the word creates Gods." It is partically impossible for *our* poets to resume some closeness with popular traditons: ten centuries of scholarly poetry separate them from such traditions. Furthermore, folkloric inspiration is drying up: at the very best, we could only imitate its simplicity from a distance. The black men of Africa, on the contrary, are still in the great period of mythical fecundity, and French-language black poets are not just using their myths as a form of diversion as we use our epic poems:* they allow themselves to be spellbound by them so that the end of the incantation, negritude—magnificently evoked—may surge forth. This is why I call this method of "objective poetry" *magic*, or charm.

Césaire, on the contrary, chose to backtrack into himself. Since this Eurydice will disappear in smoke if Black Orpheus turns around to look back on her, he will descend the royal road of his soul with his back turned on the bottom of the grotto; he will descend below words and meanings— "in order to think of you, I have placed all words on the

---

* Sartre uses the word *chansons* for what I have translated as "epic poems." He is referring, of course, to the medieval French epic poems, the *chansons de geste.—Translator.*

mountain-of-pity"—below daily activities and the plan of "repetition," even below the first barrier reefs of revolt, with his back turned and his eyes closed, in order finally to touch with his feet the black water of dreams and desire and to let himself drown in it.* Desire and dream will rise up snarling like a tidal wave; they will make words dance like flotsam and throw them pell-mell, shattered, on the shore.

> Words go beyond themselves; and just as the old geography is done for, the high and the low [words] do not allow diversion either toward heaven or toward earth . . . On the contrary, they operate on a strangely flexible range at one level: on the gaseous Level of an organism both solid and liquid, black and white day and night.†

One recognizes the old surrealistic *method* (automatic writing, like mysticism, is a method: it presupposes an apprenticeship, exercises, a start along the way). One must dive under the superficial crust of reality, of common sense, of reasoning reason, in order to touch the very bottom of the soul and awaken the timeless forces of desire: desire which makes of man a refusal of everything and a love of everything: desire, the radical negation of natural laws and of the possible, a call to miracles; desire which, by its mad cosmic energy, plunges man back into the seething breast of Nature and, at the same time, lifts him above Nature through the affirmation of his Right to be unsatisfied. Furthermore, Césaire is not the first Negro to take this road. Before him, Etienne Léro had founded *Légitime Défense.*

---

* Sartre seems to have confused his images here, since Orpheus was instructed not to look back while he was *ascending* from Hades, *after* he had retrieved Eurydice from Pluto.—*Translator.*

† The French notion of "automatic writing" was so completely untranslatable that I have tried simply to give an English *approximation* of its sense. For those who care to consult the original French text, it runs as follows: "Les mots se dépassent, c'est bien vers un ciel et une terre que le haut et le bas ne permettent pas de distraire, c'en est fait aussi de la vieille géographie . . . Au contraire, un étagement curieusement respirable s'opère réel mais au niveau. Au Niveau gazeux de l'organisme solide et liquide, blanc et noir jour et nuit."—*Translator.*

"*Légitime Défense*," says Senghor, "was more a cultural movement than a review. Starting from the Marxist analysis of the society of the "Islands," it discovered, in the Antilles, descendants of African Negro slaves, who had been kept in the dulling condition of the proletarian for three centuries. It affirmed that only surrealism could deliver him from his taboos and express him in his entireness."

However, if one compares Léro with Césaire, one cannot help being struck by their dissimilarities, and this comparison may allow us to measure the abyss that prevents a black revolutionary from utilizing white surrealism. Léro was the precursor; he invented the exploitation of surrealism as a "miraculous weapon" and an instrument for reconnaissance, a sort of radar with which one probes the depths of the abyss. But his poems are student exercises, they are mere imitations: they do not go beyond themselves; rather, they close in on each other:

> The ancient heads of hair
> Glue to the branches floors of empty seas
> Where your body is only a memory
> Where Spring trims its nails
> Helix of your smile thrown far away
> On the houses we will have nothing to do with . . .

"The helix of your smile," "the spring which trims its nails": we recognize in these the preciousness and gratuitousness of surrealistic imagery, the eternal process that consists of throwing a bridge between two extremely unrelated or separated terms and hoping—without really believing—that this "throw of the dice" will uncover some hidden aspect of Being. It does not seem to me that, either in this poem or in the others, Léro demands the liberation of the black man: at the very most he lays claim to a categorical liberation of the imagination. In the completely abstract game, no combination of words evokes Africa even remotely. If these poems were taken out of the anthology and the name of their author hidden, I would defy anyone at all, white or black, not to attribute them to a European contributor to *La Révolution surréaliste* or *Le Minotaure*. The purpose of Surrealism is to rediscover—beyond race and condition, beyond class, behind the fire of language—dazzling silent darknesses which are no longer opposed to anything, not even to day, because day and night and all opposites are blended in them and suppressed; consequently, one might speak of the impassiveness and the impersonality of the Surrealist poem, just as there is a Parnassian impassiveness and impersonality.

A poem by Césaire, on the contrary, bursts and wheels around like a rocket; suns turning and exploding into new suns come out of it: it is a perpetual going-beyond. It is not a question of the poem's becoming part of the calm unity of opposites, but rather of making *one* of the opposites in the "black-white" couple expand like a phallus in its opposition to the other. The density of these words thrown into the air like stones from a volcano is found in negritude, which is defined as being *against* Europe and colonization. What Césaire destroys is not *all* culture but rather *white* culture; what he brings to light is not desire for *everything* but rather the revolutionary aspirations of the oppressed Negro; what he touches in his very depths is not the spirit but a certain specific, concrete form of humanity. With this in mind, one can speak here about *engaged* and even *directed* automatic writing, not because there is any meditative intervention but because the words and images perpetually translate the same torrid obsession. The white Surrealist finds within himself the trigger; Césaire finds within himself the fixed inflexibility of demands and feeling. Léro's words are feebly organized around vague general themes through expansion and a relaxing of logical ties; Césair's words are pressed against each other and cemented by his furious passion. Between the most daring comparisons and between the most widely separated terms runs a secret thread of hate and hope. For example, compare "the helix of your smile thrown far away"—which is the product of a free play of the imagination as well as an invitation to reverie—with

and the radium mines buried in the abyss of my innocence
will jump by grains
into the feeding-trough of birds
and the stars' stere
will be the common name of firewood
gathered from the alluvium of the singing veins of night

in which the "disjecta membra" of the vocabulary are so
organized as to allow the supposition that there is a black
"Art Poétique." Or read:

Our beautiful faces like the true operative power of negation.

Also read:

Seas lousy with islands cracking in the roses' fingers
flame-thrower and my lightning-struck body intact.

Here we find the apotheosis of the fleas of black misery
jumping in the water's hair, islands in a stream of light,
cracking under the fingers of the celestial delouser: dawn with
rose-colored fingers, the dawn of Greek and Mediterranean
culture—snatched from the sacrosanct Homeric poems by a
black thief—whose enslaved princess's fingernails are suddenly controlled by a Toussaint L'Ouverture in order to crack
the triumphant parasites of the black sea; the dawn, which
suddenly rebels and is metamorphosed, which opens fire like
that savage weapon of white men, the flame-thrower, the
weapon of scientists, the weapon of executioners, strikes the
tall black Titan with its white fire, and he arises intact and
eternal in order to begin the assault on Europe and heaven.
In Césaire, the great Surrealist tradition is realized, it takes
on its definitive meaning and is destroyed: Surrealism—that
European movement—is taken from the Europeans by a black
man who turns it against them and gives it a rigorously
defined function. I have pointed out elsewhere how the whole
of the proletariat completely shut itself off from the destructive poetry of Reason: in Europe, Surrealism languishes and
pales, rejected by those who could have given it a transfusion

of their own blood. But at the very moment when it is losing contact with the Revolution, it is, in the Antilles, grafted onto another branch of the universal Revolution; it develops into an enormous somber flower. Césaire's originality lies in his having directed his powerful, concentrated anxiety as a Negro, as one oppressed, as a militant individual, into this world of the most destructive, free, and metaphysical poetry at the moment when Eluard and Aragon were failing to give political content to their verse. And finally, *negritude-object* is snatched from Césaire like a cry of pain, of love, and of hate. Here again he follows the Surrealist tradition of *objective* poetry. Césaire's words do not describe negritude, they do not designate it, they do not copy it from the outside like a painter with a model: they *create* it; they compose it under our very eyes. Henceforth it is a thing which can be observed and learned; the subjective method which he has chosen joins the objective method we spoke about earlier: he ejects the black soul from himself at the very moment when others are trying to interiorize it; the final result is the same in both cases. Negritude is the far-away tam-tam in the streets of Dakar at night; voodoo shouts from some Haitian cellar window, sliding along level with the roadway; the Congolese mask; but it is also this poem by Césaire, this slobbery, bloody peom full of phlegm, twisting in the dust like a cut-up worm. This double spasm of absorption and excretion beats out the rhythm of the black heart on every page of this collection.

What then, at present, is this negritude, sole anxiety of these poets, sole subject of this book? It must first be stated that a white man could hardly speak about it suitably, since he has no inner experience of it and since European languages lack words to describe it. I ought then to let the reader encounter it in the pages of this collection and draw his own conclusions about it. But this introduction would be incomplete if, after having indicated that the quest for the Black Grail represented—both in its original intention and in its methods—the most authentic synthesis of revolutionary aspirations and poetic anxiety, I did not show that this complex notion is essentially pure Poetry. I shall

therefore limit myself to examining these poems objectively
as a cluster of testimonies and to pointing out some of their
principal themes. Senghor says, "What makes the *negritude*
of a poem is less its theme than its style, the emotional
warmth which gives life to words, which transmutes the
word into the Word." It could not be more explicitly stated
that negritude is neither a state nor a definite ensemble of
vices and virtues or of intellectual and moral qualities, but
rather a certain affective attitude toward the world. Since
the beginning of this century, psychology has renounced its
great scholastic distinctions. We no longer believe that the
"facts" of the soul are divided into volitions or actions,
knowledge or perceptions, sentiments or blind passiveness.
We know that a feeling is a definite way of establishing our
rapport with the world around us, that it involves a certain
comprehension of this universe. It is a tension of the soul,
a choice of oneself and of another, a way of going beyond the
raw facts of experience; in short, a *plan* quite like the
voluntary act. To use Heidegger's language, negritude is
the Negro's being-in-the-world.

Furthermore, here is what Césaire tells us about it.

> My negritude is not a stone with its deafness flung out against the
>   clamor of the day
> My negritude is not a dead speck of water on the dead eye of the
>   earth
> my negritude is neither a tower nor a cathedral
> it plunges into the red flesh of the ground
> it plunges into the ardent flesh of the sky
> it perforates the opaque pressure of its righteous patience.

Negritude is portrayed in these beautiful lines of verse more
as an act than as a frame of mind. But this act is an *inner*
determination; it is not a question of *taking* the goods of this
world in one's hands and transforming them; it is a question
of *existing* in the middle of the world. The relation with the
universe remains an *adaptation*. But this adaptation is not
technical. For the white man, to possess is to transform. To
be sure, the white worker uses instruments which he does

not possess. But at least his techniques are his own: if it is true that the personnel responsible for the major inventions of European industry comes mainly from the middle classes, at least the trades of carpenter, cabinetmaker, potter, seem to the white workers to be a true heritage, despite the fact that the orientation of great capitalist production tends to remove their "joy in work" from them. But it is not enough to say that the black worker uses instruments which are lent to him: techniques are also lent to him.

Césaire refers to his black brothers as

> Those who have invented neither powder nor compass
> those who have never tamed either steam or electricity
> those who have not explored the seas and the sky . . .

But this haughty claim of nontechnicalness reverses the situation: what could pass as a deficiency becomes a *positive* source of wealth. A technical *rapport* with Nature reveals Nature as simple quantity, inertia, exteriority: Nature dies. By his haughty refusal to be *homo faber*, the Negro gives it life again. As if the passiveness of one of the members of the "man-nature" couple necessarily produced the other's activity. Actually, negritude is not passiveness, since it "perforates the flesh of the sky and of the earth": it is "patience," and patience appears like an active imitation of passiveness. The Negro's act is first of all an act on himself. The black man stands erect and immobilizes himself like a bird-charmer, and things come to perch on the branches of this fake tree. A magic inveigling of the world—through silence and rest—is involved here: the white man, by acting first of all on Nature, loses himself when he loses Nature; the Negro, by acting first of all on himself, claims to win Nature while winning himself.

> Seized, they abandon themselves to the essence of every thing
> ignorant of the surfaces but seized by the movement of every thing
> heedless of counting, but playing the world's game
> truly the elder sons of the world
> porous to all the breaths of the world . . .

flesh of the world's flesh palpitating from the very movement of the world.

Upon reading this, one can hardly help thinking of the famous distinction between intelligence and intuition established by Bergson. Césaire rightly calls us

Omniscient and naïve conquerors . . .

Because of his tools, the white man knows all. But he only scratches the surface of things; he is unaware of the duration of things, unaware of life. Negritude, on the contrary, is comprehension through instinctive congeniality. The black man's secret is that the sources of his existence and the roots of Being are identical.

If one wanted to give a sociological interpretation of this metaphysic, one would say that an agriculturist poetry is here opposed to an engineer prose. Actually, it is not true that the black man has no techniques: the *rapport* between any human group and the exterior world is always technical in one way or another. And inversely, I shall say that Césaire is imprecise: Saint Exupéry's airplane folding the earth below like a carpet is a means of disclosure. However, the black man is first of all a peasant; agricultural technique is "righteous patience"; it trusts in life; it waits. To plant is to impregnate the earth; after that, you must remain motionless and watch: "each atom of silence is a chance for ripe fruit," each instant brings forth a hundred times more than man gave, whereas the worker finds in the manufactured product only as much as he put into it; man grows along with his wheat: from minute to minute he goes beyond himself and becomes more golden; he intervenes in his watchful wait before the fragile swelling belly, only to protect. Ripe wheat is a microcosm because the cooperation of sun, wind, and rains was needed for it to grow; a blade of wheat is both the most natural thing and the most improbable chance. Techniques have contaminated the white peasant, but the black peasant remains the great male of the earth, the world's sperm. His existence is great vegetal patience; his work is the yearly repetition of holy coitus. Creating and nourished because he creates. To till, to plant, to eat, is to make love with Nature. The sexual pantheism of these poets is undoubtedly what will impress us first of all: it is in this that they join the dances and the phallic rites of the Negro-Africans.

> Oho! Congo lying in your bed of forests, queen of tamed Africa
> May the phalli of the mountains carry your banner high
> For, through my head, through my tongue, through my belly,
>   you are a woman,

writes Senghor. Also:

> and so I shall mount again the soft belly of the dunes
> and the gleaming thighs of the day . . .

and Rabéarivelo:

> the earth's blood, the stone's sweat and the sperm of the world

and Laleau:

> The conical drum laments under the sky
> And it is the very soul of the black man
> Sultry spasms of men in rut, lover's sticky sobs
> Outraging the calm of the evening.

Here, we are far from Bergson's chaste asexual intuition. It is no longer a matter of being congenial with life, but rather of being in love with all its forms. For the white technician, God is first of all an engineer. Jupiter orders chaos and prescribes its laws; the Christian God conceives the world through his understanding and brings it into being through his will: the relation between the created and the creator is never carnal, except for a few mystics whom the Church looks upon with a great deal of suspicion. Even so, erotic mysticism has nothing in common with fecundity: it is the completely passive wait for a sterile penetration. We are *steeped* in alluvium: statuettes come from the *hands* of the divine sculptor. If the manufactured objects surrounding us could worship their ancestors, they would undoubtedly adore us as we adore the All-powerful. For our black poets, on the contrary, Being comes out of Nothingness like a penis becoming erect; Creation is an enormous perpetual delivery; the world is flesh and the son of flesh; on the sea and in the sky, on the dunes, on the rocks, in the wind, the Negro finds the softness of human skin; he rubs himself against the sand's belly, against the sky's loins: he is "flesh of the flesh of this world"; he is "porous to all its breaths," to all its pollens; he is both Nature's female and its male; and when he makes love with a woman of his race, the sexual act seems to him to be the celebration of the Mystery of Being. This spermatic religion is like the tension of a soul balancing between two complementary tendencies: the dynamic feeling of being an erect phallus, and that more deaf, more patient, more feminine one of being a growing plant. Thus, negritude is basically a sort of androgyny.

> There you are
> Upright and naked
> alluvium you are and remember yourself as having been
> but in reality you are the child of this parturient shadow
> feeding on lunar lactogen*
> then you slowly take the form of a bole
> on this low wall jumped over by the dreams of flowers
> and the perfume of summer at rest.
> To feel, to believe that roots are pushing your feet
> and running and twisting like thirsty serpents
> toward some subterranean spring . . .
>
> (Rabéarivelo)

And Césaire:

> Wornout mother, leafless mother, you are a *flamboyant*
> and now wear only husks. You are a calabash tree

* "Lactogen" is a neologism in the French text as well.—*Translator*.

and you are only a stand of *couis* . . .†

This profound unity of vegetal and sexual symbols is certainly the greatest originality of black poetry, especially in a period when, as Michel Carrouges has shown, most of the images used by white poets tend to mineralize the human being. Césaire, on the contrary, "vegetalizes," "animalizes" sea, sky, and stones. More precisely, his poetry is a perpetual coupling of men and women who had been metamorphosed into animals, vegetables, stones, with stones, plants, and beasts metamorphosed into men. Thus the black man attests to a natural Eros; he reveals and incarnates it; to find a point of comparison in European poetry, one must go back to Lucretius, the peasant poet who celebrated Venus, the mother goddess, when Rome was not yet much more than a large agricultural market. In our time, only Lawrence seems to me to have had a cosmic feeling for sexuality. Even so, this feeling remains very literary in his works.

However, although negritude seems basically to be this immobile springing-forth, a unity of phallic erection and plant growth, one could scarcely exhaust it with this single poetic theme. There is another motif running through this collection, like a large artery:

> Those who have invented neither powder nor compass . . .
> They know the most remote corners of the country of suffering . . .

To the absurd utilitarian agitation of the white man, the black man opposes the authenticity gained from his suffering; the black race is a chosen race because it has had the horrible privilege of touching the depths of unhappiness. And even though these poems are anti-Christian from beginning to end, one might call negritude a kind of

† *Flamboyant*: a plant found in semitropical countries, especially in the Antilles; a poinciana, or peacock flower. *Couis:* apparently some kind of tree found in the Antilles.—*Translator.*

Passion: the black man who is conscious of himself sees himself as the man who has taken the whole of human suffering upon himself and who suffers for all, even for the white man.

> On the judgment day, Armstrong's trumpet will be the interpreter of man's sufferings.
>
> (Paul Niger)

Let us note immediately that this in no way implies a resigned suffering. A while ago I was speaking about Bergson and Lucretius; I would be tempted now to quote that great adversary of Christianity, Nietzsche, and his "Dionysianism." Like the Dionysian poet, the Negro attempts to penetrate the brilliant phantasm of the day, and encounters, a thousand feet under the Apollonian surface, the inexpiable suffering which is the universal essence of man. If one wished to systematize, one would say that the black man blends with the whole of nature inasmuch as he represents sexual congeniality with Life and inasmuch as he claims he is Man in his Passion of rebellious suffering. One will feel the fundamental unity of this double movement if one considers the constantly tighter relationship which psychiatrists establish between anguish and sexual desire. There is only one proud upheaval which can be equally well described as a desire plunging its roots into suffering or as suffering fixed like a sword across a vast cosmic desire. This "righteous patience" that Césaire evokes is both vegetal growth and patience against suffering; it resides in the very muscles of the Negro; it sustains the black porter going a thousand miles up the Niger under a blinding sun with a fifty-pound load balanced on his head. But if in a certain sense, one can compare the fecundity of Nature to a proliferation of suffering, in another sense—and this one is also Dionysian—this fecundity, by its exuberance, goes beyond suffering, drowns it in its creative abundance which is poetry, love, and dance. Perhaps, in order to understand this indissoluble unity of suffering, eros, and joy, one must have seen the black men of Harlem dance frenetically to the rhythm of "blues," which are the saddest sounds in the world. In effect, rhythm cements the multiple aspects of the black soul, communicates its Nietzschean lightness with heavy Dionysian intuitions. Rhythm—tam-tam, jazz, the "bounding" of these poems—represents the temporality of Negro *existence*. And when a black poet prophesies to his brothers a better future, he portrays their deliverance to them in the form of rhythm:

> What?
> rhythm
> sound wave in the night across the forests, nothing
>   —or a new soul
> timbre
> intonation
> vigor
> dilation
> vibration which flows out by degrees into the marrow
> revulses* in its progression an old sleeping body, takes
> it by the waist
> and spins it
> and turns
> and once more vibrates in its hands, in its loins, its
> sexual member, its thighs, its vagina . . .

But one must go still further: this basic experience of suffering is ambiguous; through it, black conscience is going to become historical. In effect, whatever may be the intolerable iniquity of his present condition, it is not to that condition that the black man first refers when he proclaims that he has touched the heart of human suffering. He has the horrible benefit of having known bondage. For these poets, most of whom were born between 1900 and 1918, slavery—abolished half a century earlier—lingers on as a very real memory:

> Each of my todays looks on my yesterday
> with large eyes rolling with rancor with

* *Revulses*: referring to the medical term *revulsion*, a counterirritant.—*Translator*.

shame
Still real is my stunned condition of the past
of
blows from knotted cords of bodies calcinated
from toe to calcinated back
of dead flesh of red iron firebrands of arms
broken under the whip which is breaking loose . . .

writes Damas, poet from Guiana. And the Haitian, Brierre:

. . . Often like me you feel stiffnesses
Awaken after murderous centuries
And old wounds bleed in your flesh . . .

During the centuries of slavery, the black man drank the cup of bitterness to the last drop; and slavery is a past fact which neither our authors nor their fathers have actually experienced. But it is also a hideous nightmare from which even the youngest of them are not yet sure of having awakened. From one end of the earth to the other, black men—separated by languages, politics, and the history of their colonizers—have a *collective* memory in common. This will not be surprising if one only recalls the French peasants who, in 1789, were still aware of the panicky terrors that went back to the Hundred Years' War. Thus, when the black man goes back to his principal experience, it is suddenly revealed to him in two dimensions: it is both the intuitive seizure of the human condition and the still-fresh memory of a historical past. Here, I am thinking of Pascal, who relentlessly repeated that man was an irrational composite of metaphysics and history, his greatness unexplainable if he comes from the alluvium, his misery unexplainable if he is still as God made him; that in order to understand man, one had to go back to the simple basic fact of man's downfall. It is in this sense that Césaire calls his race "the fallen race." And in a certain sense I can see the *rapprochement* that can be made between black conscience and Christian conscience: the brazen law of slavery evokes that law of the Old Testament, which states the consequences of the *Fault*. The abolition of slavery recalls this *other historical fact:*

Redemption. The white man's insipid paternalism after 1848 resembles that of the white God after the Passion. The difference being, however, that the expiable fault that the black man discovers in the back of his memory is not his own; it belongs to the white man. The first fact of Negro history is certainly a kind of original sin; but the black man is the innocent victim of it. This is why his concept of suffering is radically opposed to white "dolorism." If these poems are for the most part so violently anti-Christian, it is because the white man's religion is more clearly a hoax in the eyes of the Negro than in the eyes of the European proletariat: this religion wants to make him share the responsibility for a crime of which he is the victim; it wants to persuade him to see the kidnappings, the massacres, the rapes, and the tortures which have covered Africa with blood as a legitimate punishment, deserved tests. Will you say that it also proclaims equality for all men before God? *Before God*, yes. Only yesterday I was reading in *Esprit* these lines from a correspondent in Madagascar:

> I am as certain as you that the soul of a Malagasy is worth the soul of a white man . . . Just as, before God, the soul of a child is worth the soul of his father. However, if you have an automobile, you don't let your children drive it.

One can hardly reconcile Christianity and colonialism more elegantly. In opposition to these sophisms, the black man—by a simple investigation of his memory as a former slave—affirms that suffering is man's lot and that it is no less deserved for all that. He rejects with horror Christian stagnation, melancholy sensual pleasure, masochistic humility, and all the tendentious inducements to his submission; he lives the absurdity of suffering in its pure form, in its injustice and in its gratuitousness; and he discovers thereby this truth which is misunderstood or masked by Christianity: suffering carries within itself its own refusal; it is by nature *a refusal to suffer*, it is the dark side of negativity, it opens onto revolt and liberty. The black man promptly *transforms himself into history* inasmuch as the intuition of suffering confers on him a collective past and assigns to him a goal in the future. Only a short while ago, he was a sheer *present* surging of timeless instincts, a simple manifestation of universal and eternal fecundity. Now he calls to his colored brothers in quite another language:

Negro peddler of revolt
you have known the paths of the world
ever since you were sold in Guinée . . .

And:

Five centuries have seen you with weapons in your hands
and you have taught the exploiting races
passion for liberty.

There is already a black epic:* first the golden age of Africa, then the era of dispersion and captivity, then the awakening of conscience, the heroic and somber times of great revolts, of Toussaint L'Ouverture and black heroes, then the *fact* of the abolition of slavery—"unforgettable metamorphosis," says Césaire—then the struggle for definitive liberation:

You are waiting for the next call
the inevitable mobilization
for that war which is yours has known only truces
for there is no land where your blood has not flowed
no language in which your color has not been insulted
You smile, Black Boy,
you sing
you dance
you cradle generations
which go out at all hours to the
fronts of work and pain
which tomorrow will assault bastilles

* The French here reads *geste*, as in *chanson de geste*. Sartre is comparing the Negro epic with the themes of medieval French epic poetry.— *Translator*.

onward toward the bastions of the future
in order to write in all languages
on the clear pages of all skies
the declaration of your rights unrecognized
for more than five centuries . . .

Strange and decisive turn: *race* is transmuted into *historicity*, the black Present explodes and is temporalized, negritude—with its Past and its Future—is inserted into Universal History, it is no longer a *state*, nor even an existential attitude, it is a "Becoming." The black contribution to the evolution of Humanity is no longer savor, taste, rhythm, authenticity, a bouquet of primitive instincts: it is a dated enterprise, a long-suffering construction and also a future. Previously, the black man claimed his place in the sun in the name of *ethnic* qualities; now, he establishes his right to life on his mission; and this mission, like the proletariat's, comes to him from his historical position: because he has suffered from capitalistic exploitation more than all the others, he has acquired a sense of revolt and a love of liberty more than all the others. And because he is the most oppressed, he necessarily pursues the liberation of all, when he works for his own deliverance:

Black messenger of hope
you know all the hymns of the world
even those of the timeless building-works of the Nile.

But, after that, can we still believe in the interior homogeneousness of negritude? And how can one say that it exists? Sometimes it is lost innocence which had its existence in some faraway past, and sometimes hope which can be realized only within the walls of the future City. Sometimes it contracts with Nature in a moment of pantheistic fusion and sometimes it spreads itself out to coincide with the whole history of Humanity; sometimes it is an existential attitude and sometimes the objective ensemble of Negro-African traditions. Is it being discovered? Is it being created? After all, there are black men who "collaborate"; after all, in the prefaces he writes for the works of each poet, Senghor seems to distinguish between degrees of negritude. Does the poet who would be the Prophet for his colored brothers invite them to *become* more Negro, or does he disclose to them what they *are*, by a sort of poetic psychoanalysis? Is negritude necessity or liberty? For the authentic Negro, is it a matter of conduct deriving from essences, as consequences derive from a principle, or is one a Negro in the way that the religious faithful are believers, that is to say, in fear and trembling, in anguish, in perpetual remorse for never sufficiently being what one would like to be? Is it a given fact or a value? The object of empirical intuition or of a moral concept? Is it a conquest of meditation? Or does meditation poison it? Is it never authentic except when unmeditated and in the immediate? Is it a systematic *explanation* of the black soul, or a Platonic Archetype which one can approach indefinitely without ever attaining? Is it, for black men, like our engineer's common sense, the most widely shared thing in the world? Or do some have it, like grace; and if so, does it have its chosen ones? One will undoubtedly answer this question by saying that it is all of these at once, and still other things. And I agree: like all anthropological notions, negritude is a shimmer of being and of needing-to-be; it makes you and you make it: both oath and passion. But there is something even more important in it: the Negro himself, we have said, creates a kind of antiracist racism. He wishes in no way to dominate the world: he desires the abolition of *all* kinds of ethnic privileges; he asserts his solidarity with the oppressed of every color. After that, the subjective, existential, ethnic notion of negritude "passes," as Hegel says, into that which one has of the proletariat: objective, positive, and precise. Senghor says: "For Césaire, 'White' symbolizes capital, just as Negro symbolizes work. . . . When writing about the black men of his race, he is writing about the worldwide proletarian struggle." It is easy to say, not so easy to think. And it is certainly not just by accident that the most ardent cantors of negritude are also militant Marxists. Nevertheless, the notion of race does not mix with the notion of class: the former is concrete and particular; the latter, universal and abstract. One belongs to what Jaspers calls comprehension, and the other to intellection; the first is the product of a psychobiological syncretism, and the other is a methodical construction starting with experience. In fact, negritude appears like the upbeat [unaccented beat] of a dialectical progression: the theoretical and practical affirmation of white supremacy is the thesis; the position of negritude as an antithetical value is the moment of negativity. But this negative moment is not sufficient in itself, and these black men who use it know this perfectly well; they know that it aims at preparing the synthesis or realization of the human being in a raceless society. Thus, negritude is *for* destroying itself; it is a "crossing to" and not an "arrival at," a means and not an end. A poem by Jacques Roumain, a black communist, furnishes the most moving evidence of this new ambiguity:

Africa I have held on to your memory Africa
you are in me
Like a thorn in a wound
like a guardian mascot in the center of the village
make of me the stone of your sling
of my mouth the lips of your wound
of my knees the broken columns of your humbling
however
I want to be only of your race
peasant workers of all countries.

With what sadness he still retains for the moment what he has decided to abandon. With what pride as a *man* he will strip his pride as a Negro for other men! He who says both that Africa is in him like "a thorn in a wound," and that he *wants* to be only of the universal race of the oppressed, has not left the empire of afflicted consciousness. One more step and negritude will disappear completely: the Negro himself makes of what was the mysterious bubbling of black blood a geographic accident, the inconsistent product of universal determinism:

Is it all that climate extended space
which creates clan tribe nation
skin race gods
our inexorable dissimilarity.*

But the poet does not completely have the courage to accept the responsibility for this *rationalization* of the racial concept; one sees that he limits himself to questioning; a bitter regret is visible beneath his will to unite. Strange road: humiliated and offended, black men search deep within themselves to find their most secret pride; and when they have found it at last, it challenges its own right to exist. Through supreme generosity they abandon it, just as Philoctetes abandoned his bow and arrows at Neoptolemus. Thus, the rebel Césaire finds the secret of his revolts in the bottom of his heart: he is of royal blood:

it is true that there is in you something which has
never been able to yield, an anger, a desire, a sadness,
an impatience, in short a scorn, a violence . . . and now
your veins carry gold, not mud; pride, not servitude.
King you have been King in the past.

But he immediately thrusts aside this temptation:

There is a law that I cover up with a chain unbroken
as far as the confluence of fire which violates me
which purifies me and burns me with my prism of amal-
gamated gold . . . I shall perish. But one. Whole.

It is perhaps this ultimate nudity of man that has snatched from him the white rags that were concealing his black armor, and that now destroys and rejects that very armor; it is perhaps this colorless nudity that best symbolizes negritude: for negritude is not a state, it is a simple going-beyond-itself, it is love. It is when negritude renounces itself that it finds itself; it is when it accepts losing

---

* Although the poem itself and Sartre's interpretation of it suggest that there should be a question mark here, there is none in the text from which this was translated.—*Translator.*

that it has won: the colored man—and he alone—can be asked to renounce the pride of his color. He is the one who is walking on this ridge between past particularism—which he has just climbed—and future universalism, which will be the twilight of his negritude; he is the one who looks to the end of particularism in order to find the dawn of the universal. Undoubtedly, the white worker also becomes conscious of his class in order to deny it, since he wants the advent of a classless society: but once again, the definition of class is objective; it sums up only the condition of the white worker's alienation; whereas it is in the bottom of his heart that the Negro finds race, and he must tear out his heart. Thus, negritude is dialectical; it is not only nor above all the blossoming of atavistic instincts; it represents "going beyond" a situation defined by free consciences. Negritude is a sad myth full of hope, born of Evil and pregnant with future Good, living like a woman who is born to die and who feels her own death even in the richest moments of her life; it is an unstable rest, an explosive fixity, a pride which renounces itself, an absolute that knows it is transitory: for whereas it is the Announcer of its birth and of its death agony, it also remains the existential attitude chosen by free men and lived *absolutely*, to the fullest. Because it is tension between a nostalgic Past into which the black man can no longer enter completely and a future in which it will be replaced by new values, negritude adorns itself with a tragic beauty that finds expression only in poetry. Because it is the living and dialectical unity of so many opposites, because it is a Complex defying analysis, negritude is only the multiple unity of a hymn that can reveal both it and the flashing beauty of the Poem which Breton calls *"explosante-fixe."* Because any attempt to conceptualize its various aspects would necessarily end up showing its relativity—even though it is lived in the absolute through royal consciences—and because the poem is an absolute, it is poetry alone that will allow the unconditional aspect of this attitude to be fixed. Because it is subjectivity written in the objective, negritude must take form in a poem, that is to say, in a subjectivity-object; because it is an Archetype and a Value, it will find its most transparent symbol in aesthetic values; because it is a call and a gift, it will make itself heard and offer itself only by means of a work of art which is both a call to the spectator's liberty and absolute generosity. Negritude is the content of the poem, it is the poem like a thing of the world, mysterious and open, obscure and suggestive; it is the poet himself. One must go still further; triumph of Narcissism and Narcissus' suicide, tension of the soul beyond culture, beyond words and beyond all psychic facts, luminous night of unknowing, deliberate choice of the *impossible* and of what Bataille calls "torture" [*supplice*], intuitive acceptance of the world and refusal of the world in the name of "the law of the heart," double contradictory postulation, demanding retraction, expansion of generosity—negritude is, in essence, Poetry. For once at least, the most authentic revolutionary plan and the purest poetry come from the same source.

And if the sacrifice is achieved one day, what will happen then? What will happen if, casting off his negritude for the sake of the Revolution, the black man no longer wishes to consider himself only a part of the proletariat? What will happen if he then allows himself to be defined only by his objective condition? If, in order to struggle against white capitalism, he undertakes to assimilate white technics? Will the source of poetry run dry? Or in spite of everything, will the great black river color the sea into which it flows? That does not matter: each era has its poetry; in each era, circumstances of history elect a nation, a race, a class to take up the torch, by creating situations that can be expressed or that can go beyond themselves only through Poetry. Sometimes the poetic *élan* coincides with the revolutionary *élan*, and sometimes they diverge. Let us greet today the historic chance that will permit black men to

> shout out the great Negro cry so hard that the
> world's foundations will be shaken.[3]

Translated by John MacCombie

Notes

A Note on the Texts

Index

Notes

What Is Literature?

1. At least in general. The greatness and error of Klee lie in his attempt to make a painting both sign and object.
2. I say 'create', not 'imitate', which is enough to squelch the bombast of M. Charles Estienne, who has obviously not understood a word of my argument and who is dead set on tilting at shadows.
3. This is the example cited by Bataille in *Expérience intérieure*.
4. If you wish to know the origin of this attitude towards language, the following are a few brief indications.

Originally, poetry creates the *myth,* while the prose-writer draws its *portrait.* In reality, the human act, governed by needs and urged on by the useful, is, in a sense, a *means.* It passes unnoticed, and it is the result which counts. When I extend my hand *in order* to take up my pen, I have only a fleeting and obscure consciousness of my gesture; it is the pen which I see. Thus, man is alienated by his ends. Poetry reverses the relationship: the world and things become inessential, become a pretext for the act which becomes its own end. The vase is there so that the girl may perform the graceful act of filling it; the Trojan War, so that Hector and Achilles may engage in that heroic combat. The action, detached from its goals, which become blurred, becomes an act of prowess or a dance. Nevertheless, however indifferent he might have been to the success of the enterprise, the poet, before the nineteenth century, remained in harmony with society as a whole. He did not use language for the end which prose seeks, but he had the same confidence in it as the prose-writer.

With the coming of bourgeois society, the poet puts up a common front with the prose-writer to declare it unliveable. His job is always to create the myth of man, but he passes from white magic to black magic. Man is always presented as the absolute end, but by the success of his enterprise he is sucked into a utilitarian collectivity. The thing that is in the background of his act and that will allow transition to the myth is thus no longer success, but defeat. By stopping the infinite series of his projects like a screen, defeat alone returns him to himself in his purity. The world remains the inessential, but it is now there as a pretext for defeat. The finality of the thing is to send man back to himself by blocking the route. Moreover, it is not a matter of arbitrarily introducing defeat and ruin into the course of the world, but rather of having no eyes for anything but that. Human enterprise has two aspects: it is both success and failure. The dialectical scheme is inadequate for reflecting upon it. We must make our vocabulary and the frames of our reason more supple. Some day I am going to try to

334 | *Notes to Page 34*

describe that strange reality, History, which is neither objective, nor ever quite subjective, in which the dialectic is contested, penetrated, and corroded by a kind of antidialectic, but which is still a dialectic. But that is the philosopher's affair. One does not ordinarily consider the two faces of Janus; the man of action sees one and the poet sees the other. When the instruments are broken and unusable, when plans are blasted and effort is useless, the world appears with a childlike and terrible freshness, without supports, without paths. It has the maximum reality because it is crushing for man, and as action, in any case, generalizes, defeat restores to things their individual reality. But, by an expected reversal, the defeat, considered as a final end, is both a contesting and an appropriation of this universe. A contesting, because man *is worth more* than that which crushes; he no longer contests things in their 'little bit of reality', like the engineer or the captain, but, on the contrary, in their 'too full of reality', by his very existence as a vanquished person; he is the remorse of the world. An appropriation, because the world, by ceasing to be the tool of success, becomes the instrument of failure. So there it is, traversed by an obscure finality; it is its coefficient of adversity which serves, the more human in so far as it is more hostile to man. The defeat itself turns into salvation. Not that it makes us yield to some 'beyond', but by itself it shifts and is metamorphosed. For example, poetic language rises out of the ruins of prose. If it is true that the word is a betrayal and that communication is impossible, then each word by itself recovers its individuality and becomes an instrument of our defeat and a receiver of the incommunicable. It is not that there is *another thing* to communicate; but the communication of prose having miscarried, it is the very meaning of the word which becomes the pure incommunicable. Thus, the failure of communication becomes a suggestion of the incommunicable, and the thwarted project of utilizing words is succeeded by the pure disinterested intuition of the word. Thus, we again meet with the description which we attempted earlier in this study, but in the more general perspective of the absolute valorization of the defeat, which seems to me the original attitude of contemporary poetry. Note also that this choice confers upon the poet a very precise function in the collectivity: in a highly integrated or religious society, the defeat is masked by the State or redeemed by Religion; in a less integrated and secular society, such as our democracies, it is up to poetry to redeem them.

Poetry is a case of the loser winning. And the genuine poet chooses to lose, even if he has to go so far as to die, in order to win. I repeat that I am talking of contemporary poetry. History presents other forms of poetry. It is not my concern to show their connection with ours. Thus, if one absolutely wishes to speak of the commitment of the poet, let us say that he is the man who commits himself to lose. This is the deeper meaning of that tough-luck, of that curse with which he always claims kinship and which he always attributes to an intervention from without; whereas it is his deepest choice, the source and not the consequence of his poetry. He is certain of the total defeat of the human enterprise and arranges to fail in his own life in order to bear witness, by his individual defeat, to human defeat in general. Thus, he challenges, as we shall see, which is what the prose-writer does too. But the challenge of prose is carried on in the name of a greater success; and that of poetry, in the name of the hidden defeat which every victory conceals.

5. It goes without saying that in all poetry a certain form of prose, that is, of success, is present; and, vice versa, the driest prose always contains a bit of poetry, that is, a certain form of defeat; no prose-writer is *quite* capable of expressing what he wants to say; he says too much or not enough; each phrase is a wager, a risk assumed; the more cautious one is, the more attention the word attracts; as Valéry has shown, no one can understand a word to its very bottom. Thus, each word is used simultaneously for its clear and social meaning and for certain obscure resonances—let me say, almost for its physiognomy. The reader, too, is sensitive to this. At once we are no longer on the level of concerted communication, but on that of grace and chance; the silences of prose are poetic because they mark its limits, and it is for the purpose of greater clarity that I have been considering the extreme cases of pure prose and pure poetry. However, it need not be concluded that we can pass from poetry to prose by a continuous series of intermediate forms. If the prose-writer is too eager to fondle his words, the *eidos* of 'prose' is shattered and we fall into highfalutin nonsense. If the poet relates, explains, or teaches, the poetry complex becomes *prosaic;* he has lost the game. It is a matter of structures—impure, but well-defined.

6. The same is true in different degrees regarding the spectator's attitude before other works of art (paintings, symphonies, statues, etc.).

7. In *practical life* a means may be taken for an end as soon as one searches for it, and each end is revealed as a means of attaining another end.

8. This last remark may arouse some readers. If so, I'd like to know a single good novel whose express purpose was to serve oppression, a single good novel which has been written against Jews, negroes, workers, or colonial people. 'But if there isn't any, that's no reason why someone may not write one some day.' But you then admit that you are an abstract theoretician. You, not I. For it is in the name of your abstract conception of art that you assert the possibility of a fact which has never come into being, whereas I limit myself to proposing an explanation for a recognized fact.

9. Etiemble: 'Happy the writers who die for something.' *Combat,* January 24, 1947.

10. Today his public is spread out. He sometimes runs into a hundred thousand copies. A hundred thousand copies sold means four hundred thousand readers. Thus, for France, one out of a hundred in the population.

11. Dostoyevsky's famous 'If God does not exist, all is permissible' is the terrible revelation which the bourgeoisie has forced itself to conceal during the one hundred and fifty years of its reign.

12. This was somewhat the case of Jules Vallès, though a natural magnanimity constantly struggled within him against bitterness.

13. I am not unaware that workers defended political democracy against Louis Napoleon Bonaparte much more than did the bourgeois, but that was because they thought that by means of it they would be able to bring about structural reforms.

14. I have so often been accused of being unfair to Flaubert that I cannot

resist the pleasure of quoting the following texts, which anyone can verify in the correspondence:

'Neo-Catholicism on one hand and socialism on the other have stultified France. Everything moves between the Immaculate Conception and the workers' lunch-boxes' (1868).

'The first remedy would be to put an end to universal suffrage, the shame of the human mind' (September 1871).

'I'm worth twenty Croisset voters' (1871).

'I have no hatred for the communards for the reason that I don't hate mad dogs' (Croisset, Thursday, 1871).

'I believe that the crowd, the herd, will always be hateful. The only ones important are a small group of spirits, always the same, who pass the torch from hand to hand' (Croisset, September 8, 1871).

'As to the Commune, which is on its last legs, it's the last manifestation of the Middle Ages.'

'I hate democracy (at least what it is taken to mean in France)—that is, the exaltation of grace to the detriment of justice, the negation of law: in short, anti-sociability.'

'The Commune re-instates murderers.'

'The populace is an eternal minor, and it will always be at the bottom of the scale since it is number, mass, the unbounded.'

'It's not important for a lot of peasants to know how to read and no longer listen to their priest, but it's infinitely important that a lot of men like Renan or Littré live and be listened to. Our salvation is now in a *legitimate aristocracy*. I mean by that a majority which will be composed of something other than mere figures' (1871).

'Do you believe that if France, instead of being governed, in short, by the mob, were in the power of the mandarins, we would be in this mess? If, instead of having wanted to enlighten the lower classes, we had been concerned with educating the upper ones?' (Croisset, Wednesday, August 3, 1870).

15. In *The Devil on Two Sticks,* for example, Le Sage *novelizes* the characters of La Bruyère and the maxims of La Rochefoucauld; that is, he binds them together by the slender thread of a plot.

16. The procedure of writing the novel in the form of letters is only a variation of what I have just indicated. The letter is the subjective recital of an event; it refers back to the one who wrote it and who becomes both actor and witnessing subjectivity. As to the event itself, although it is recent, it is already re-thought and explained: the letter always supposes a lag between the fact (which belongs to a recent past) and its recital, which is given subsequently and in a moment of leisure.

17. This is the reverse of the vicious circle of the surrealists, who try to destroy painting by painting. In this case one wants to have literature's letters of credit given by literature.

18. When Maupassant writes *Le Horla,* that is, when he speaks of the madness which threatens him, the tone changes. It is because at last something—something horrible—is going to happen. The man is overwhelmed, crushed; he no longer understands; he wants to drag the reader along with him into his terror. But the twig is bent; lacking a

technique adapted to madness, death, and history, he fails to move the reader.

19. Among these procedures I shall first cite the curious recourse to the style of the theatre that one finds at the end of the last century and the beginning of this one in Gyp, Lavedan, Abel Hermant, etc. The novel was written in dialogue form. The gestures of the characters and their actions were indicated in italics and parenthetically. It was evidently a matter of making the reader contemporaneous with the action as the spectator is during the performance. This procedure certainly manifests the predominance of dramatic art in polite society around 1900. In its way it also sought to escape the myth of primary subjectivity. But the fact that it was abandoned shows sufficiently that it did not solve the problem. First, it is a sign of weakness to ask for help from a neighbouring art, a proof that one lacks resources in the very domain of the art one practises. Then, the author did not thereby prevent himself from entering into the consciousness of his characters and having the reader enter with him. He simply divulged the intimate contents of the consciousness in parentheses and italics, with the style and typographical methods that are generally used for stage directions. In effect, it was an attempt without a future. The authors who used it had a vague feeling that new life could be put into the novel by writing it in the present. But they had not yet understood that it was not possible if one did not first give up the *explanatory attitude*.

More serious was the attempt to introduce the interior monologue of Schnitzler. (I am not speaking here of that of Joyce, which has quite different metaphysical principles. Larbaud, who, I know, harks back to Joyce, seems to me much rather to draw his inspiration from *Les Lauriers sont couplés* and from *Mademoiselle Else*.) In short, it was a matter of pushing the hypothesis of a primary subjectivity to-the limit and of passing on to realism by leading idealism up to the absolute.

The reality which one shows to the reader without intermediary is no longer the thing itself—the tree, the ashtray—but the consciousness which sees the thing; the 'real' is no longer only a representation, but rather the representation becomes an absolute reality since it is given to us as an immediate datum. The inconvenient aspect of this procedure is that it encloses us in an individual subjectivity and that it thereby lacks the intermonadic universe; besides, it dilutes the event and the action in the perception of one and then the other. Now, the common characteristic of the fact and the action is that they escape subjective representation, which grasps their results but not their living movement. In short, it is only with a certain amount of faking that one reduces the stream of consciousness to a succession of words, even deformed ones. If the word is given as an intermediary *signifying* a reality which in essence transcends language, nothing could be better; it withdraws itself, is forgotten, and discharges consciousness upon the object.

But if it presents itself as the *psychic reality,* if the author, by writing, claims to give us an ambiguous reality which is a sign, objective in essence—that is, in so far as it relates to something outside itself—and a thing, formal in essence—that is, as an immediate psychic datum—then he can be accused of not having participated and of disregarding the rhetorical law which might be formulated as follows: in literature, where one uses signs, it is not necessary to use *only* signs; and if the *reality* which one wants to signify is *one word*, it must be given to the reader by other words. He can be charged, besides, with having forgotten that the greatest riches of the psychic life are *silent*. We know what has happened to the internal monologue: having become *rhetoric,* that is, a poetic transposition of the inner life—silent as well as verbal—it has today become one method *among others* of the novelist. Too idealistic to be true, too realistic to be complete, it is the crown of the subjectivist technique. It is within and by means of this technique that the literature of today has become conscious of itself; that is, the literature of today is a double surpassing, towards the objective and towards the rhetorical, of the technique of the internal monologue. But for that it is necessary that the historical circumstance change.

It is evident that the writer continues today to write in the past tense. It is not by changing the tense of the verb but by revolutionizing the techniques of the story that he will succeed in making the reader contemporary with the story.

20. American literature is still in the stage of regionalism.

21. When I was passing through New York in 1945, I asked a literary agent to get the translation rights of *Miss Lonelyhearts,* a work by Nathanael West. He did not know the book and came to a gentleman's agreement with the author of a certain *Lonlyheart,* an old maiden lady who was very surprised that someone was thinking of translating her book into French. He learned of his mistake and, continuing his search, finally found West's publisher, who admitted that he did not know what had become of the author. I urged them to investigate and finally they learned that West had died several years earlier in an automobile accident. It seems that he still had a bank account in New York and the publisher was still sending him cheques from time to time.

22. In Jouhandeau the bourgeois souls have the same quality of the marvellous; but often this marvellous changes sign; it becomes negative and satanic. As you might well imagine, the Black Masses of the bourgeoisie are still more fascinating than its permissible displays.

23. To make oneself the clerk of violence implies that one deliberately adopts violence as a method of thought, that is, one has common recourse to intimidation, to the principle of authority; one haughtily refuses to demonstrate and discuss. This is what gives the dogmatic texts of the surrealists a purely formal but disturbing resemblance to the political writings of Charles Maurras.

24. A resemblance to L'Action Française, of which Maurras was able to say that it was not a party but a conspiracy. And don't the punitive expeditions of the surrealists resemble the pranks of the young royalist henchmen?

25. These passionless remarks have stirred up impassioned whirlwinds. However, far from convincing me, the defences and the attacks have made me more convinced than ever that surrealism has lost—perhaps temporarily—its timeliness. As a matter of fact, I find that most of its defenders are eclectics. It is made out to be a cultural phenomenon 'of high

importance', an 'exemplary' attitude, and an attempt is being made to integrate it, on the quiet, into bourgeois humanism. If it still had any life in it, would it be willing to spice the slightly stale rationalism of M. Alquié with the Freudian pepper? In the last analysis, it is a victim of the idealism which it has so fought against; the *Gazette des lettres, Fontaine,* and *Carrefour* are stomachs which just can't wait to digest it.

If a Desnos could have read in 1930 the following lines of M. Claude Mauriac, a young sparkplug of the Fourth Republic: 'Man fights against man without realizing that the joint effort of all minds should first be brought to bear against a certain skimpy and false conception of man. But surrealism has known this and has been crying it aloud for twenty years. As an enterprise of knowledge, it proclaims that everything about the traditional modes of thinking and feeling has to be re-invented,' he would certainly have protested; surrealism was not an 'enterprise of *knowledge*'; he specifically quoted Marx's famous phrase: 'We do not want to understand the world; we want to change it'; he never wanted this 'joint effort of minds' which pleasantly recalls the Rally of the French People [General de Gaulle's Rassemblement Populaire Français—*Translator*]. Against this rather silly optimism he always affirmed the strict connection between inner censorship and oppression; if there had to be a joint effort of all minds (that expression *minds,* in the plural, is hardly surrealistic!) it would come after the Revolution. In his heyday he would not have tolerated anyone's brooding over him that way in order to understand him. He considered—like the Communist Party in this respect—that everything that was not totally and exclusively for him was against him. Is he aware today of the way he is being manœuvred? In order to enlighten him, I shall therefore reveal to him that M. Bataille, before publicly informing Merleau-Ponty that he was withdrawing his article from us, had notified him of his intentions in a private conversation. [M. Merleau-Ponty is a member of the editorial board of *Les Temps Modernes* of which M. Sartre is editor-in-chief and in which the present work was originally serialized—*Translator*.] This champion of surrealism had then declared, 'I have serious charges to make against Breton, but we must unite against communism.' That should be sufficient! I think that I show more esteem for surrealism by harking back to the time of its ardent life and by discussing its aim than by slyly trying to assimilate it. It is true that it is not going to thank me for it, for, like all totalitarian parties, it affirms the continuity of its views in order to mask their perpetual change and therefore does not at all like anyone to hark back to its previous declarations. Many of the texts I meet with today in the catalogue of the surrealist exhibition (*Surrealism in* 1947) and which are approved by the chiefs of the movement are closer to the gentle eclecticism of M. Claude Mauriac than to the bitter revolt of the first surrealism. Here, for example, are a few lines of M. Pastoureau: 'The political experiment of surrealism which has caused it to revolve round the Communist Party for some ten years is very plainly conclusive. To attempt to continue it would be to lock itself up in the dilemma of compromise and ineffectualness. To follow the Communist Party in the way of the collaboration of classes to which it is committed is contradictory to the motives which in the past pushed surrealism into undertaking political action and which are as much

immediate demands in the domain of the mind and especially in that of morals as
the pursuit of the distant end which is the total liberation of man. And yet,
it is obvious that the politics on which one might base the hope of seeing
the aspirations of the proletariat realized is not that of the so-called left
opposition to the Communist Party nor that of the little anarchist
groups. . . . 'Surrealism, whose appointed rôle is to demand innumerable
reforms in the domain of the mind, and, in particular, ethical reforms, can
no more participate in a political action which is necessarily immoral in
order to be effective than it can participate, unless by renouncing the
liberation of man as a goal to be attained, in a political action which is
necessarily ineffectual because respectful of principles which it thinks it
does not have to violate. Thus, it retires into itself. Its efforts will again
tend to fulfil the same demands and to hasten the liberation of man, but *by
other means.'*

(Analogous texts and even identical phrases will be found in 'Rupture
inaugurale', a declaration adopted June 21, 1947, by the group in France.)

The reader will note, in passing, the word 'reform' and the extraordinary recourse to morals. Will we some day read a periodical entitled
'Surrealism in the Service of Reform'? But above all, this text established
surrealism's break with Marxism: everybody now agrees that one can act
on superstructures without the economic substructure's being modified.
An *ethical* and *reformist* surrealism wanting to confine its action to
changing ideologies: that smacks dangerously of idealism. What these
'other means' are remains to be determined. Is surrealism going to offer us
new scales of values? Is it going to produce a new ideology? Not a bit;
surrealism is going to busy itself, 'pursuing its old-time objectives, in
weakening Christian civilization and in preparing the conditions for the
coming of the eventual *Weltanschauung'*. It is still, obviously, a matter of
negation. Western civilization—even Pastoureau admits it—is moribund;
a tremendous war threatens it and will attend to burying it; our time calls
for a new ideology which permits man to live; but surrealism will
continue to attack the 'Christian-Thomist stage' of civilization. And how
can it be attacked? By the pretty lollipop of the 1947 Exhibition? Let's
rather go back to the *real* surrealism, that of the *Point du Jour,* of *Nadja,*
of *The Communicating Vessels.*

Alquié and Max-Pol Fouchet stress above everything else the fact that it
was an attempt at liberation. According to them, it is a matter of asserting
the rights of the human totality without omitting anything, be it the
unconscious, the dream, sexuality, or the imaginary. I am in complete
agreement with them. That is what surrealism *wanted;* that is certainly the
greatness of its enterprise. It should again be noted that the 'totalitarian'
idea is typical of the age; it animates the Nazi, the Marxist, and, today, the
'existentialist' attempt. It must certainly go back to Hegel as the common
source of all these efforts. But I discern a serious contradiction at the origin
of surrealism: to use Hegelian language, this movement had the *concept* of
totality (that is what is striking in Breton's famous phrase, 'freedom, colour
of man') and *realized* something quite different in its concrete manifestations. The totality of man is, indeed, necessarily a synthesis, that is, the
organic and schematic unity of all his secondary structures. A liberation

which proposes to be *total* must start with a total knowledge of man by himself (I am not trying to show here that it is possible; it is known that I am profoundly convinced that it is). That does not mean that we must know—or that we can know—*a priori*, the whole anthropological content of human reality, but that we can *first* reach ourselves in both the deep and manifest unity of our behaviour, our emotions, and our dreams. Surrealism, the fruit of a particular epoch, was embarrassed at the start by anti-synthetic survivals: first, the analytic negativity which is practised on *everyday reality*. Hegel writes of scepticism: 'Thought becomes perfect thought annihilating the being of the world in the *multiple variety of its determinations,* and the negativity of free self-consciousness at the heart of this multiform configuration of life becomes real negativity . . . scepticism corresponds to the realization of this consciousness, to the negative attitude in regard to the being who is the other; thus, it corresponds to desire and to work.' As a matter of fact, what appears to me essential in surrealist activity is the descent of the negative spirit *into work:* sceptical negativity *becomes concrete;* Duchamp's pieces of sugar as well as the fox-table are *works,* that is, concrete and painstaking destruction of what scepticism destroys only in words. I shall have as much to say for *desire,* which is one of the essential structures of surrealist love, and which is, as we know, desire of consuming, of destroying. We see the distance that has been covered; it exactly resembles the Hegelian avatars of consciousness: bourgeois analytics and idealistic destruction of the world by digestion. The attitude of the *rallié* writers deserves the name Hegel gave to stoicism: 'It is only a concept of negativity; it raises itself above this life like the spirit of the master.' Surrealism, on the contrary, 'penetrates this life like the spirit of the slave'. This is certainly its value and, without any doubt, that is the way it can hope to join hands with the worker who experiences his freedom in work. However, the worker destroys in order to construct. By destroying the tree he constructs beams and boards. Thus, he learns the two aspects of freedom, which is a constructive negativity. Surrealism, borrowing methods from bourgeois analysis, inverts the process: instead of destroying in order to construct, it constructs in order to destroy. Its construction is always alienated; it is compounded in a process whose end is annihilation. However, as the construction is real and the destruction is symbolic, the surrealist object may also be directly conceived as an end in itself. It is 'marble sugar' or a contestation of sugar, according to the way one looks at it. The surrealist object is necessarily iridescent because it represents the human order as topsy-turvy and because, as such, it contains within itself its own contradiction. That is what permits its constructor to claim that he is both destroying the real and is poetically creating a super-reality beyond reality. In fact, the super-real thus constructed becomes one object among others in the world, or it is only the crystallized indication of the possible destruction of the world. The fox-table of the last Exhibition is as much a syncretic effort to imbue our flesh with a vague sense of woodiness as it is a reciprocal challenge of the inert by the living and the living by the inert. The effort of the surrealists aims to present these two aspects of their production in the unity of the same movement. But the synthesis is lacking; the reason is that our authors do not want it. They are content with presenting the two moments as blended in an essential unity and, at the same time, as being each essential, which does not remove the contradiction. And doubtless the expected result is achieved: the created object arouses a tension in the mind of the spectator, and it is this tension which is, strictly speaking, the surrealist *instant;* the *given* thing is destroyed by internal challenge, but the challenge itself and the destruction are in turn contested by the positive character and the concrete *being-there* of the creation. But this irritating iridescence of the impossible is, at bottom, *nothing,* unless it be the irreconcilable divergence between the two terms of a contradiction. We have a case of technically provoking Baudelairean *dissatisfaction.* We have no revelation, no intuition of a new object, no seizure of matter or content, but only the *purely formal* consciousness of the mind as a surpassing, an appeal, and an emptiness. I shall again apply to surrealism Hegel's formula on scepticism: 'In [surrealism] consciousness actually experiences itself as a consciousness contradicting itself within itself.' Will it at least turn in on itself? Will it bring about a philosophical conversion? Will the surrealist object have the concrete efficiency of the hypothesis of the evil genius? But a second preconception of surrealism intervenes at this point: I have shown that it utterly rejects subjectivity as the free arbiter. Its deep love of materiality (the object and the unfathomable support of its destructions) leads it to profess materialism. Thus, it immediately covers up the consciousness which it for a moment discovered; it substantiates contradiction. It is no longer a matter of tension of subjectivity but of an objective structure of the universe. Read *The Communicating Vessels:* the title as well as the text shows the regrettable absence of any mediation; dream and waking are communicating vessels; that means that there is a merging, an ebb and flow but not a synthetic unity. I know perfectly well what will be said: 'But this synthetic unity has to be made and that is precisely the aim which surrealism sets up for itself.' 'Surrealism', says Mezer, 'starts from realities distinct from the conscious and the unconscious and goes towards the synthesis of those components.' All well and good; but *with what* does it propose to do it? What is the instrument of mediation?

To see a whole merry-go-round of fairies whirling round a pumpkin (even if it is possible, which I doubt) is to *mix* dream and reality; it is not to unify them in a new form which would retain within it, transformed and surpassed, elements of the dream and the real. In fact, we are always on the level of contestation; the *real* pumpkin supported by the entire real world contests these fading fairies which run about its rind; and vice versa, the fairies contest the gourd. There remains consciousness, the only witness, the only recourse, of this reciprocal destruction; but it is not wanted. Whether we paint or sculpt our dreams, it is sleep which is eaten by waking: the scandalous object, retrieved by the electric lights, presented in a closed room, in the midst of other objects, two yards and ten inches from one wall and three yards and fifteen inches from another, becomes a thing of the world (I place myself here in the surrealist hypothesis which recognizes *the same nature* in the use as in the perception; it is evident that there would not even be any use in discussing the matter if one thought, as I do, that these natures are radically distinct) in so far as it is a positive creation and only escapes in so far as it is a pure negativity. Thus, surrealist man is an addition, a mixture, but never a synthesis.

It is no accident that our authors owe so much to psycho-analysis; it offered them under the name of 'complexes' precisely the model of those contradictory and multiple interpretations which they everywhere make use of and which are without real cohesion. It is true that 'complexes' exist. But what has not been sufficiently observed is that they can exist only on the foundation of a previously given synthetic reality. Thus, for surrealism the total man is only the sum total of all his manifestations. Lacking the synthetic idea, they have organized whirligigs of contraries; this flutter of being and non-being might have been able to reveal subjectivity, just as the contradiction of the sensible sent Plato back to intelligible forms; but their rejection of the subjective has transformed man into a plain haunted house: in that vague atrium of consciousness there appear and disappear self-destructive objects which are exactly similar to things. They enter by the eyes or by the back door. Powerful disembodied voices ring out like those which announced the death of Pan. This odd *collection* brings to mind American neo-realism even more than it does materialism. After this, as a substitute for the synthetic unifications which are effected by consciousness, one will conceive, by participation, a sort of magical unity which manifests itself capriciously and which will be called objective chance. But it is not the inverted image of human activity. One does not liberate a collection; one makes an inventory of it. And surrealism is just that—an inventory. It is only a matter of fighting against the discredit into which certain portions of the human condition have fallen. Surrealism is haunted by the ready-made, the solid; it abhors geneses and births; it never regards creation as an emanation, a passing from the potential to the act, a gestation; it is the surging up *ex nihilo,* the abrupt appearance of a completely formed object which enriches the collection. At bottom, a *discovery.* So how could it 'deliver man from his monsters'? It has perhaps killed the monsters, but it has also killed man. It will be said that there remains desire. The surrealists have wanted to liberate human desire, they have proclaimed that man was desire. But that is not quite true; they have proscripted a whole category of desires (homosexuality, vices, etc.), without ever justifying this proscription. Then, they have judged it conformable to their hatred of the subjective never to come to know desire except by its products, as psycho-analysis does too. Thus, desire is still a *thing,* a collection. But instead of referring back from things (abortive acts, objects of oneiric symbolism, etc.) to their subjective source (which, strictly speaking, is desire) the surrealists remain fixed upon the thing. At bottom, desire is paltry and does not in itself interest them, and then it represents the rational explanation of the contradictions offered by complexes and their products. One will find very few and rather vague things in Breton about the unconscious and the libido. What interests him a great deal is not raw desire but crystallized desire, what might be called, to borrow an expression of Jaspers, the emblem of desire in the world. What has also struck me among the surrealists or ex-surrealists whom I have known has never been the magnificence of their desires or of their freedom. They have led lives which were modest and full of restraints; their sporadic violence made me think rather of the spasms of a maniac than of a concerted action; as for the rest, they were solidly harpooned by powerful complexes. As far as freeing desire goes, it has always seemed to me that the great roaring boys of the Renaissance or even the Romantics did a great deal more. You may say that, at least, they are great poets. Fine; there we have a meeting-ground. Some naïve people have said that I was 'anti-poetic' or 'against poetry'. What an absurd phrase! As well say that I am *against* air or *against* water. On the contrary, I recognize in no uncertain terms that surrealism is the *only* poetic movement of the first half of the twentieth century; I even recognize that in a certain way it contributes to the liberation of man. But what it liberates is neither desire nor the human totality, but pure imagination. Now, the fact is that the purely imaginary and *praxis* are not easily reconciled. I find a touching admission of this in a surrealist of 1947, whose name seems predisposed to the utmost honesty:

'I must recognize (and probably I am not alone among those who are not easily satisfied) that there is a divergence between my feeling of rebellion, the reality of my life, and the fields of the battle of poetry which I may be waging, which the works of those who are my friends help me to wage. Despite them, despite myself, I hardly know how to live.

'Does recourse to the imaginary, which is a criticism of the social order, which is a protestation and a hastening of history, risk burning the bridges which connect us with other men and, at the same time, with reality? I know that there can be no question of freedom for man himself' (Yves Bonnefoy, *Surrealism in 1947*, p. 68). [Bonnefoy (*la bonne foi*)—good faith, honesty. This will explain M. Sartre's play on words in the sentence immediately preceding the quotation.—*Translator*.]

But between the two wars surrealism spoke in a quite different tone. And it's something quite different that I attacked above concerning the surrealists' singing political manifestoes, their bringing judgement to bear against those among them who did not stick to the line, their defining a method of social action, their entering the C.P. and leaving it with a flourish, their *rapprochement* with Trotsky, and their concern about clarifying their position with regard to Soviet Russia. It's hard for me to believe that they thought they were acting as poets. It may be objected that man is a whole and that he is not to be divided up into a politician and a poet. I agree, and I will even add that I am more at ease for knowing that there are authors who make poetry a product of automatism and politics a conscious and reflective effort. But after all it is a truism; it is both true and false. For if man is one and the same, if, in a way, his mark is found everywhere, that does not at all mean that the *activities* are identical; and if, in each case, they bring the whole mind into question, one need not conclude that they do so in the same way, nor that the success of one justifies the failures of the other. Besides, does one think that one would be flattering the surrealists by telling them that they have been carrying on political activity as poets?

Still, it is reasonable for a writer who wants to mark the unity of his life and his work to show by a *theory* the community of aims of his poetry and his practice. But the fact is that this theory can itself only *belong to prose*. There is a surrealist prose, and that is the only thing I was considering in the pages that are under attack. But surrealism is hard to pin down; it is *Proteus*. Sometimes it presents itself as completely involved in reality, struggle, and life; and if you call it to account, it starts screaming that it's pure poetry and that you're murdering it, and that you don't know what poetry is all about. This is shown rather clearly in the following anecdote which everyone knows but which is pregnant with meaning: Aragon had written a poem which rightly appeared as a provocation to murder; there was talk of legal prosecution; whereupon, the whole surrealist group solemnly asserted the irresponsibility of the poet; the products of automatism were not to be likened to concerted undertakings. However, to anyone who had some experience with automatic writing, it was apparent that Aragon's poem was of a quite different kind. Here was a man quivering with indignation, who, in clear and violent terms, called for the death of the oppressor; the oppressor was stirred to action, and all at once he found before him nothing more than a poet who woke up and rubbed his eyes and was amazed that he was being blamed for his dreams. This is what has just happened again: I attempted a critical examination of the totality of the fact 'surrealism' as a commitment in the world, in so far as surrealists were attempting, *by means of prose,* to make its meanings clear. I was answered that I am harming poets and that I misunderstand their 'contribution' to the inner life. But really, they didn't give a rap about the inner life; they wanted to shatter it, to break down the walls between subjective and objective, and to wage the Revolution on the side of the proletariat.

To conclude: surrealism is entering a period of withdrawal; it is breaking with Marxism and the C.P. It wants to demolish the Christian-Thomist edifice stone by stone. Very well, but I should like to know what public it expects to reach. In other words, *in what souls* it expects to ruin western civilization. It has said over and over again that it could not affect the workers directly and that they were not yet accessible to its action. The facts show that they are right: how many workers visited the 1947 Exhibition? On the other hand, how many bourgeois? Thus, its purpose can only be negative: to destroy the last remnants of the Christian myths in the minds of the bourgeois who form their public. That was what I wanted to show.

26. Which has particularly characterized them for the last hundred years because of the misunderstanding which has separated them from the public and has obliged them to decide upon the marks of their talent themselves.

27. Prévost declared, more than once, his sympathy for Epicureanism as revised and corrected by Alain.

28. If I did not speak of Malraux or Saint-Exupéry earlier, it is because they belong to our generation. They were writing before we were and are doubtless a little older than we. But whereas we needed the urgency and the physical reality of a conflict in order to discover ourselves, Malraux had the immense merit of recognizing as early as his first work that we were at war and of producing a war literature when the surrealists and even Drieu were devoting themselves to a literature of peace. As to Saint-Exupéry, against the subjectivism and the quietism of our predecessors he was able

to sketch the chief features of a literature of work and tool. I shall show later that he is the precursor of a literature of construction which tends to replace the literature of consumption. War and construction, heroism and work, doing, having and being—it will be seen, at the end of this chapter, that these are the chief literary and philosophical themes of today. Consequently, when I say 'we', I believe that I can speak of them too.

29. What are Camus, Malraux, Koestler, etc. now producing if not a literature of extreme situations? Their characters are at the height of power or in prison cells, on the eve of death or of being tortured or of killing. Wars, *coups d'état*, revolutionary action, bombardments, massacres. There you have their everday life. On every page, in every line, it is always the whole man who is in question.

30. Of course, some minds are richer than others, more intuitive, or better qualified for analysis or synthesis. Some of them are even prophetic and some are in a better position to foresee because they hold certain cards in their hand or because they discern a broader horizon. But these differences are *a posteriori* and the evaluation of the present and the near future remains conjectural. For *us* too the event appears only through subjectivities. But its transcendence comes from the fact that it exceeds them all because it extends through them and reveals to each person a different aspect of itself and of himself.

Thus, our technical problem is to find an orchestration of consciousnesses which may permit us to render the multi-dimensionality of the event. Moreover, in giving up the fiction of the omniscient narrator, we have assumed the obligation of suppressing the intermediaries between the reader and the subjectivities—the viewpoints of our characters. It is a matter of having him enter into their minds as into a windmill. He must even coincide successively with each one of them. We have learned from Joyce to look for a second kind of realism, the raw realism of subjectivity without mediation or distance. Which leads us to profess a third realism, that of temporality. Indeed, if without mediation we plunge the reader into a consciousness, if we refuse him all means of surveying the whole, then the time of this consciousness must be imposed upon him without abridgement. If I pack six months into a single page, the reader jumps out of the book.

This last aspect raises difficulties that none of us has resolved and which are perhaps partially insoluble, for it is neither possible nor desirable to limit all novels to the story of a single day. Even if one should resign oneself to that, the fact would remain that devoting a book to twenty-four hours rather than to one, or to an hour rather than to a minute, implies the intervention of the author and a transcendent choice. It will then be necessary to mask this choice by purely aesthetic procedures, to practise sleight of hand, and, as always in art, to lie in order to be true.

31. From this viewpoint, absolute objectivity, that is, the story in the third person which presents characters solely by their conduct and words without explanation or incursion into their inner life, while preserving strict chronological order, is rigorously equivalent to absolute subjectivity. Logically, to be sure, it might be claimed that there is at least a witnessing consciousness, that of the reader. But the fact is that the reader forgets to

see himself while he looks and the story retains for him the innocence of a virgin forest whose trees grow far from sight.

32. I sometimes wonder whether the Germans, who had at their disposal a hundred means of knowing the names of the members of the National Writers' Committee, did not spare us. We were pure consumers for them too. Here the process is inverted. The diffusion of our newspapers was highly limited. It would have been more inexpedient in regard to the supposed politics of collaboration to arrest Eluard or Mauriac than dangerous to let them whisper in freedom. The Gestapo doubtless preferred to concentrate its efforts on the underground forces and the members of the Maquis whose acts of real destruction troubled it more than our abstract negativity. Doubtless, they arrested and shot Jacques Decour. But at the time Decour was not yet very well known.

33. See particularly *Wind, Sand and Stars.*

34. Like Hemingway, for example, in *For Whom the Bell Tolls.*

35. But don't let us exaggerate. *In gross,* the situation of the writer has improved. But, as will be seen, chiefly by extra-literary means (radio, cinema, journalism) which were not available formerly. He who can't or won't have recourse to these means must practise a second profession or have a tough time of it. 'It is extremely rare for me to have coffee to drink and enough cigarettes,' writes Julien Blanc ('Grievances of a Writer', *Combat,* April 27, 1947). 'Tomorrow I won't put any butter on my bread, and the chemist's price for the phosphorous which I lack is preposterous . . . since 1943 I have undergone five serious operations. Very shortly I am going to have a sixth, a very serious one. Being a writer, I have no social security. I have a wife and child. The state remembers me only to ask for excessive taxes on my trifling royalties. . . . It is going to be necessary for me to take steps to reduce my hospital expenses. . . . And the Society of Men of Letters and the Authors' Fund? The first will back me up; the second, having given me a gift last month of four thousand francs . . . Let's forget it.'

36. Aside, of course, from Catholic 'writers'. As for the so-called Communist 'writers', I speak about them later on.

37. I admit without difficulty the Marxist description of 'existentialist' anguish as a historical and class phenomenon. Existentialism, in its contemporary form, appears with the decomposition of the bourgeoisie, and its origin is bourgeois. But that this decomposition can *disclose* certain aspects of the human condition and make possible certain metaphysical intuitions does not mean that these intuitions and this disclosure are illusions of the bourgeois consciousness or mythical representations of the situation.

38. The worker has joined the C.P. under the pressure of circumstances. He is less suspect because his possible choices are more limited.

39. In Communist literature in France, I find only one genuine writer. Nor is it accidental that he writes about mimosa and beach pebbles.

40. They have caused Hugo to be read. More recently they have spread the work of Giono in certain areas.

41. I except the abortive attempt of Prévost and his contemporaries. I have spoken of them above.

348 | Notes to Pages 220–330

42. This contradiction is met with everywhere, particularly in communist *friendship*. Nizan had many friends. Where are they? Those he was most fond of belonged to the C.P. These are the ones who revile him today. The only ones who remain faithful are not in the Party. The reason is that the Stalinist community with its excommunicative power is present in love and friendship which are person-to-person relationships.

43. And the idea of freedom? The fantastic criticisms that have been made of existentialism prove that people no longer mean anything by it. Is it their fault? Here is the P.R.L., antidemocratic and antisocialist, recruiting former fascists, former collaborators and former P.S.F.'s. Yet it calls itself the Republican Party of Freedom (*Parti républicain de la liberté*). If you are against it, it means that you are therefore against freedom. But the communists also refer to freedom; only it is Hegelian freedom, which is an assumption of necessity. And the surrealists too, who are determinists. A young simpleton said to me one day, 'After *The Flies,* in which you spoke splendidly about the freedom of Orestes, you betrayed yourself and you betrayed us by writing *Being and Nothingness* and by failing to set up a deterministic and materialistic humanism.' I understand what he meant: that materialism delivers man from his myths. It is a liberation, I agree, but in order the better to enslave him. However, from 1760 on, some American colonists defended slavery in the name of freedom: if the colonist, citizen, and pioneer wants to buy a negro, isn't he free? And having bought him, isn't he free to use him? The argument has remained. In 1947 the proprietor of a public swimming pool refused to admit a Jewish captain, a war hero. The captain wrote letters of complaint to the newspapers. The papers published his protest and concluded: 'What a wonderful country America is! The proprietor of the pool was *free* to refuse admittance to a Jew. But the Jew, a citizen of the United States, was *free* to protest in the press. And the press, which, as everybody knows, is free, mentions the incident without taking sides. Finally, everybody is free.' The only trouble is that the word *freedom* which covers these very different meanings—and a hundred others—is used without anyone's thinking that he ought to indicate the meaning he gives it in each case.

44. Because, like Mind, it is of the type of what I have elsewhere called 'detotalized totality'.

45. Camus's *The Plague,* which has just been published, seems to me a good example of a unifying movement which bases a plurality of critical and constructive themes on the organic unity of a single myth.

Black Orpheus

1. Stéphane Mallarmé, "Magie," in *Oeuvres complètes* (Paris: Pléiade, 1945), p. 400.
2. Aimé Césaire, "Tam-Tam II," in *Les Armes miraculeuses,* 2nd ed. (Paris: Gallimard, 1946), p. 69.
3. Césaire, "Et les chiens se taisaient," in *Les Armes miraculeuses,* p. 156.

A Note on the Texts

"Qu'est-ce que la littérature?" was originally published in six installments in *Les Temps modernes* 17–22 (February–July 1947). It subsequently appeared in *Situations II* (Paris: Gallimard, 1948), along with "Présentation des *Temps modernes*" and "La Nationalisation de la littérature," and was published separately by Gallimard in 1964. The translation used here, published by the Philosophical Library (New York) in 1949, was the first to appear in English and has been reproduced with a small number of corrections. The final section of the essay, "Ecrire pour son époque," was first published in Alexandria in the periodical *Valeurs* 7–8 (October 1946–January 1947), and was reprinted in the June 1948 issue of *Les Temps modernes*. English translations appeared in late 1946 and early 1947 in several periodicals, including *Virginia Quarterly Review* 23 (Spring 1947).

"Présentation des *Temps modernes*" was published in the inaugural issue of *Les Temps modernes* on October 1, 1945. It appeared for the first time in English as "The Case for Responsible Literature" in *Horizon* (London) 2 (May 1945), and in *Partisan Review* 12 (Summer 1945). The translation used here was commissioned especially for this volume.

"La Nationalisation de la littérature" appeared in the second issue of *Les Temps modernes*, on November 1, 1945. It is published here in English for the first time.

"Orphée Noir" appeared originally as the preface to an anthology of works by African and West Indian poets, *Anthologie de la nouvelle poésie nègre et malgache de langue français*, edited by Léopold Sédar-Senghor (Paris: Presses Universitaires de France, 1948). Excerpts were also published in *Les Temps modernes* 37 (October 1948) and *Présence africaine* 6 (April 1949), and the whole was reprinted, with a supplementary note, in *Situations III* (Paris: Gallimard, 1949). It first appeared in English in *Présence africaine* (1951). Its first American publication was in the *Massachusetts Review* 6, no. 1 (1965), and it is that text which has been reprinted here.

Index

Adorno, Theodor, 16–17, 18
Aesthetic joy, 39, 63–65, 219
Africa, 298–299
Alain (Emile Chartier), 165, 167, 172, 345n27; *The Citizen versus the Powers That Be,* 262
Alienation, 56, 72, 73, 134–137, 192
Alquiré, Ferdinand, 338n25
Anouilh, Jean, 197
Aragon, Louis (Louis Andrieux), 144, 284, 338n25; *Aurélien,* 219
Aristotle, 254
Arland, Marcel, 151; *L'Ordre,* 150; *Terres Etrangères,* 150
Aron, Raymond, 5
Art: formal, 62; realistic, 62, 66, 67, 78, 119, 249. *See also* Literature; Poetry; Poetry, black; Writing
Artistic creation, 25–28, 48–52. *See also* Author; Writing
Art object: as appeal to freedom, 16–17, 56–69; as absolute end, 55–56, 104, 191, 213, 221, 249; in bourgeois society, 105–107. *See also* Literature; Poetry; Poetry, black; Writing
Assouline, Pierre: *L'Epuration des intellectuels,* 5n
Audience: historicity of, 15, 70–75, 222; in feudal society, 82–85; in 17th century, 85–93; in 18th century, 93–103; in 19th century, 103–130, 250; con-

temporary, 166–168, 195–204, 214–215, 218–224, 253–254. *See also* Public; Reading
Augier, Emile, 108
Author: remuneration of, 8, 80–130, 164, 249–250, 347n35; class origins of, 8, 93, 99–103, 141–145, 155–156, 187–188, 204, 223–224, 249–250; historicity of, 9, 68–69, 70–80, 134–137, 175–178, 180, 182–187, 251–255, 277–279; commitment of, 34–41, 46–47, 68–69, 77–80, 192–196, 215–238, 243–245, 251–255, 265–267, 286–287; function of, 38–39, 228–235, 255; relation of, to reader, 50–58, 60–63, 65–68, 70–75, 78; freedom of, 58, 60–69, 72, 77, 92, 100, 191–192, 195, 213–214, 222–224; bad conscience of, 82, 135; in feudal society, 82–85; cooption of, 82–93; in 17th century, 85–93, 96–97; in 18th century, 93–103; and the bourgeoisie, 96, 99–100, 103–109, 113–130, 223–224; pretensions of, to class independence, 97–103, 111–120, 155–157, 249–250; in 19th century, 103–130; and the proletariat, 109–113, 121–122, 130–132; situation of contemporary, 132–140, 184–192, 195–196, 279–280, 287–288;

356 | *Index*

358 | Index

Novel (*continued*)
tional, 182–183, 185. *See also*
Literature; Prose; Writing

Occupation. *See* German occupation of France
Oeuvre, L', 167
Ohnet, George, 108
Ollivier, Albert, 5
Oppression: and writing, 12, 72, 76–77, 300–307; and inner censorship, 338n25
Order, 125–127, 149, 150, 273–274
Orpheus, 300
Other, the, 79, 92

Pailleron, Edouard, 108
Painting, 26, 27–30, 62–63, 274
Parain, Brice, 38, 127, 227, 228, 295
Pascal, Blaise, 46, 85, 108, 272, 322; *Provincial Letters*, 40
Pastoureau, Henri, 338n25
Paulhan, Jean, 5, 135, 250; *The Flowers of Tarbes*, 10–11
Péguy, Charles, 146
Peret, Benjamin, 161
Pétain, Henri, 75, 203
Philo, 155
Philoctetes, 328
Philosophy, 14–15
Phrase-object, 32
Picasso, Pablo, 28, 31, 32
Plato, 42
"Plea for Intellectuals, A," 18–19
Pluto, 300
Poe, Edgar Allan, 114
Poetry, 28–35, 143, 173, 250, 293–295, 308, 313, 319; non-instrumental language of, 11–12, 28–34, 333n4, 335n5; and commitment, 12–13, 34–35, 258, 333n4; and subjectivity, 295, 297–298. *See also* Poetry, black

Poetry, black, 297–330; revolutionary potential of, 297–298, 303, 311, 329–330; subjectivity in, 297–298, 303, 329–330; mystical geography in, 298–299; theme of exile in, 298–299; theme of slavery in, 298–299, 321–323; Orphic, 300; *tam-tam*, 307–308; epic, 308, 324; Nature in, 315–316, 320; sexual imagery in, 316–319; Passion imagery in, 319–321; Dionysian, 320–324; anti-Christian, 322–323
Poincaré, Henri, 273
Politzer, Georges, 156, 212
Pouillon, Jean, 4
Praxis, 12, 194–196, 204, 295; literature of, 14–16, 19, 233–234
Prévost, Marcel, 108, 164, 167, 193, 283, 345n26, 347n41
Proletariat, 73, 107, 121–122, 130–132, 166, 199–201, 211, 257, 265, 295–296, 329; emergence of, 109–111; culturelessness of, 112–113; and Surrealism, 158–160; as revolutionary public, 204–207, 263
Propaganda, 226–228, 232; literature as, 213, 227, 258, 285–286; of fraternity, 255–258; Nazi, 261–262
Prose: instrumentality of, 11–12, 28, 30, 31–32, 34–40, 46–47; remnants of poetry in, 335n5. *See also* Literature; Writing
Proudhon, P.-J., 5, 112, 196
Proust, Marcel, 8–9, 12, 51, 146, 151, 258–259, 280
Psychoanalysis, 116, 152, 165–166, 338n25
Public, reading: real, 82, 85, 93, 95, 136; virtual, 82, 88, 112, 137, 204, 209, 215–216; in

Seignobos, Charles, 254
Senghor, Léopold, 12, 15, 310,
314, 326
Shakespeare, William, 42
Shelley, Percy Bysshe, 145
Significance, 25–26, 27, 28. *See
also* Meaning
Signs, 25–26, 29, 30, 34–38. *See
also* Language; Meaning
Situation, 36–37, 72, 79, 260–
261, 264–265; author's, 132–
140, 184–192, 195–196, 279–
280, 287–288; in travel
writing, 162–163; contemporary discovery of, 175–178; and
oppression, 188–189; and love,
259–260. *See also* Historicity
Socialism, 5; bourgeois, 110; and
race, 296–297. *See also* Bour-
geoisie; Class; Proletariat
Socialist Party, 158
Society: bourgeois conception of,
255–259; Sartre's conception
of, 259–263
Soday, Paul, 198
Solidarity, 76, 167, 258, 287
Soviet Union, 158, 287; and
United States, 205, 234, 235–
236; internal problems of, 205–
207; violence in, 230, 231
Spinoza, Baruch, 132
Sprinker, Michael: *Imaginary Relations*, 14
Steinbeck, John, 141
Stendhal, 45, 114; *Armance*, 53
Stoicism, 168
Subjectivity, 124–125, 151–152,
295, 346n30; black, 297–330
Surrealism, 120, 151–164, 176,
250, 273, 279, 303, 306, 311,
312–313; and the Communist
Party, 7, 157–160, 174; failure
of, 12, 13, 120–121, 154–
157, 312–313, 338n25; subjec-
tivity and objectivity in, 152–

154; the marvellous in, 155;
violence in, 159, 163–164,
206; gamma point in, 161,
163; language in, 228; and
Marxism, 338n25; and psycho-
analysis, 338n25
Switzerland, 285
Synthetic anthropology, 13–15,
261

Talent, 105, 275, 294
Tam-tam poetry, 307–308
Temp modernes, Les, 3, 6–7, 12,
18, 28
Terre des hommes, 6
Terrorism, literary, 10–11, 135,
271
Thérive, André, 281
Thibaudet, Albert, 151
Tintoretto, 27
Tito (Josip Broz), 144
Torricelli, Evangelista, 182, 236
Torture, 178–181
Truth, 94, 98, 306
Turenne, Henri de La Tour d'Au-
vergne, vicomte de, 285

United States of America, 206,
228, 230; and Soviet Union,
205, 234, 235–236; and European literature, 274, 284, 285
Utilitarianism: bankruptcy of,
104, 147–148, 231; surrealism's rejection of, 151; in Communist Party, 213

Vaché, Jacques, 158
Valéry, Paul, 35, 42, 285, 335n5
Valles, J., 91
Van Gogh, Vincent, 63
Vauvenargues, Luc de Clapiers,
108
Vercors (Jean-Marcel Bruller),
144; *The Silence of the Sea*, 73–
75, 137